Codel W

American Political Institutions and Public Policy

FIVE CONTEMPORARY STUDIES

Edited by

Allan P. Sindler
Cornell University

Little, Brown and Company Boston

Preface:
The Purposes of This Casebook

This book consists of five original case studies intended to complement the customary coverage in courses in American government, politics, and public policy. The case study, as a type of analysis and reporting, possesses both potential strengths and limitations, of which the reader should be apprised.

As compared to a textbook or to a "readings book" collection of articles and book excerpts, the casebook device emphasizes selective probes and depth of treatment rather than comprehensive coverage. We have been careful, therefore, to choose for exploration topics specifically relevant to any course on American government and politics. Our case studies treat the major institutions of American national government—presidency, Congress, Supreme Court, the bureaucracy, and the parties—as they grappled with problems of high contemporary importance. One study, focusing on the Congress, deals with the contentious development of Medicare. A second examines the presidency during the critical decision-making period in American involvement in Vietnam. The evolution of antipoverty policy, with its controversial Office of Economic Opportunity, is the subject of a third study on the role of the bureaucracy. The difficulties facing the minority party in our political system are illustrated by examining the Republican party in the House of Representatives after Johnson's landslide victory in 1964. And the final study depicts innovation in Constitutional interpretation, stressing the interaction of the Supreme Court and political forces in setting new standards for state legislative apportionment.

Our decision to focus on central and representative rather than peripheral or untypical aspects of the American political process is carried through in each author's treatment of his subject. Each concentrates on the interaction of a policy and an institution, yet all are sensitive to the broader political interplay that characterizes the making of public policy in America. Each author, accordingly, adds to his primary emphasis by giving attention to other influential factors and actors. For example, all the cases, and not just the one on Medicare, which concentrates on the Congress, comment on the Congress and on its specific committees, procedures, and legislators. Quite deliberately, then, each author seeks to depict the complex diversity that surrounds American policy making and to avoid a misleading "tunnel" perspective that might result from examining the one institution that is his principal subject.

Each contributor consciously tries to move beyond the particulars of his subject to general theoretical problems important to political scientists and students alike. Issues dealing with, among others, congressional-presidential, presidential-bureaucratic, national government-state government, judicial-congressional, interest groups-public officials, congressional-bureaucratic, and majority party-minority party relations are identified and discussed at many points in this volume. By such explicit attention we seek not to obscure the forest by undue attention to the trees.

In the same vein, the studies have been written with an eye to provoking informed classroom discussion. Each author raises questions and offers general interpretations; the editor's epilogue highlights some cross-chapter themes to the same end. But each author tries to avoid overstructuring or overinterpreting; we wish the instructor and the student to have plenty of room to propose other questions and to suggest competing interpretations. If readers react to these chapters with diverse analytic and normative judgments, and ground their views on evidence drawn from the studies, this aspect of our intentions will be well served.

Finally, and surely not among the least of its virtues, a case study presents special opportunities for an intimate and dramatic account of political forces, personalities, and events. All the contributors have the familiarity and involvement with their areas of analysis requisite to exploiting this possibility fully. Thus the treatment is rich in detail and is supported by interviews and quotations from major participants in the events. Avoiding the tone and scope associated with textbooks, each study spells out less familiar aspects of American politics when useful for the reader's grasp of the narrative. Each, in other words, attempts to be a self-sufficient story aiming to involve the reader's active interest as a sensible precondition to stimulating his thought.

These case studies are, then, specifically designed and crafted for a special group of college readers. At their simplest, they are meant to be attractive "yarns" about political subjects, told with flavor and insight. More ambitiously and critically, the authors seek to probe problems considered important enough to warrant exploring under different, varying, actual political conditions. They seek to discuss political reality in its interlocking complexity. They seek to provoke consideration of general and representative issues among informed students of American politics. Above all, they seek to engage the reader's attention and thought in ways more direct and intense than textbooks or "readings book" collections are likely to do. These are our purposes in collaborating on this volume, and we gratefully welcome comments by its classroom users so that we may narrow the gap between intention and performance.

A final word on the relative responsibilities of authors and editor for this casebook. The editor takes the responsibility for the conception of the volume, the broad design of each study, the recruiting of the five authors and cases, and the relation of the parts to the whole. Each contributor chose his own topic and developed his own case, being guided by a common understanding of the volume's purposes as here described and by his continued awareness of the coverage and emphases of the other studies. Although the responsibility of each author, therefore, is essentially limited to his own study, it should be apparent that the congenial collaboration of each underlies the coherence of the volume.

Allan P. Sindler

About the Contributors

THEODORE MARMOR, with B.A. and Ph.D. degrees from Harvard University, is currently an assistant professor of political science and a research associate at the Institute for Research on Poverty, both at the University of Wisconsin. Since 1966 he has been a consultant to the Office of Assistant Secretary for Program Coordination, Department of Health, Education and Welfare. The general subject of his study continues to be his primary interest, and he presently is completing research for a volume on the politics of medical remuneration in England, Sweden, and the United States.

EUGENE EIDENBERG completed his undergraduate work at the University of Wisconsin and his graduate training at Northwestern University. A specialist in the American political process, since 1965 he has been at the University of Minnesota, where he is currently an associate professor of political science. No stranger to practical politics, he served in 1964–65 as a Congressional Fellow of the American Political Science Association, working in the office of the Majority Whip (Representative T. Hale Boggs of Louisiana) and of the Vice-President (Hubert H. Humphrey). He currently is on leave from his academic post to serve as administrative deputy to the mayor of Minneapolis.

RICHARD BLUMENTHAL earned a B.A. in government from Harvard University in 1967. His study in this casebook is based on his undergraduate thesis, which was awarded highest honors. His undergraduate activity included a year's stint as editorial chairman of the student daily newspaper, the *Harvard Crimson*. In 1967–68, he attended Trinity College, Cambridge University, and also worked for *Newsweek* and the *Washington Post*. After a few months as assistant to the president of the *Washington Post*, he became a staff assistant to Daniel P. Moynihan, Chairman of the Council on Urban Affairs in the Nixon administration.

ROBERT L. PEABODY was awarded his B.A. by the University of Washington and his Ph.D. by Stanford University. He is associate professor of political science at Johns Hopkins University, at which he has taught since 1961. A specialist in legislative, administrative, and party politics, he co-edited *New Perspectives in the House of Representatives* (1963), wrote *Organizational Authority* (1964), and has contributed articles to the professional journals. He has been associate director of the American Political Science Association's study of Congress, a subject of continuing professional interest to him.

ANDREW HACKER, an Amherst College and Oxford University B.A. and a Princeton University Ph.D., is professor of government at Cornell University, where he has taught since 1955. His broad and varied interests in political science include a special devotion to American politics and political sociology. His publications include *Political Theory: Philosophy, Ideology, Science* (1961), *Congressional Districting: The Issue of Equal Representation* (1963), and *The Study of Politics* (1963). He is also a frequent contributor to both learned journals and general magazines, and has served as consultant to a variety of private and public bodies.

ALLAN P. SINDLER earned his undergraduate and graduate degrees at Harvard University and, in 1965, after service at Duke and Yale universities, joined Cornell University as professor of government. His interests focus on American national and state politics, especially political parties. Among his publications are *Huey Long's Louisiana: State Politics, 1920–1952* (1956); as editor, *Change in the Contemporary South* (1963); and *Political Parties in the United States* (1966).

Contents

decisions. The bombing decision. The troop decisions. Some general lessons. Conclusion. Sources. Further reading.

The Durham example: marching on the City Council. The "guerrillas." A structural view of poverty. Three views of community action. A basic disagreement. President Kennedy gives the go-ahead. From CEA to BOB. President Johnson says "Move!" Legerdemain. Departmental infighting. The BOB's outlines, January, 1964. Unresolved questions and differing perspectives. The task force decides. Drafting the legislation. Congressional action. Implementation by the task force. Some closing interpretations. Sources. Further reading.

Ford defeats Halleck. Reasons for Halleck's loss. Initial tests of Ford's leadership. Out-party legislative strategies. The House minority leader's external relations. The effects of leadership change. The congressional election, 1966. Some major themes reconsidered. Sources. Further reading.

Eleven angry men. Recourse to the courts. The state of the states. Baker rebuffed. The professor's precedent. 1946 vs. 1959. Baker at the bar. Lobbying and litigation. The decision. Frankfurter's dissent. Applying the principles. Unfinished business: standards are specified. What about voluntary underrepresentation? The Court becomes controversial. Congress vs. the Court. Changing the Constitution. Pressure for passage. Call for a convention. An ivory tower tribunal? Some concluding observations. Sources. Further reading.

American Political Institutions and Public Policy

FIVE CONTEMPORARY STUDIES

STUDY

1

The Congress:
Medicare Politics and Policy

Theodore R. Marmor

On July 30, 1965, President Johnson flew to Independence, Missouri, to sign the Medicare bill in the presence of former President Harry S Truman. The new statute—technically Title 18 of the Social Security Amendments of 1965—included two related insurance programs to finance substantial portions of the hospital and physician expenses incurred by Americans over the age of 65. The bill-signing ceremony in Missouri was attended by hundreds of government officials, health leaders, and private citizens, many of whom had participated in the long, bitter fight for social security health insurance during the administrations of Presidents Roosevelt, Truman, Eisenhower, Kennedy, and Johnson. That afternoon, Johnson reviewed the two decades which had culminated in the Medicare legislation, and observed that the surprising thing was not "the passage of this bill . . . but that it took so many years to pass it."

President Johnson's remark underscored the obvious fact that good health, like peace and prosperity, is a laudable goal, widely shared by Americans. Yet the president was too astute a practitioner of politics to be really surprised by the delay in devising an acceptable federal health insurance program. Public attempts to improve

3

American health standards typically have precipitated bitter debate, even as the issue has shifted from the professional and legal status of physicians to the availability of hospital care, from quackery among doctors and druggists to providing public health programs. The beginning of the American Medical Association itself (1847) was part of the broader effort to define the legitimate medical practitioner and to raise the educational standards expected of him. Later in the nineteenth century, licensing of physicians by the states and the regulation of drugs were fought for by the AMA. Hospital care, once almost exclusively supported by private institutions, became politically controversial once general hospitals grew with the support of local tax funds. Sanitation measures, disease control through mass inoculation, state regulation of hospitals—all commanded increasing public attention as Americans left the countryside to congregate in large urban centers after the Civil War.

It was not until the twentieth century, however, that medical care problems, always of concern to local government, generated interest in national politics. That interest, particularly after World War II, focused on three features of the American system of medical care: medical research, hospital construction, and federal health insurance programs. Since 1945, the federal government has massively increased its support of medical research (primarily through the National Institutes of Health), and, under the Hill-Burton Act of 1946, has subsidized a significant portion of the nation's postwar hospital construction. By 1960, federal, state, and local governments together expended almost $7 billion of the $29 billion Americans spent in that year for health services. "In few fields," concluded the *Congressional Quarterly*, "were there more new federal programs established in the postwar era, or more significant changes made, than in health."

Americans have been no less concerned about expanding the federal government's role in providing health insurance, but in this controversial area postwar government action has not paralleled the rapid expansion of support for research and hospital facilities. This inaction has persisted despite public sentiment to the contrary. Opinion surveys from 1943 to 1965 have shown a relatively stable two-thirds majority of Americans favoring government assistance in the financing of personal health services.

Courtesy of Scott Long and the *Minneapolis Tribune*, 1965

"The operation is a failure! . . .
The patient is going to live!"

The legislative activity of the United States Congress, however, is never simply a matter of ratifying public opinion polls. For controversial legislation to be enacted, the public must be sufficiently organized to make its views felt. Beyond that, the support of executive agencies is normally required in framing complex legislative proposals. Bills must have sponsors and floor managers in both houses of the Congress, and they must pass through a maze of obstacles: committee hearings, placement on the agenda by the House Rules Committee, votes in both houses, and, if successfully passed, a conference committee in which differences between House and Senate versions are ironed out. It was not until 1965 that a health insurance bill for the aged emerged from the congressional maze to become public law. Understanding how that bill became law enables us to recognize some of the typical patterns by which divisive public issues run the obstacle course in American politics from initial demands to statutory enactment.

Twentieth Century Medicine: The Paradoxes of Progress

By the close of the first decade in this century, medical science had reached, in the words of a distinguished Harvard professor, a "Great Divide" when "for the first time in human history, a random patient with a random disease consulting a doctor chosen at random stands a better than 50/50 chance of benefiting from the encounter."* Subsequent developments have fully borne out this prediction of remarkable advances in medical science, technology, and therapy. One by one, dread diseases—tuberculosis, cholera, diphtheria, pneumonia, smallpox, polio—have been controlled. Surgical and drug therapy have dramatically reduced the impact of diseases and maladies unconquered by preventive medicine. These changes, along with substantial improvements in the general American standard of living, have not resulted in diminished morbidity (illness), but have startlingly altered mortality rates. The newborn child in 1900 had a life expectancy of 47 years; by 1950 the average was 70 years. In what Herman and Anne Somers have called the "paradox of medical progress," however,

---

*Professor Lawrence Henderson, cited in Richard Harris, *A Sacred Trust* (New York: New American Library, 1966), p. 5.

"as we preserve life at all age levels, there is more illness, more enduring disability, for the population as a whole."[*]

The demand for medical care has increased both through improved capacity and heightened expectations among longer-living populations. Changes in the organization of medical care have accompanied the rapid increase in utilization. Since 1930, the average number of patient visits to the doctor has more than doubled, increasing from 2.6 to 5.3 visits per year. The type of doctors Americans visit also has changed: whereas in 1930, two-thirds of American physicians were general practitioners, two-thirds were specialists three decades later.[†] The focus of medical activity has shifted to the hospital, and the costs of those activities have steadily increased. Between 1953 and 1963, expenditures for health services more than doubled. The price of hospital beds rose 90 per cent while physicians' fees increased 37 per cent. The mean expenditure of American families for medical care during this decade grew by 70 per cent. Figures on mean expenditures fail to show, however, the uneven distribution of illness throughout the society, and its financial implications. In fact, a recent study concluded, people with illness "requiring hospitalization account for one-half of all private expenditures, but amount to only 8 per cent of the population."[**]

The combination of increased medical competence, heightened consumer expectations and utilization, and rising costs have shaped the environment for public policy demands. But these experiences, common to western industrial countries, have not predetermined either the proposals for government action or their fate. Bismarck's Germany initiated health insurance for industrial workers as early as 1883; in 1911, England incorporated health insurance for low-income workers into a social security program providing pensions, unemployment compensation, and sickness benefits. By 1940, no western European country was without a government health insurance program for at least its low-income workers, though there were substantial differences in beneficiaries, benefits, and financing mechanisms. The enactment of Medicare in 1965 illustrated Amer-

[*]Herman and Anne Somers, *Doctors, Patients, and Health Insurance* (New York: Doubleday & Co., 1962).

[†]United States Department of Health, Education and Welfare, *Health Manpower Source Book* (Washington, D.C., 1960), Section 9, p. 27.

[**]Ronald Anderson and Odin W. Anderson, *A Decade of Health Services* (Chicago: University of Chicago Press, 1967), pp. 122ff.

ica's late entry into compulsory health insurance, and its restriction to the aged alone was quite unlike the patterns established in other industrial countries.

Origins of the Government Health Insurance Issue

Demands in America for government involvement in health insurance date back to the first decade of the twentieth century. The impetus in these early efforts came from academics, lawyers, and other professionals, organized in the American Association for Labor Legislation. During the years 1915–1918, this group made a concerted effort to shepherd its model medical care insurance bill through several state legislatures, but with no success. The American Medical Association, whose officials had initially co-operated with the AALL, found local medical societies adamantly opposed to the state health insurance bills, and in 1920 the AMA House of Delegates announced

its opposition to the institution of any plan embodying the system of compulsory contributory insurance against illness, or any other plan of compulsory insurance which provides for medical service to be rendered contributors or their dependents, provided, controlled, or regulated by any state or federal government.[*]

Even more disappointing to the labor reformers was the unequivocal opposition of Samuel Gompers, the president of the American Federation of Labor, to the model bills. The strength of the opposition prevented America from following England's example of insuring low-income workers against illness. During the 1920's, a variety of groups undertook studies of health care financing in the United States, and attention turned to the feasibility of group medical practice and of prepayment medical plans. But it was not until the Great Depression began, in an atmosphere of general concern for economic insecurity, that a sustained interest in government health insurance reappeared. The evolution of the 1965 Med-

[*]Odin W. Anderson, "Compulsory Medical Care Insurance, 1910–1950," *The Annals of the American Academy of Political and Social Science*, CCLXXIII (January, 1951), 106–113. Reprinted in Eugene Feingold (ed.), *Medicare: Policy and Politics* (San Francisco: Chandler Publishing, 1966), p. 89.

icare Act reaches back to this New Deal period. To understand the particular form of the Medicare legislation, and to explain the two decades of controversy and delay at which President Johnson expressed surprise, one must begin the story here.

The source of renewed interest in government health insurance was President Roosevelt's advisory Committee on Economic Security, created in 1934 to draft a social security bill providing a minimum income for the aged, the unemployed, the blind, and the widowed and their children. The result was the Social Security bill of 1935, which, in addition to providing for insurance against potential loss of income, broached the subject of a government health insurance program. Edwin Witte, a former professor of economics at the University of Wisconsin who was executive director of the committee, described the extent of the committee's involvement with health insurance and the response:

When in 1934 the Committee on Economic Security announced that it was studying health insurance, it was at once subjected to misrepresentation and vilification. In the original social security bill there was one line to the effect that the Social Security Board should study the problem and make a report to Congress. That little line was responsible for so many telegrams to the members of Congress that the entire social security program seemed endangered until the Ways and Means Committee unanimously struck it out of the bill.[*]

Roosevelt's fears that the controversial issue of government health insurance would jeopardize the Social Security bill and, later, his chances for re-election, kept him from vigorously sponsoring the proposal. For many of his advisors in the Committee on Economic Security, however, the discussions in Washington in the mid-thirties marked the beginning of an active interest in the subject. The divorce of compulsory health insurance from the original Social Security program of 1935 had alerted the critics within the medical world to the possibility of attempts to enlarge the partial government program to "get a foot-in-the-door for socialized medicine." In response they reversed their former opposition to private health insurance alternatives; in an effort to forestall federal action, the AMA began to promote Blue Cross and commercial hospital insurance, and, in the case of state Blue Shield plans, actively to

[*]Ibid., footnote 6, p. 90.

organize private insurance plans for surgical and medical expenses. In the meantime, passage of the Social Security Act had freed advocates of compulsory health insurance from their concerns about providing income protection for the aged, the blind, and dependent women and children. Their attention was now directed to the broad social question of how equitably medical care was distributed in post-Depression America. From 1939 onward, their activities were reflected in the annual introduction of congressional bills proposing compulsory health insurance for the entire population. An orphan of the New Deal, government medical care insurance was to become one of the most prominent aspirations of Harry Truman's "Fair Deal."

Universal Health Insurance Proposals in the Fair Deal

Although the government health insurance issue was originally raised in conjunction with social security income protection, New Deal-Fair Deal champions of medical care proposals did not view it primarily as a measure to further income security but as a remedy for the inequitable distribution of medical services. The proponents of Truman's compulsory insurance program took for granted that financial means should not determine the quality and quantity of medical services a citizen received. "Access to the means of attainment and preservation of health," flatly stated the 1952 report of Truman's Commission on the Health Needs of the Nation, "is a basic human right." The health insurance problem in this view was the degree to which the use of health services varied with income (and not simply illness). In contrast, for those who considered minimum accessibility of health services a standard of adequacy, the provision of charity medicine in doctors' offices and general hospitals represented a solution, and the problem was to fill in where present charity care was unavailable.

The Truman solution to the problem of unequal accessibility to health services was to remove the financial barriers to care through government action. As set forth in his State of the Union message in 1948, his goal was "to enact a comprehensive insurance system which would remove the money barrier between illness and therapy ... [and thus] protect all our people equally ... against ill health." Bills embracing such goals had been introduced as early as 1935, but the first to receive widespread public attention was S. 1620, introduced by Senator Robert Wagner (D., N.Y.) in 1939. A decade later, in Truman's term, it was S. 1679 which Senator Wagner, Senator Murray (D., Mont.) and Representative Dingell (D., Mich.) presented for congressional consideration. By 1949, the introduction of a Wagner-Murray-Dingell bill had become an annual event which was invariably followed by congressional refusal to hold hearings on the bill.

Throughout the decade, public opinion polls continued to report favorable reactions to federal involvement in health insurance. However, although from 1939 to 1946 the Democrats controlled both houses of Congress, the partisan majority did not make up an issue majority. There were too few legislative supporters to bring the repeatedly introduced bills through the stages of committee hearings, committee approval, and congressional passage. By 1945, officials within the Federal Security Agency* had secured presidential endorsement of the Wagner-Murray-Dingell proposal, but the advantage of Truman's support was offset by the congressional elections the following year, which returned Republican majorities in both the House and the Senate. This Congress, it has been observed, "was generally at loggerheads with Truman in domestic affairs," and in the campaign of 1948, the President used its inaction, on health insurance and other domestic issues, to berate the "do-nothing Republican 80th Congress." The election of 1948, returning the presidency to Truman and control of the Congress to the Democrats, left Truman and his advisors with high hopes for enactment of the domestic proposals that had highlighted his "Fair Deal" campaign against Dewey.†

Early in 1949, in keeping with his recent campaign pledges, the president requested congressional action on medical care insurance. The specifications of the proposal repeated those of previous Wagner-Murray-Dingell bills:

the insurance benefits would cover all medical, dental, hospital and nursing care expenses.

---

*The three key officials—Arthur Altmeyer, Wilbur Cohen, and I. S. Falk— worked for the Social Security Board, a division of the Federal Security Agency. The FSA, created in 1939 to oversee the Board, the Public Health Service, and the Office of Education, was in 1953 replaced by the Cabinet-rank Department of Health, Education and Welfare.

†*Congress and the Nation, 1945–1964* (Washington, D.C.: Congressional Quarterly Service, 1965), pp. 4, 7.

beneficiaries would include all contributors to the plan and their dependents, and for the medical needs of a destitute minority which would not be reached by the contributory plan, provisions were made for federal grants to the states.

the financing mechanism would be a compulsory 3 per cent payroll tax divided equally between employee and employer.

administration would be in the hands of a national health insurance board within the Federal Security Agency.

to minimize the degree of federal control over doctors and patients, it was specified that doctors and hospitals would be free not to join the plan; patients would be free to choose their own doctors and doctors would reserve the right to reject patients whom they did not want; doctors who agreed to treat patients under the plan would be paid for their services by the national health board, and the question of whether they would be paid on a stated-fee, per capita, or salary basis would be left to the majority decision of the participating practitioners in each health service area.

The bill's reception in the 81st Congress was bitterly disappointing to the Truman administration. Although the Democrats had gained 75 seats in the House, a coalition of anti-Truman southern Democrats and Republicans blocked most of Truman's major domestic proposals. Despite some success in housing and social security legislation, the federal aid to education bill floundered, and the administration's health insurance plan was not reported out of committee in either house.

The Democrats had their House majority reduced from 263–171 to 235–199 in the elections of 1950, and barely maintained control of the Senate by a margin of two. Attempts to leave doctors' participation in the national health insurance plan voluntary had failed to placate the American Medical Association. The organization had been roused to a nationwide propaganda campaign, directed by the California public relations firm, Whitaker and Baxter, and financed by "taxing" every AMA member $25. The doctors had enlisted hundreds of voluntary organizations and pressure groups to oppose compulsory health insurance, holding out horrific visions of a socialized America ruled by an autocratic federal government. Ignoring the stipulations that doctors would remain free to choose their own patients, and patients to choose their own doctors, he

AMA campaign pictured an impersonal medical world under the national health plan in which patients and doctors were forced unwillingly upon each other. In 1950, the AMA took the issue of "socialized medicine" to both the primary and general elections, and their propaganda was credited with the defeat of some of the Senate's firmest supporters of health insurance, including Claude Pepper (D., Fla.), Frank Graham (D., N.C.), Elbert Thomas (D., Utah), and Glen Taylor (D., Idaho).

Although Truman persisted in requesting compulsory health insurance in 1950, 1951, and 1952, his advisors agreed that after 1949 the prospects for such a broad program were bleak. Among those advisors were two Federal Security Agency officials, Wilbur J. Cohen and I. S. Falk,* who had had the most to do with the drafting of health insurance proposals since 1935. Recognizing the need to "resurrect health insurance" in a dramatically new and narrower form, Cohen and Falk worked out a plan that would limit health insurance to the beneficiaries of the Old Age and Survivors Insurance program. Oscar Ewing, head of the Federal Security Agency, considered this approach "terrific," and it shaped the entire strategy of health insurance advocates in the period after 1951. Thus the stage was set in early 1951 for the programs that have come to be called "Medicare." Millions of dollars spent on propaganda, the activation of a broad cleavage in American politics, the framing of choice in health insurance between socialism and "the voluntary way," the bitter, personally vindictive battle between Truman's supporters and the AMA-led opposition—these comprised the legacy of the fight over general health insurance and provided the setting for the emergence of Medicare as an issue.

The Politics of Incrementalism:
Turning Toward the Aged

Major shifts in the demands brought to the Congress seldom derive from dispassionate analysis of contemporary social

*Wilbur J. Cohen, who in 1965 was Under-Secretary of the Department of Health, Education and Welfare, became HEW Secretary in March, 1968. Cohen was a member of the staff of the original committee that drafted the Social Security Act of 1935. He was, in 1950–52, on the staff of the Social Security Board with the Federal Security Agency, as was I. S. Falk. Falk recently retired as Professor of Public Health at Yale University.

conditions. The decision to pare down President Truman's health insurance aims to a more modest hospitalization insurance program for the aged was no exception to this pattern. In 1951 and 1952 extended discussions took place among Truman's social security advisors about how to deal with congressional reluctance to enact his administration's health program. In October of 1951 presidential assistant David Stowe outlined for Truman three ways of responding to the bleak legislative prospects for general health insurance: "softpedal the general health issue; push some peripheral programs in the area but not general insurance; or appoint a study commission to go over the whole problem." Three days later Truman accepted his staff's recommendation to create a study commission and charged them with finding "the right people." But the effort to "push some peripheral programs" had already begun, with the president's passive acquiescence. In June, 1951, Oscar Ewing, acting on the suggestions of Cohen and Falk, announced a new plan to insure the 7 million aged social security beneficiaries for 60 days of hospital care a year. "It is difficult for me to see," said Ewing to an assembled corps of reporters, "how anyone with a heart can oppose this [type of program]."

Ewing, Cohen, and Falk assumed the administration could most easily build an issue majority in the Congress by narrowing previous demands and tailoring them to meet the objections of congressmen and critical pressure groups. The major objections to the Truman health program which the Medicare strategists felt they had to meet included charges that: (1) general medical insurance was a "give-away" program which made no distinction between the deserving and undeserving poor; (2) that it would substantially help too many well-off Americans who did not need financial assistance; (3) that it would swell utilization of existing medical services beyond their capacity, and (4) that general medical insurance would produce excessive federal control of physicians, and would constitute a precedent for socialism in America. In connection with the latter objection, there was the widespread fear, grounded in the bitter, hostile propaganda of the AMA, that physicians would refuse to provide services under a national health insurance program.

To meet these objections, the proponents of "peripheral programs" turned from the health problems of the general population to those of the aged. As a group, the aged could be presumed to be both needy and deserving because, through no fault of their own, they had lower earning capacity and higher medical expenses than any other adult age group. Since the proponents wished to avoid imposition of a means test to determine eligibility within the ranks of the aged, they limited the beneficiaries to those persons over 65 (and their spouses) who had contributed to the social security program during their working life. As an additional advance concession to spike the guns of those opponents who could be counted on to assault the program as a "give-away," benefits were limited to 60 days of hospital care. Finally, physician services were excluded entirely from the plan in hopes of softening the hostility of the medical profession. What had begun in the 1930's as a movement to redistribute medical services for the entire population turned into a proposal to help defray some of the hospital costs of social security beneficiaries only.

The Appeal of Focusing on the Aged

The selection of the aged as the problem group is easily comprehensible in the context of American politics, however distinctive it appears in comparative perspective. No industrial country in the world has begun its government health insurance program with the aged. The typical pattern has been the initial coverage of low-income workers, with subsequent extensions to dependents and then to higher-income groups. Insuring low-income workers, however, involves use of means tests, and the cardinal assumption of social security advocates in America has been that the stigma of such tests must be avoided. In having to avoid both general insurance and the humiliating means test, the Federal Security Agency strategists were left with finding a socio-economic group whose average member could be presumed to be in need. The aged passed this test easily; everyone intuitively knew the aged were worse off. Cohen was later to say that the subsequent massing of statistical data to prove the aged were sicker, poorer, and less insured than other adult groups was like using a steamroller to crush an ant of opposition.

Everyone also knew that the aged—like children and the disabled —commanded public sympathy. They were one of the few population groupings about whom one could not say the members should take care of their financial-medical problems by earning and saving more money. The American social security system makes unemployment (except for limited part-time work) a condition for the receipt of pensions, and a fixed retirement age is widely accepted as desirable public policy. In addition, the postwar growth in private health insurance was uneven, with lower proportions of the aged covered, and the extent of their insurance protection more limited than that enjoyed by the working population. Only the most contorted reasoning could blame the aged for this condition by attributing their insurance status to improvidence. Retirement forces many workers to give up work-related group insurance, and the aged cannot easily shift to individual policies because, as a high-risk group, insurance companies are reluctant to cover them, except at high premium rates. The aged thus were subject to inadequate private coverage at a time when their medical requirements were greatest and their financial resources were lowest. Under these circumstances many of the aged fell back upon their children for financial assistance, thus giving the Medicare emphasis upon the aged additional political appeal. The strategists expected support from families burdened by the requirement, moral or legal, to assume the medical debts of their aged relatives.

The same strategy of seeking broad public agreement was evident in the benefits and financial arrangements chosen. The 1951 selection of hospitalization benefits reflected the search for a narrower and less disputable "problem" than Truman's 1949 proposals. General health insurance was a means for solving the problem of the unequal distribution of medical care services; its aim was to make health care more equally accessible by removing all financial barriers to utilizing those services, an aim broadly similar to that of the British National Health Service. In contrast, a program of hospital insurance identifies the aged's problem not as the inaccessibility of health services, but as *the financial consequences of using those services*. The hospital benefit was designed not so much to cope with the health problems of the elderly as to reduce their most onerous financial difficulties. Medicare proponents were well aware that this shift in emphasis left gaping inadequacies when compared with earlier insurance proposals; but in the political context of the early 1950's they took for granted that broader conceptions of the aged's health problems were less likely to receive legislative backing.

The differences between making health services more accessible and coping with the financial consequences of medical utilization were continually revealed in the next fifteen years. The statistical profiles of the aged—first provided by the Truman health commission of 1952—uniformly supported the popular conception of the aged American as sicker, poorer, and less insured than his compatriots. For example, in 1958, the median income of families whose head was 64 or younger was $5,455, and over 75 per cent of this age category had some form of sickness insurance. By contrast, the median income of families whose head was 65 or older was $2,666; roughly half had some form of health insurance, but it was usually expensive and limited. One national survey of hospital patients found that insurance did not meet more than one-fourteenth of the total cost for all the aged, their incidence of illness, chronic disabilities, and hospitalization was twice that of younger age groups, and their average yearly medical expenses were twice as high. There could be no question that the aged faced the most serious problems coping with health expenses, though it was easy to point out that averages conceal the variation in illness, income, and insurance coverage *among* the aged.

For those who saw Medicare as prevention against financial catastrophe, the vital question was not what health care the aged could buy with their limited income, but which bills were the largest for any spell of illness. The ready answer was hospital care. One in six aged persons enters a hospital in a given year, and his total medical costs are four to five times those incurred by the non-hospitalized. Hospitalization insurance was, according to this information, a necessity which the aged had to have to avoid financial catastrophe. It should be pointed out, however, that by limiting the insurance coverage to 60 days and excluding custodial nursing home care altogether, the Medicare protection against catastrophic medical bills was incomplete. Ewing and his advisors were aware of the gap between the problem and the proposed remedy, but they feared that unlimited coverage would inflate the estimated costs of the program to a point where the price tag would become a major political liability.

The concentration on the burdens of the aged was a ploy for

sympathy. The disavowal of aims to change fundamentally the American medical system was a sop to AMA fears, and the exclusion of physician services benefits was a response to past AMA hysteria. The focus on the financial burdens of receiving hospital care took as given the existing structure of the private medical care world, and stressed the issue of spreading the costs of using available services within that world. The organization of health care, with its inefficiencies and resistance to cost reduction, was a fundamental but politically sensitive problem which consensus-minded reformers wanted to avoid when they opted for 60 days of hospitalization insurance for the aged in 1952 as a promising "small" beginning.

Focusing on Social Security Contributors

The financing of the Truman health program had deliberately been left vague by its backers; the Wagner-Murray-Dingell bill of 1949 mentioned a 3 per cent payroll tax, equally divided between worker and employer, and administered by a new division within the Federal Security Agency. In the 1951 promotion of a Medicare program, the financing of hospital insurance was to be through the already established Old Age and Survivors Insurance system (OASI), enacted as part of the Social Security package in 1935. The use of social security funding was an obvious effort to tap the widespread legitimacy which OASI programs enjoyed among all classes of Americans. Yet social security financing would in 1952 have restricted Medicare benefits to seven million pensioners out of the twelve and one-half million persons over 65, thus overlooking five and one-half million aged whose medical and financial circumstances had been used to establish the "need" for a Medicare program in the first place. Nonetheless, social security financing offered so many other advantages that its advocates were prepared to live with this incomplete coverage.

The notion that social security recipients pay for their benefits is one traditional American response to the charge that government assistance programs are "give-aways" which undermine the willingness of individuals to save and take care of their own problems. The Ewing group thought they had to squash that charge if they were both to gain mass public support and to shield the aged from the indignity of a means test. The contributory requirement of social security—the limitation of benefits to those having paid social security taxes—gives the system a resemblance to private insurance. Thus, social security members would appear to have paid for hospital insurance. In fact, social security beneficiaries are entitled to pensions exceeding those which, in a strict actuarial sense, they have "earned" through contributions. But this is a point generally lost in the avalanche of words about how contributions, as a commissioner of Social Security, Robert Ball, remarked, "give American workers the *feeling* they have earned their benefits." The notion that contributions confer rights analogous to those which premiums entail within private insurance was one which deeply permeated the advocacy of Medicare.

The public legitimacy granted the social security program made it an ideal mechanism for avoiding the stigma attached to most public welfare programs. The distinction between public assistance for the poor and social security rights for contributors is, in fact, less clear in law than might be expected. Rights are prescriptions specified in law, and welfare legislation—for any class of persons—confers rights in this sense. But those who insist on the distinction between public assistance and social security focus less on the legal basis of rights than on the different ways in which these programs are viewed and administered. Social security manuals insist on treating beneficiaries as "claimants," and stress that the government "owes" claimants their benefits. The stereotype of welfare is comprised of legacies from charity and the notorious Poor Laws, a combination of unappealing associations connected with intrusive investigation of need, invasion of privacy, and loss of citizenship rights. The unfavorable stereotype of welfare programs thus supports the contention that social security funds are the proper financing instrument for providing benefits while safeguarding self-respect.

Ewing and his aides were concerned about securing the support of governmental elites as well as the support of interest groups and the electorate. They proposed social security financing partly because of the political advantages it offered a president sympathetic to health insurance, but also concerned about levels of administrative spending. Social security programs are financed out of separate trust funds that are not categorized as executive expenditures; the billions of dollars spent by the Social Security

Administration each year are not included in the annual budget the president presents to Congress, a political advantage not likely to be lost on Democratic presidents worried about the perennial charge of reckless federal spending. (After 1967, SSA expenditures were included in the executive budget.)

These structural features of the politics of social welfare in America largely account for the type of "incremental" health insurance strategy adopted at the end of the Truman administration. They help explain why the postwar Truman plans of comprehensive government health insurance gave way to a proposal to help defray some of the hospital costs of Americans over 65 who participated in the social security system. The strategy of the incrementalists after 1952 was consensus-mongering: the identification of less disputed problems and the advocacy of modest solutions which ideological conservatives would have difficulty in attacking. "In the beginning," recalled Wilbur Cohen, one of the co-authors of the first Medicare bill, "we looked at [its introduction in 1952] as a small way of starting something big."*

Pressure Groups and Medicare: The Lobbying of Millions

Serious congressional interest in special health insurance programs for the aged developed in 1958, six years after the initial Medicare proposal. From 1958 to 1965, the Committee on Ways and Means held annual hearings, which became a battleground for hundreds of pressure groups. The same intemperate debate of the Truman years (and often the same debaters) reappeared. The acrimonious discussion of the problems, prospects, and desires of the aged illustrated a lesson of the Truman period: the federal government's role in the financing of personal health services is one of the small class of public issues which can be counted on to activate deep, emotional, and bitter cleavages between what political commentators call "liberal" and "conservative" pressure groups. In the press, commentators felt compelled to write blow-by-blow descriptions of pressure group harangues and congressional responses. Within the Congress, clusters of Republicans and conservative southern Democrats allied to oppose "government

*Quoted in Richard Harris, *A Sacred Trust* (New York: New American Library, 1966), p. 55.

medicine" and to declare war against this "entering wedge of the socialized state." The president of the AMA captured the mood of Medicare's critics in testifying before the Ways and Means Committee in 1963; hospital insurance for the aged, he said, was "not only unnecessary, but also dangerous to the basic principles underlying our American system of medical care."

For all the important differences in scope and content between the Truman general health program and the Medicare proposals, the lineup of proponents and opponents was strikingly similar. Among the supporters organized labor was the most powerful source of pressure. The AMA sparked the opposition and framed its objections in such a way that disparate groups only tenuously involved with medical care or the aged could rally around their leadership. A small sample, representing a fraction of the groups involved in the lobbying, illustrates the continuity between the broad economic and ideological divisions of the Truman fight and that over health insurance for the aged:*

For	*Against*
AFL-CIO	American Medical Association
American Nurses Association	American Hospital Association
Council of Jewish Federations & Welfare Funds	Life Insurance Association of America
American Association of Retired Workers	National Association of Manufacturers
National Association of Social Workers	National Association of Blue Shield Plans
National Farmers Union	American Farm Bureau Federation
The Socialist Party	The Chamber of Commerce
American Geriatrics Society	The American Legion

Three features of this pressure group alignment merit mention. First, the adversaries who are "liberal" and "conservative" on that issue are similarly aligned on other controversial social policies, e.g., federal aid to education and disability insurance. Second, the extreme ideological polarization promoted by these groups has remained markedly stable despite significant changes in the actual objects in dispute, such as the much narrower scope of health

*Health Services for the Aged Under the Social Security Insurance System (H.R. 4222), Hearings Before the Committee on Ways and Means, House of Representatives, 87th Congress, 1st Session, July–August, 1961.

insurance proposals since 1952. Proposals for incremental change in a disputed social policy typically fail to avoid disagreement about "first principles." Finally, public dispute continued to be dominated by the AFL-CIO and the AMA, lobbying organizations capable of expending millions in the effort to shape the scope of debate and to influence legislative results. Since the 1940's these two chief adversaries have engaged in what *The New York Times* characterized as a "slugging match," a contest of invectives. Aaron Wildavsky's description of the conflict between public and private power advocates in America is just as apt for the contestants over Medicare:

[They] have little use for one another. They distrust each other's motives; they question each other's integrity; they doubt each other's devotion to the national good. Each side expects the other to play dirty, and each can produce substantiating evidence from the long history of their dispute.*

The AMA is an organization with conflicting roles. As a type of trade union, it is committed to improving the status of physicians. As a scientific organization, the AMA sponsors research and regulates medical practice to improve the quality of health care available to American consumers. As a pressure group, the AMA has fused these roles, linking, and, to some extent, confusing the issues on which physicians speak as scientific authorities and as self-interested professionals. Seeking to convince the American public that physicians are the sole proper authority to determine the organization, financing, and regulation of medical care practice, the AMA has framed the Medicare dispute so that proponents of federal action would meet the widest range of ideological objections. They have rallied groups against Medicare behind the slogans of freedom of choice, individualism, distaste for bureaucracy, hatred of the welfare state, collectivism, and higher taxes. Under such banners have trooped organizations distantly related to health insurance legislation: professional organizations, business and fraternal groups, farm organizations, and various right-wing protest groups.

The confusion of roles in the AMA has adversely affected the credibility of either role. Physicians enjoy both high status and high income (more than $34,000 median income after expenses in 1964), and the image of the tireless and selfless practitioner has

---

*Aaron Wildavsky, *Dixon-Yates: A Study in Power Politics* (New Haven: Yale University Press, 1962), pp. 5–6.

enhanced the authority of medical organizations in public discourse. Yet recent trends, accompanying the lobbying activities of the AMA, have weakened the claims of medical doctors to disinterested community leadership. Increased specialization (and with that the gradual disappearance of the general practitioner), rising fees, the greater impersonality of medical practice in the modern hospital setting—all have increased public dissatisfaction with physicians. The persistent AMA involvement with public policy issues since World War II has increased the risks that an image of the rich and greedy physician will replace that of the noble general practitioner and thus undermine the widely accepted role of the AMA (and its local affiliates) as controllers of medical practice. In these areas, organizations like the AFL-CIO feel less tension; their straightforward championing of the interest of wage-earners means that opponents have little opportunity to dwell upon the gap between the pronouncements of selflessness and the practice of self-interested maneuvering.

Both the AFL-CIO and the AMA have the membership, resources, and experience to engage in multi-million dollar lobbying. Their members are sufficiently spread geographically to make congressional electioneering and pressure relatively easy to organize. In 1965, the AMA had 159,000 dues-paying members, and expended a budget of approximately $23 million. The AFL-CIO's 129 affiliated unions represented in the mid-1960's over thirteen million workers. Lobbying—personal contact between organization officials and members of the government*—keeps substantial full-time staffs of each busy in Washington, but the largest organizational expenditures are for what is euphemistically called "public education." In 1965, the AMA lobbyists spent just under $1 million, of which $830,000 went for the newspaper, radio, and television campaign against the Medicare bill. Both organizations control legally separate political bodies that try to influence elections and mobilize members for political action. The AFL-CIO's Committee on Political Education (COPE) and the AMA's Political Action Committee

*This restrictive definition of lobbying accounts for the discrepancy between what pressure groups report as lobbying expenses and the larger amount they actually spend in all their efforts to influence public policy. United States law (the Federal Regulation of Lobbying Act, 1946) defines lobbying as "personal contact between interested parties and government officials," and requires only that sums expended for that purpose be reported. Hence the large expenditures for propaganda in the mass media go officially unrecorded.

(AMPAC) are financed by voluntary contributions, and most of their funds are used in election campaigns. In 1964, COPE made campaign contributions of almost $1 million.

During the debates of the 1940's and early 1950's, the AMA and its allies in big business and big agriculture tellingly focused the debate on the evils of collectivism and socialized medicine. The narrowing of health insurance proposals from universal coverage to the aged, however, set new constraints on the anti-Medicare campaigns. The aged themselves began to organize into such pressure groups as the Senior Citizens Councils and the Golden Ring Clubs. Although the financial and membership resources of these groups were slim compared to the better organized lobbies, the AMA could hardly afford to engage in open warfare with them as it had with the powerful AFL-CIO. AMA reiteration of stock ideological objections to Medicare would run the risk of the AMA being labeled the enemy of America's senior citizens. One effect was the appearance of a conservative willingness to offer alternatives, which in turn helped shape congressional responses, especially in the early 1960's.

Medicare Under a Republican President: The Politics of Legislative Impossibility

At no time during the Eisenhower administrations (1953–60) did the Medicare bills have a chance of congressional enactment. Hospital insurance for the aged lacked the political sponsorship required to transmute controversial proposals into law. President Eisenhower had campaigned in 1952 against "socialized medicine," by which he meant both the Truman health plan and the more modest proposals for the aged. In addition, members of the tax committees responsible for social security bills (Ways and Means in the House, the Finance Committee in the Senate) were in the main uninterested or hostile. Among congressmen generally there was not an intensely committed majority disposed to force those committees to report health insurance legislation. Even when the Democrats regained control of the Congress in 1954, the partisan majority did not comprise a favorable Medicare majority. In fact, the legislative prospects were so slight that no committee hearings were held until 1958.

Despite the decline of Medicare as a legislative issue under Eisenhower, a group of men who had played important roles in the Truman health insurance efforts pursued their strategy of gradualism. Annually from 1952 to 1960 modest Medicare bills were introduced in the Congress, not with any hopes for enactment, but simply to keep alive the idea of health insurance under social security. At the same time, these promoters turned their energies toward other social insurance reforms. Wilbur Cohen, director of research for the Social Security Administration until 1956, actively campaigned for disability insurance covering workers over the age of 50. He did so on the assumption that by slowly expanding the number of impoverishing conditions insured against by social security, the risk of catastrophic health expenses would be left as the obvious major omission within the social insurance program requiring remedial legislation.

Once disability insurance was enacted in 1956, the strategists of gradualism concentrated once more on Medicare. The four most active members of this group included Cohen, in 1956 about to become a professor of welfare administration at the University of Michigan; I. S. Falk, then a consultant to the United Mine Workers; Nelson Cruikshank, head of the AFL-CIO's Department of Social Security; and Robert Ball, a highly respected career official in the Social Security Administration. They sought to prompt congressional interest in Medicare by persuading a well-placed congressman to sponsor the bill, and to elicit wide public concern about the health and finances of the aged through an AFL-CIO propaganda campaign. They were successful in both efforts.

Although the three most senior members of the Ways and Means Committee rebuffed the Cohen group's entreaties to sponsor its bill, the fourth-ranking Democrat, Aime Forand, from Rhode Island, responded. In 1958, hearings were held on the Forand bill. Organized labor, which through most of the early 1950's had concentrated on securing health insurance for its members through collective bargaining, whipped up a campaign for Medicare in anticipation of the Forand hearings. The holding of hearings prompted the AMA into action as well; it raised its 1958 lobbying budget fivefold, and spent a quarter of a million dollars criticizing the Forand bill. The propaganda battle of the 1940's resumed, with each side matching the other in press releases, speeches, pamphlets, and harangues. Since the hassle inevitably directed public attention toward health insurance for the aged, Congressman Forand was accurate when he facetiously expressed his indebtedness to the "American Medical Association for publicizing my bill so well." Nonetheless, in 1959 the Ways and Means Committee rejected the proposal by a decisive 17–8 vote.

The Forand Bill vs. the Welfare Approach

The debate over the Forand bill revealed a pattern of disagreement which would continue to limit the alternatives facing the Congress. Both the problems defined as warranting public action and the type of proffered solution remained relatively stable from the time of Medicare's first introduction in 1952. The information gathered on illness, income, insurance status, and health care utilization almost invariably fell into the simple categories of the aged and the non-aged. When Forand's critics attacked his bill, they, too, shared the common focus of attention on the aged. Their argument from the Truman days that all Americans are not equally poor enough to warrant compulsory government health insurance turned into the argument that not all the aged are poor. That there were substantial health and financial problems among the aged was no longer disputed by the late 1950's. But the extent of those problems among the aged, and the means of remedy, remained the controversial subjects provoking polarized positions.

The disagreement over the merits of the Forand bill illustrated the persistent divergent approaches to problems of social welfare in American politics. One, the so-called social insurance approach, seeks partial solutions to commonly recognized problems through a financing mechanism that is regressive in character. That is, equal rates of taxes are paid by all contributors irrespective of level of income, with the result that lower-income persons pay a larger proportion of their income in social security taxes than do higher-paid workers. It selects beneficiaries not through tests of destitution, but by tests of presumptive need: the orphaned, the widowed, the disabled, and the aged are *presumed* to be in need of assistance. Contribution to the social security system thus entails automatic payments of benefits to all those who fall into recognized circumstances of risk, regardless of income.

The alternative approach is that of private and public charity, based on the assumption that most members of a society protect themselves against unfortunate contingencies through savings and insurance. The remaining needs are those of the improvident, the impoverished, and the unlucky, for which the appropriate remedies are private charity, or failing that, local, state, and sometimes, federal "charity" programs. Levels of payments under these programs are determined individually, by measuring the gap between the financial resources and the needs of the beneficiary. And the means of financing the benefits are either, in the case of private charity, the largesse of the successful, or, in the case of government welfare programs, the general revenues of the federal treasury and/or state funds. General revenue funding in principle provides a more progressive tax base than that of social security in that, under general revenue taxing procedures, the higher the income the higher the tax that is levied. The social security approach relies upon federal action; the welfare view is that the resort to federal action is the least desirable alternative.

This ideological division revealed itself in the Forand controversy on a variety of issues, but particularly over the questions of who needed help, what aid the needy required, and which financing and administrative mechanisms were most appropriate to the remedy.

1. *On the question of who needed help*, the Forand bill specified all the aged participating in the social security system, irrespective of their present income. Statistical profiles of the aged which were mustered in support of social security coverage emphasized

the high proportion of low-income persons among the aged (United States Census data indicated that in 1958, about three-fifths of persons aged 65 and over had less than $1,000 in money income, while another one-fifth received $1,000–$2,000).

the greater incidence of illness among the aged (one indication was the National Health Survey finding that the aged received approximately twice as much hospitalization as those under 65).

the inadequacy of private insurance coverage in meeting the needs of the elderly (Social Security administrators claimed that 53.9 per cent of the non-institutionalized aged were without any form of hospital insurance in 1959, although it was admitted that coverage among this high-risk group was increasing. Forand backers, however, stressed the shortcomings of private insurance in meeting the total medical costs of the policy holders).

The critics frequently contested these and similar statistics on the aged, but their main theme was the numbers of aged who enjoyed good health, secure incomes, and private health insurance policies. Conceding that widespread health and financial problems did exist amongst the elderly, advocates of a welfare approach argued that the Forand bill did not address itself exclusively or effectively to those "who really need help," the very poor among the aged.

2. *The problem to which Forand directed attention* was the catastrophic effects of large hospital and surgical bills; hence his benefits were limited to those expenses associated with expensive hospitalization and in-hospital doctor's care. Welfare approach opponents emphasized the inadequacy of surgical-hospital insurance for those whose means had been exhausted and who required out-patient care and drugs. They stressed the need for comprehensive benefits for those aged who could not deal with health expenses through savings, private insurance, medical charity, or state and local assistance.

3. *On the question of administration and financing,* the Forand bill called for a federal program financed by social security taxes, emphasizing the contributory nature of OASI and the desirability of not forcing the elderly to submit to the humiliation of a means test. Many conservative critics, who conceded that federal funds might be necessary to assist the indigent aged, nonetheless argued that expansion of federal power was undesirable. A more palatable alternative, to their way of thinking, was to share the financing of any medical assistance program with the states, reserving to the latter the role of administration and of setting standards according to local needs.

The irony of the dispute should now be evident. The social security approach advocated by most liberals in Congress had several features which appeared less generous than the alternatives suggested by conservative proponents of the welfare method. What led liberals to support the Forand bill was a skepticism that a means-tested, state-administered assistance program would actually be generously implemented. The table below illustrates the major differences in approach:

	Forand social security approach	*Welfare approach*
Beneficiaries:	The aged who were covered under social security	Persons over 65 whose resources were insufficient to meet their medical expenses
Benefits:	Hospitalization, nursing home, and in-hospital surgical insurance (Medicare bills introduced after 1959 excluded surgical insurance)	Comprehensive benefits for physicians' services, dental care, hospitalization, prescribed drugs, and nursing home care
Source of financing:	Social security taxes	Federal income tax revenues, plus state matching funds
Administration and setting of standards:	Uniform national standards administered by the Social Security Administration	Standards varying by state, administered by state and local officials

The Kerr-Mills Bill of 1960

The welfare perspective on the health and financial problems was reflected in three stages. An initial skepticism about the extent of the crisis among the aged subsequently gave way to hope that the substantial health costs of the aged could be coped with by the private insurance industry. Finally, there was the acceptance of the need for federal action. The Kerr-Mills bill of 1960 reflected the conception of appropriate federal responses which conservative congressional leaders felt compelled to offer as a substitute for Medicare proposals. The beneficiaries would be limited to those in severe financial need, but the benefits were subject to few limits. The question of standards of need would be left to the various states, and the funding would be grants-in-aid, from general treasury funds, to state administrations that agreed to provide their share of the funds for "medical assistance to the aged." These were the characteristics of the bill which Senator Robert Kerr of Oklahoma and Representative Wilbur Mills of Arkansas offered as a substitute for the Forand bill. In 1960, that alternative was adopted by both tax committees of the Congress and ultimately passed as Public Law 86–778.*

The Kerr-Mills program was broad and generous in theory. The federal government would provide between 50 and 80 per cent of the funds states used in medical assistance for the aged, with the higher percentages going to the poorer states. Such arrangements, in the opinion of the Senate Finance Committee, would "enable every state to improve and extend medical services to aged persons." The expectation was that the 2.4 million persons on old-age assistance and the estimated 10 million medically indigent would share in the program. Senator Pat McNamara (D., Mich.) was more prescient. "The blunt truth," he told the Senate in August of 1960, "is that it would be the miracle of the century if all of the states— or even a sizeable number—would be in a position to provide the matching funds to make the program more than just a plan on paper." Three years later, McNamara's predictions were confirmed by a report of the special Senate Committee on Aging. In 1963, 32 of the 50 states had programs in effect, and the provision of funds was widely disparate among the states. Five large industrial states—California, New York, Massachusetts, Michigan, and Pennsylvania—were receiving nearly 90 per cent of the Kerr-Mills funds, and yet their aged populations represented only 32 per cent of the total population over 65.

These outcomes were not, of course, apparent to the promoters of medical assistance to the aged in 1960. Both Mills and Kerr were concerned about solving the worst problem—the health costs of the very poor among the aged—as a way of avoiding Medicare programs in the future. Both were quick to point out that their program allowed for more generous benefits than alternative social security proposals. In a later interview with a national business magazine, Kerr insisted on this contrast:

The Kerr-Mills program provides greater benefits to those over 65 who

*Wilbur J. Cohen, a lifelong advocate of health insurance under social security, wrote much of what became the Kerr-Mills law. Experts like Cohen were so familiar with the localistic, means-test approach to social problems that Kerr and Mills, who both had had long experience with Cohen, rather naturally called him from the University of Michigan to help draft their bill.

need those benefits. The benefits include doctors, surgeons, hospitalization, nurses and nursing care, medicines and drugs, dentists and dental benefits—even false teeth. Each state can provide what is needed by the people within the state. The . . . social security approach for aged care would provide mainly hospital and nursing home payments.*

Few states in fact were to provide such broad benefits; by 1963, only four states were providing the full range of care allowed for in the Kerr-Mills bill, and most programs imposed strict limitations on the conditions for care and the extent of care. But the program satisfied both those who genuinely believed in the desirability of state rather than uniform national administration and those who hoped even an unsuccessful Kerr-Mills program would head off the demand for Medicare.

The AMA, though originally opposed to the Kerr-Mills bill, soon came to understand its political virtues. In 1961, President E. Vincent Askey, M.D., urged the states to "implement [the Kerr–Mills program] for the needy and near-needy." Many of the state medical societies did not join in Askey's enthusiasm, but the cause of the AMA's alarm was clear. The election of John F. Kennedy, who had pledged to promote enactment of a compulsory health insurance law for aged social security beneficiaries, had returned Medicare proposals to the front pages of the nation's newspapers. In late 1960, Kennedy recalled Cohen to Washington to head a health task force asked to draft a Medicare bill for introduction in the first session of the 87th Congress. When a policy has presidential sponsorship and favorable reactions in public polls, and the partisan alignments in the Congress support the president, the chances of legislative adoption improve. The election of 1960 thus marked a pronounced shift for Medicare from the politics of legislative impossibility characteristic of the previous eight years to the politics of possibility.

The Politics of Legislative Possibility: Medicare, 1961

Kennedy had labeled his platform "The New Frontier," and included within it a variety of proposals for domestic change which he said "would get this country moving again." As a part of

---

Nation's Business (September, 1962); cited in American Medical Association, *Federalized Health Care for the Aged* (1963), pp. 52–53.

the New Frontier, Kennedy prominently included a hospital insurance program for the aged. Shortly after his inauguration as president, Kennedy made good on that campaign promise. On February 9, 1961, a presidential message to the Congress called for the extension of social security benefits for 14 million Americans over 65* to cover hospital and nursing home costs, but not, in contrast to the Forand bill, surgical expenses. These benefits were to be financed by a one-quarter of 1 per cent increase in social security taxes.

The New York Times headlined the proposal and forecast a "STIFF FIGHT" over the Forand bill's successor. The narrowing of benefits was but one obvious indication that the president and his advisors were aware of the strong opposition to his bill and that they concurred with the strategy long used by Wilbur Cohen. That strategy, designed to modify congressional intractability, softpedaled the innovative character of the program in an attempt to widen agreement on the legitimacy of government involvement in health insurance. "The program," President Kennedy reiterated, "is not socialized medicine. . . . It is a program of prepayment for health costs with absolute freedom of choice guaranteed. Every person will choose his own doctor and hospital."

Senator Clinton Anderson of New Mexico and Representative Cecil King of California—high-ranking Democratic members of the Senate Finance Committee and the House Ways and Means Committee respectively—simultaneously and enthusiastically introduced the president's bill the second week in February. Neither, however, was regarded as the pre-eminent Democrat on his committee, and presidents typically try to have controversial bills introduced by dominant figures like Senator Kerr or House Ways and Means Committee chairman Mills. The lesser prominence of Kennedy's sponsors, coupled with the fact that the Kerr-Mills

*The 14 million figure was an estimate for 1963, the first full year in which the Kennedy Medicare program could have operated. The projection of 14 million social security beneficiaries, out of a total aged population of 17 3/4 million in 1963, left an estimated 3 3/4 million aged uncovered by the Kennedy proposal. The proportion of the aged ineligible for social insurance benefits has been sharply declining since the original Medicare bill. Between 1950 and 1960 the number of aged receiving social insurance benefits more than quadrupled, from 2.7 million to 11.6 million. In 1961, approximately 4 million were ineligible for social security benefits.

program was in its first year of operation as an alternative to Medicare, left no one in doubt that Kerr and Mills would prove formidable obstacles to the president's Medicare hopes. The ideological composition of the tax committees provided additional basis for skepticism about likely enactment. That the skepticism was well-founded was illustrated by the way in which Ways and Means dealt with the King-Anderson bill.

The Obstacle Course in Congress:
First Try with Ways and Means

Kennedy's Democratic majority in the Congress presaged no clear majority favorable to Medicare, and only a majority vote of the entire House could extract the bill from a hostile Ways and Means Committee. Legislative liaison officials within the Department of Health, Education and Welfare counted only 196 House members certain to vote for Medicare in 1961—twenty-three votes short of a simple majority. The House decision on Medicare thus would rest with Ways and Means.

The composition, style, and leadership of that committee provided ample grounds for predicting Medicare's defeat at the first stage of the formal legislative process. The 17–8 defeat of the Forand bill in 1960 indicated the combined strength of the southern Democrats and conservative Republican bloc on the committee. Kennedy's Medicare strategists would have to confront this coalition: in 1961, sixteen Ways and Means committeemen were known to oppose the bill, including chairman Wilbur Mills (D., Ark.), whose influence within the committee was formidable. Under those circumstances, the Gallup poll findings that "two out of three persons interviewed would be in favor of increasing the social security tax to pay for old-age medical insurance" provided little comfort to President Kennedy. Four votes—either of southern Democrats or northern Republicans—would have to change for the president to have a Medicare majority within the committee, and the prospects were not good.

Of twenty-five Ways and Means committeemen, fifteen were Democrats, eight of whom were from southern or border states. Among the Democrats, there was a clear ideological division between six of the southern members and the others. *The New*

Republic, a liberal weekly committed to a much expanded social welfare role for the federal government, annually evaluates congressional voting behavior. On twelve roll-call votes during the first session of the 87th Congress (1961), *The New Republic* found nine of the Democrats in perfect agreement with the magazine's position. The six other Democrats—all from southern or border states—voted in accord with the magazine's position 60 per cent of the time or less. Among the ten Republicans on the committee, seven were in disagreement with the magazine's position 100 per cent of the time; the remaining three, 75 per cent of the time. The officially nonpartisan *Congressional Quarterly* studies bear out *The New Republic's* characterization of a substantial partisan cleavage, with a swing group of six southern and border state Democrats. Although the *Congressional Quarterly* analyses of the 87th and 88th Congress found Ways and Means Democrats and Republicans to be "more liberal" and "less liberal," respectively, than their party colleagues in the House, the Democratic showing was traced to the nine generally urban, pro-labor members on the committee. Thus, despite the high average support among the Democrats for "liberal" measures, the coalition of ten partisan Republicans and the six more conservative southern Democrats easily comprised a negative majority on bills expanding the social welfare role of the federal government.*

100% average approval	*with 60% approval or less*
King (California)	Mills (Arkansas)
Karsten (Missouri)	Harrison (Virginia)
Burke (Massachusetts)	Herlong (Florida)
Keough (New York)	Frazier (Tennessee)
O'Brien (Illinois)	Ikard-Thompson (Texas)
Boggs (Louisiana)	Watts (Kentucky)
Machrowicz-Griffiths (Michigan)	
Green (Pennsylvania)	
Ullman (Oregon)	

The conservative coalition opposing Medicare in 1961 was not a happenstance, but a predictable result of the committee's process of recruitment. Democrats on Ways and Means enjoy a unique source of influence, since they also comprise their party's Committee on Committees, the group which makes all Democratic

---

*Evaluation of Ways and Means Democrats, 87th Congress, First Session, "Key Votes—87th Congress," *The New Republic* (October 27, 1962).

committee assignments. By convention, however, when new Democratic members of the Ways and Means Committee are to be chosen, the Committee on Committees defers the choice to regional party caucuses. During the first session of the 87th Congress, two Democratic openings on the committee occurred through resignation: Thaddeus Machrowicz of Michigan and Frank Ikard of Texas. Their successors illustrated the pattern of geographical continuity: Martha Griffiths of Michigan replaced Machrowicz and Clark Thompson of Texas replaced Ikard. This customary practice has frozen the existing geographical distribution favoring southern representation and thereby prevented additions to the urban, pro-labor group among the Democrats.

Further, most Ways and Means members enjoyed an independence which made it unlikely that the president and the party could effectively pressure them into changing their votes. Widely regarded as one of the most prestigious House committees, Ways and Means attracts senior and influential members. Members stay on this pre-eminent committee a long time, and are more likely than other representatives to feel insulated from external pressures. Among the 1961 Democrats, Frazier, Mills, and Herlong had served continuously since the Truman administration and many of the southern Democrats, including chairman Mills, had run unopposed as often as opposed in their districts. In the 1960 congressional elections, when twenty-one fewer Democrats were returned to the House than in 1958, no Democratic incumbent of Ways and Means lost his seat. Ways and Means is thus a kind of old-timers' club within the House; its members are beyond the range of pressure from House and Executive leaders which younger congressmen, particularly those who need party help with re-election, may face.

As a rule, the committee is far more responsive to the wishes of the House of Representatives than it is to other sources of pressure. When a bill which is before the Ways and Means Committee has a strong majority on the floor waiting to enact it, its members usually feel a responsibility to report it. When, however, a controversial bill faces a bitter and close floor fight, the House frequently depends on the committee to "save it from itself." This gives Ways and Means the option of not reporting the bill at all or, if it chooses to report the measure, of writing partisan compromises into it first.

The success which chairman Mills has in satisfying the House of

Representatives is reflected in the reception which Ways and Means bills have had there. The bills reported by Ways and Means are generally voted on under a "closed rule," that is, no amendments are permitted, only limited debate, and acceptance or rejection. This convention gives the committee great discretionary power in deciding what to write into its reported bills. House members go along with the convention because many of them have neither the time nor the expertise to master the complex technical details involved in tax, trade, and social security bills and because they prefer to avoid the pressure from interest-group lobbies which those bills generally elicit. Maintaining the closed-rule convention for Ways and Means bills does, however, constrain the committee to deal responsibly with legislative proposals. Thus, despite the deep partisan cleavages on the committee, Mills has maintained a reputation for not allowing partisan considerations to interfere unduly with its collective judgment on the technical merits of bills it handles. When partisan conflict is unavoidable, Mills takes pains to contain it by compromises which seek to prevent massive Republican or Democratic defections from the bill as it is reported from committee. The pride which Ways and Means members take in the regular House acceptance of their reported bills further ensures their cautious handling of controversial measures like Medicare.

The Southern Democrats

The chairman of Ways and Means had a pivotal role in the fate of the 1961 Medicare legislation. In less than a year after his own bill, cosponsored with Senator Kerr, had become public law, Mills again faced hospital insurance proposals he had helped to defeat in the previous session and which threatened now to displace the Kerr-Mills program. At the same time, his influence within the Ways and Means Committee was such that, could he be persuaded to support Medicare, it was likely that he could carry the committee with him.

When it came to dealing with Mills over the King-Anderson bill of 1961, Kennedy was in a difficult position. Medicare was only one of several major items on the administration's agenda. The president had initiated trade and tax bills of high priority to his domestic program, and these also fell within the jurisdiction of

Mills' committee. Since Mills had agreed to introduce these bills in the House, and his support was requisite to their enactment, Kennedy and the House party leaders were at a disadvantage in pressing demands on him to back Medicare as well.

Mills' position in 1961 was affected by an election threat back home. The 1960 census returns required that Arkansas lose two of its six congressional seats, and in the redistricting it appeared that Mills would have to oppose Dale Alford in the district which included the whole of Little Rock. Alford was one of the two most conservative and anti-administration of the Arkansas congressmen. A contest with him would have been the most serious Mills had faced in a House career dating back to the New Deal. It seemed reasonable to suppose that Mills would be disinclined to support legislation, such as Medicare, which in the minds of many Little Rock voters would be too closely associated with an excessive role for the federal government in social welfare policy.

In addition to the chairman, five other southern Democrats on Ways and Means were opposed to the King-Anderson bill. The president needed at least thirteen pro-Medicare votes to have the bill reported to the floor, and took for granted that none of the ten Republicans on the committee would defect from his party's position. Hence, four affirmative votes were required from among those southern and border state Democrats who had voted against the Forand bill in 1960.

The 1961 Congress strikingly illustrated a key difference between the legislative politics of America and those of a cabinet-parliamentary system like that of England. Party, executive, and legislative leadership in the United States is not, as in England, in the same hands, and the platform on which a president rides into office need not reflect the aims of many of his fellow partisans whose assistance is crucial in the committee and floor stage of the legislative process. Kennedy's prospects for changing the votes of the crucial Ways and Means Democrats hinged on the House Democratic leadership: the Speaker, the party whip, the floor leader, and the relevant committee chairman, Mills. Though Speaker Rayburn was ready to support the president's Medicare proposal, he lacked formal means to enforce party discipline on recalcitrant Democrats.

Of the six Democratic opponents of Medicare, Burr Harrison of

Virginia was the least likely candidate for persuasion: a conservative southerner, he was both fixed in his ways and immune from pressure. At the other extreme was John Watts of Kentucky. He was reportedly willing to be the thirteenth vote for the King-Anderson bill if twelve others could first be mustered; he faced enough anti-administration sentiment in Kentucky to make conspicuous support of President Kennedy a personal liability. Among the other possibilities were the chairman, already a publicly announced opponent, and Herlong, Frazier, and Ikard, all of whom were at least six-term veterans of the House and had conservative predilections. Yet, since they were old acquaintances of Speaker Rayburn, they might have been expected to go along with him in the absence of special district concerns.

Unfortunately for the legislative fate of the Medicare bill, at the very time when all the resources and skills of the House leadership were needed, the Speaker himself was in failing health. Majority floor leader McCormack increasingly took on many of the informal leadership functions that Rayburn in the past exercised so skillfully. The Massachusetts Democrat, though thoroughly schooled in the norms and sentiments of House veterans, could not be expected to have Rayburn's influence, enjoying neither the Speaker's office nor the immense personal popularity Rayburn, a Texan, had with southern Democrats of the Watts and Ikard type.

The absence of Rayburn's highly personal legislative management, coupled with the past reluctance of the six "swing" Democrats to support health insurance under social security, meant that Chairman Mills' position was unlikely to be challenged within his committee. *The New York Times'* Washington correspondent, Russell Baker, judged this correctly only days after the King-Anderson bill was introduced. "The President's medical program," reported Baker, "despised by many of his own party inside the House Ways and Means Committee, was in great trouble."*

Earlier in the month, the *Times* had emphasized the equally important fact that Ways and Means faced a "heavy schedule of high-priority legislation," with the controversial Medicare bill unlikely to be discussed in hearings until late in the session.† The certain opposition of Mills and Harrison, and the probable opposi-

The New York Times, February 19, 1961.
†*Ibid.*, February 11, 1961.

tion of the four remaining members of the conservative southern group, held out dim hopes for those late-session hearings. In the meantime, the problem facing the president was not only to secure these southern votes on medical care legislation, but have this group follow party leadership on the foreign aid, depressed areas, tax, housing, and trade bills.

When, as with the King-Anderson bill of 1961, it appears that a committee will not report favorably on a presidential proposal, the president and his allies have alternative strategies. The question facing President Kennedy was whether anything could be gained by any of three possible offensive strategies.

Kennedy could concentrate his bargaining resources on medical care, taking the chance of alienating support on other high-priority bills. Since the outlook for Kennedy's trade and tax legislation was otherwise favorable, both the president and his advisors agreed it would be unwise to press the Ways and Means Committee too forcefully. Moreover, the Democratic margin in the House (263–174) did not assure passage of the King-Anderson bill even if it were somehow to get to a floor vote: sixty or more of those Democrats appeared unwilling to pass Medicare in 1961. Hence a determined bid for House action was rejected by the president.

The second possibility was to try by-passing the House with a Medicare rider to another bill. A rider is a bill which is attached as an amendment to another bill that has already passed one house. In April, 1961, an increasing number of reports suggested the administration was preparing for a move in that direction. Senator Javits (R., N.Y.) expressed "dismay at reports that the administration had decided to put off a request for Congressional action until next year," and argued that "nothing will happen unless the administration gives [Medicare] priority at this session."* The support of liberal Republican senators, coupled with broader sponsorship of Medicare among some Democratic senators, led Senator Anderson, Medicare's cosponsor, to deny late in April that legislative efforts for the session had been abandoned. The proposal was to add a Medicare amendment to the House-approved social security bill then before the Senate Finance Committee.

The Senate Democratic leadership, however, saw strong arguments against the rider tactic. Even if the composite bill passed

*The New York Times, April 2, 1961.

the Senate, it would be reviewed by a House-Senate conference committee, and Mills' bipartisan influence within his committee was sufficient to force a choice between the social security bill stripped of the Medicare amendment or no bill at all. Kennedy and his advisors discarded the rider alternative, for the time being, and press speculation faded out.

A third option for Kennedy, the one he was to choose, involved accepting the defeat of the bill for that year, but using it to attract public attention to his thwarted campaign pledge. Although he had rejected the use of arm-twisting tactics within the Congress, Kennedy hoped to put indirect pressure on legislators by going to the public with an educational campaign about the legislation denied him in 1961. Whatever its short-term effects, that strategy ultimately had prospects of beneficial consequences.

The Kennedy Administration vs. the AMA

Even before the King-Anderson bill was introduced in February, representatives of the Kennedy administration had begun castigating the AMA for trying, as Wilbur Cohen said at a Washington conference on the aged, "to thwart the will of the majority of the people" by "methods of vilification and intimidation." Although clearly the most immediate threat to enactment was the bottleneck within the Ways and Means Committee, it was the AMA and its supporters who drew most of the administration's fire.

The American Medical Association offered, to be sure, a conspicuous target. Eschewing compromise, the AMA employed every propaganda tactic it had learned from the bitter battles of the Truman era. "The surest way to total defeat," cautioned Dr. Ernest Howard, the organization's assistant executive vice-president, "is to say that the AMA should try to sit down and negotiate." Instead, AMA-sponsored newspaper advertisements and radio and television spots indicting the King-Anderson bill began appearing throughout the nation. Waving the red flag of socialism, these messages held out horrifying visions of a "new bureaucratic task force" entering "the privacy of the examination room," depriving American patients of the "freedom to choose their own doctor" and the doctor of the freedom "to treat his patients in an individual way."

The AMA simultaneously launched less publicized efforts to

mobilize local communities against the Kennedy bill. Congressional speeches criticizing H.R. 4222 were reproduced and distributed to newspapers and voluntary organizations. An "Operation Hometown" campaign began, enlisting county medical societies in a variety of lobbying tasks. The AMA equipped local medical leaders with a roster of ready-made speeches, reprints, pamphlets, sample news announcements, a "High School Debate Kit," radio tapes and scripts, and a list of guidelines for using the materials most effectively in reaching "every segment of the American public through every possible medium, [and stimulating] every voter to let his Congressman know that medicare is really 'Fedicare'—a costly concoction of bureaucracy, bad medicine, and an unbalanced budget."

Since King-Anderson supporters could do little to bring direct pressure on the pivotal congressmen in Ways and Means, they hoped their representation of the AMA as an unscrupulous and inordinately powerful interest which was successfully thwarting the public would cause congressional critics of Medicare to suffer guilt by association. In April, HEW Secretary Abraham Ribicoff debated Senator Kenneth Keating (R., N.Y.) on television over the King-Anderson bill, and used the opportunity to lash out against the "scare tactics" of "organized medicine's" campaign against compulsory health insurance for the aged.

The Ways and Means hearings of July and August provided another prominent occasion for continuing the bid for public support. The testimony of representatives from HEW linked the well-known case for the King-Anderson bill to a blistering attack on the pressure groups opposing it. The administration spokesmen, along with those of the AFL-CIO, diverted their attention from the specifications of the Medicare bill to the methods and interests of their medical, business, and hospital critics. In his testimony Secretary Ribicoff attempted to discredit AMA predictions of creeping socialism and the end of freedom by outlining again the modest character of Medicare. "The bill is designed," he said,

only to take care of the aged. It is not my intention to advocate that we take care of the medical needs and hospital needs of our entire population, and the reason is that insurance is available for younger people. Blue Cross is available and it can be paid for by our working population.

The press gave prominent coverage to the summer hearings, but the behavior of the committee members indicated that the bill's fate was a foregone conclusion. The southern Democrats, whose views were central to the outcome, were relatively quiet. Chairman Mills, who ordinarily took a dominant role in hearings over major bills, missed two of the nine sessions, and remained dispassionate during most of those he chaired. Questioning was left primarily to a few of the anti-Medicare Republicans and pro-Medicare Democrats who were amenable to joining the propaganda battle being waged by those giving testimony.

At the end of nine days, on August 4, 1961, the hearings ended undramatically. A week later *The New York Times* reported that no further action on the King-Anderson bill was contemplated for that session. Amid the national concern over Berlin and the call-up of reserve units, many Americans were unaware of the fate of what had been a campaign issue, or of the fact that Ways and Means had failed even to take a vote on the bill. Chairman Mills, unwilling as ever to highlight the partisan cleavages within the committee, and sharing with his fellow committeemen, and congressmen generally, a reluctance to clarify their public record with anything so concrete as a "yes" or "no" vote when there was little to be gained by it, preferred to let the bill die an anonymous death. If future events should force a reconsideration of the committee's position on Medicare—and Mills was aware of the possibility—a tell-tale 1961 vote might prove an embarrassment. Nor did the Kennedy administration, with an interest in future negotiations with Ways and Means, wish to burden Medicare with the legacy of a negative vote. The quietness of Medicare's burial made it easier for the bill's supporters to blame its murder on the AMA while diverting attention from the active complicity of the House committee and the passive complicity of the Kennedy administration.

Medicare's Near Miss, 1964

Between the defeat of President Kennedy's initial Medicare proposal in 1961 and the national elections of 1964, none of the major congressional obstacles to its enactment was fully altered. The Democrats maintained control of the Congress after the 1962 elections, but the pro-administration bloc was, as usual, never as large as the number of Democrats. In 1961, HEW's congressional liaison staff estimated the House Medicare breakdown as approximately twenty-three votes short of a 218 majority. The Ways and Means Committee never gave them the chance to check the accuracy of their estimates, and attempts to circumvent the committee with rider strategies proved abortive in 1962 and 1964. Each year hearings were held on Medicare, and by 1964, thirteen volumes of testimony had been compiled, totaling nearly 14,000 pages. But Wilbur Mills and his committee were not ready to report a Medicare bill.

The administration's pro-Medicare strategy included continued efforts to change votes on the committee. Two methods were employed. First, HEW officials were directed to respond to the objections of the key southern Democrats in hopes of bringing them around on the King-Anderson bill. Cohen and his staff spent far more time courting critics like Herlong, Watts, Harrison, and Mills than they did working with pro-Medicare members of the committee. The administration, acting through the influence of House Democratic leadership over members of the regional caucuses, also took steps directed to enlarge the size of the pro-Medicare group. After 1961, no new member of the committee was elected who had failed to assure the House leadership that he would vote for Medicare or, at the very least, would support its being reported out. By 1964, these efforts had brought the total of pro-Medicare Democrats to twelve, one short of a committee majority. Three of the anti-Medicare southern Democrats of 1961, Frazier, Ikard, and Harrison, had been replaced by fellow southerners who supported the King-Anderson bill, Richard Fulton, Clark Thompson, and Pat Jennings. All the other Democratic newcomers between 1961 and 1964 were, like their predecessors, firm administration supporters.

Sensing the rising support for Medicare, its opponents on Ways and Means nearly pulled off a clever legislative coup in the early summer of 1964. The ranking Republican, John W. Byrnes of Wisconsin, proposed that the 5 per cent increase in social security benefits which the committee had approved in earlier deliberations be increased to 6 per cent. This would have raised social security taxes to 10 per cent, widely accepted within Congress as the upper tax limit, and thus leave no fiscal room for Medicare in the future. The pro-Medicare committeemen realized the trap, but only eleven of their number were at the roll call vote. Mills, Herlong, and

Watts supported Byrnes' amendment, giving the anti-Medicare group what seemed a winning margin, 12–11. But the final vote cast was by Bruce Alger, an arch-conservative Republican from Dallas. Unwilling to play the game, Alger voted with the Democratic majority, explaining later that "since he opposed the entire Social Security system, consistency would not permit him to expand it," even to undermine the chances of Medicare.

Having observed their House brethren come close to catastrophe, Senate Democrats acted to attach the Medicare rider to the social security bill which the House had already passed in 1964. But Mills had anticipated that move and, fearing that Ways and Means would lose control over the content of any Medicare bill, had taken steps to thwart it. He promised pro-Medicare Democrats on the committee that Medicare would be the "first order of business" in 1965; in return he received their support in rejecting the rider in the conference committee. On October 4, the conference announced its deadlock over the entire social security bill, thus postponing both the social security cash benefit increases and Medicare until the following year.

Medicare's defeat in 1964, compared to Kennedy's failing effort in 1961, presaged its enactment in 1965. The Senate was on record favoring the King-Anderson bill, and the key bottleneck of 1961, the Ways and Means Committee, was within one vote of a health insurance majority. Wilbur Mills' promises for 1965 evidenced the weakened position of the anti-Medicare coalition. In September and December of 1964, Mills suggested to audiences in Little Rock that a soundly financed Medicare bill would gain his support in the next session of the Congress. Having already stated that medical care insurance would be the first order of business for his committee the following January, Mills expressed his concern about the discrepancies between popular conceptions of Medicare and the content of the King-Anderson proposals. "The public," Mills warned in his Little Rock speech of December 7, "must be under no illusion regarding the benefits . . . [and must understand that] Medicare does not refer to doctor services" or general out-patient medical care.

Mills' worry was not ill-founded. "Medicare," a term which originally referred to the comprehensive health program run for servicemen's families by the Defense Department, was a misleading slogan for the King-Anderson bill. "Hospicare" would have been a more appropriate epithet. Despite the accretion of support between 1961 and 1964, the King-Anderson bills had changed only slightly. After 1963, Medicare was altered to include non-social security beneficiaries for a limited period, and here and there changes were made in the level of benefits. But the bill over which the conference committee deadlocked in 1964 remained basically a hospital insurance measure. When the deadlock was announced, observers, taking their cue from Mills' promises, assumed the King-Anderson proposal would be close to passage in 1965. In the meantime, the election of November, 1964, changed practically every political consideration; and Mills' ruminations in December about the unrealistic conception Americans held of Medicare was the first sign that anyone read the electoral victory of the Democrats to mean anything more than speedy enactment of a bill providing hospitalization and nursing home insurance for the aged.

The Election of 1964 and the Assurance of Legislative Action

The electoral outcome of 1964 guaranteed the passage of legislation on medical care for the aged. Not one of the obstacles to Medicare was left standing. In the House, the Democrats gained thirty-two new seats, giving them a more than two-to-one ratio for the first time since the heyday of the New Deal. In addition, President Johnson's dramatic victory over Goldwater had some of the features of a popular mandate for Medicare. The president had campaigned on the promise of social reforms—most prominently Medicare and federal aid to education—and the public seemed to have rejected decisively Goldwater's alternatives of state, local, and private initiative.

Within the Congress, immediate action was taken to forestall recurrence of the dilatory methods previously employed against both federal aid to education and medical care bills. Liberal Democratic members changed the House rules so as to reduce the power of Republican-southern Democrat coalitions on committees to delay proposals. The twenty-one-day rule was reinstated, making it possible to dislodge bills from the House Rules Committee after a maximum delay of three weeks. On the Ways and Means Committee, the traditional majority party-minority party ratio of three-to-two was altered to the partisan ratio of the entire House (two-to-one). In 1965, that meant a shift from fifteen Democrats and ten Republicans to seventeen Democrats and eight Republicans, thereby producing a pro-Medicare majority. Enactment of the King-Anderson program, only a legislative possibility until the election of 1964, had now become a certainty. The only question remaining was what its precise form would be.

The Administration's Suggestion: H.R. 1 and S. 1

Administration leaders assumed after the election that the Ways and Means Committee would report a bill similar to the one rejected by the conference in 1964. Hence, Anderson and King introduced on January 4, 1965, in the Senate and House respectively, the standard Medicare package: coverage of the aged, limited hospitalization, nursing home insurance benefits, and social security financing. The HEW staff prepared a background guide on the bill which continued to emphasize its modest aims. The guide included assurances that the bill's coverage of hospitalization benefits "left a substantial place for private insurance for nonbudgetable health costs, [particularly for] physicians' services." It described H.R. 1 as "Hospital Insurance for the Aged through Social Security," and no doubt would have encouraged the substitution of "Hospicare" for "Medicare" as its popular name, had this been still possible by 1965.

Social Security experts within HEW, with a rich history of sponsoring unsuccessful health insurance bills, were doubly cautious now that success seemed so near at hand. Wilbur Cohen, for instance, busied himself, with Johnson's blessings, convincing congressional leadership to give Medicare the highest priority among the president's Great Society proposals: hence Medicare became H.R. 1 and S. 1. Its content, however, remained essentially unchanged. The HEW leaders, like everyone else, could read newspapers and find criticisms that Medicare's benefits were insufficient, and that the aged mistakenly thought the bill covered physicians' services. The strategists believed, however, that coverage of physicians' care could wait: the reformers' fundamental premise had always been that Medicare was only "a beginning," with increments of change set for the future.

If the 1964 elections promoted satisfaction among H.R. 1's backers with their customary position, it provoked significant shifts among Medicare's opponents. Both Republican and AMA spokesmen shifted to discussions of what one AMA official, Dr. Ernest Howard, called "more positive programs." These alternatives grew out of the familiar criticisms that the King-Anderson bills had "inadequate" benefits, would be too costly, and made no distinction between the poor and wealthy among the aged. The AMA gave the slogan "Eldercare" to its bill, and had it introduced as H.R. 3737 by Thomas Curtis (R., Mo.) and A. Sydney Herlong (D., Fla.), both Ways and Means members. In comparing its bill and H.R. 1, the AMA earnestly stressed the disappointingly limited benefits of the latter:

Eldercare, implemented by the states, would provide a wide spectrum of benefits, including physicians' care, surgical and drug costs, nursing home charges, diagnostic services, x-ray and laboratory fees and other services. Medicare's benefits would be far more limited, covering about one-quarter (25%) of the total yearly health care costs of the average person . . . Medicare would *not* cover physicians' services or surgical charges. Neither would it cover drugs outside the hospital or nursing home, or x-ray or other laboratory services not connected with hospitalization.*

Claiming their "program offered more benefits for the elderly at less cost to the taxpayers," the AMA charged, as did some Republicans, that the public had been misled by the connotations of the "Medicare" epithet. Seventy-two per cent of those questioned in an AMA-financed survey during the first two months of 1965 agreed that doctors' bills should be insured in a government health plan. Sixty-five per cent of the respondents preferred a selective welfare program which would "pay an elderly person's medical bill only if he were in need of financial help" to a universal social security plan which would "pay the medical expenses of everyone over 65, regardless of their income." Armed with these figures, the AMA once again launched a full-scale assault on the King-Anderson bill, hoping to head it off with what amounted to an extension of the Kerr-Mills program.

*American Medical Association, "Why Eldercare Offers Better Care Than Medicare" (March, 1965).

By February, the issue was once again before the Ways and Means Committee. Pressure groups—medical, labor, hospital, and insurance organizations primarily—continued to make public appeals through the mass media, but they also made certain their viewpoints were presented to the committee. Ways and Means had before it three legislative possibilities: the administration's H.R. 1, the AMA's Eldercare proposal, and a new bill sponsored by the ranking Republican committee member, John Byrnes.

The Ways and Means Committee and the House Take Action, January–April

For more than a month Ways and Means worked on H.R. 1, calling witnesses, requesting detailed explanation of particular sections, and trying to estimate its costs and benefits. Executive sessions closed to the press, one mark of serious legislative intention, began on February 17. The atmosphere was businesslike and deliberate; members assumed the administration bill would pass, perhaps with minor changes, and there was little disposition to argue the broad philosophical issues that had dominated hearings in the preceding decade. When spokesmen for the AMA invoked their fears of socialized medicine, they infuriated committee members intent on working out practical matters, and chairman Mills refused to permit AMA representatives to attend further sessions of the hearings.

Mills led his committee through practically every session of hearings on the administration bill, promising to take up the Byrnes bill (H.R. 4351) and the Eldercare bill in turn. By March 1, there had been continued reference to the exclusions and limits of the King-Anderson bill, with the charges of inadequacy coming mostly from the Republicans. On March 2, announcing his concern for finding "some degree of compromise [that] results in the majority of us being together," Mills invited Byrnes to explain his bill to the committee.

The Byrnes bill was ready for discussion because the Republicans on the committee following the 1964 election wanted to prevent the Democrats from taking exclusive credit for a Medicare law. The Republican staff counsel, William Quealy, had explained this point in a confidential memorandum in January, reminding the

Republican committeemen that they had to "face political realities."
Those realities included the certain passage of health insurance
legislation that session and excluded the strategy of substituting
an expanded Kerr-Mills program. "Regardless of the intrinsic merits
of the Kerr-Mills program," Quealy wrote, "it has not been accepted
as adequate . . . particularly by the aged, [and a] liberalization of
it will not meet the political problem facing the Republicans in
this Congress." That problem was the identification of Republican
with diehard AMA opposition to Medicare, which some Republican
leaders thought contributed heavily to their 1964 electoral catastrophe.

Byrnes emphasized that his bill, which proposed benefits similar
to those offered in the Aetna Life Insurance Company's health
plan for federal employees, would cover the major risks overlooked
by H.R. 1, particularly the costs of doctors' services and drugs.
He also stressed the voluntary nature of his proposal; the aged
would be free to join or not, and their share of the financing would
be "scaled to the amounts of the participants' social security cash
benefits," while the government's share would be drawn from general revenues. The discussion of the Byrnes bill was spirited and
extended; the AMA's Eldercare alternative, not promoted vigorously
by even its committee sponsors, was scarcely mentioned.

Increasingly, the Byrnes and King-Anderson bills were discussed
as mutually exclusive alternatives. HEW officials—Cohen, Ball,
Irwin Wolkstein of the Social Security Administration, and several
others—were exhausted from weeks of questioning and redrafting,
and viewed the discussion of the Byrnes bill as a time for restful
listening. But Mills, instead of posing a choice between the two
bills, unexpectedly suggested a combination which involved extract-
ing Byrnes' benefit plan from his financing proposal. On March 3,
Mills turned to HEW's Wilbur Cohen and calmly asked whether
such a "combination" was possible. "Stunned," Cohen was initially
suspicious that the suggestion was a plot to kill the entire administration proposal. Cohen had earlier argued for what he called a
"three-layer cake" reform by Ways and Means: H.R. 1's hospital
program first, private health insurance for physicians' coverage, and
an expanded Kerr-Mills program "underneath" for the indigent
among the aged. Mills' surprise proposition to come up with a
"medi-elder-Byrnes bill" posed for Cohen an innovative and un-

foreseen possibility. That night, in a memorandum to the president, Cohen reflected on Mills' "ingenious plan," explaining that a proposal which put "together in one bill features of all three of the major" alternatives before the committee would make Medicare "unassailable politically from any serious Republican attack." Convinced now that Mills' strategy was not destructive, Cohen was delighted that Republican charges of inadequacy against H.R. 1 had been used by Mills to prompt the expansion of that bill.

Byrnes himself was reluctant to approve the dissection of his proposal, humorously referring to his bill as "bettercare." Nonetheless, from March 3 to March 23, when the committee finished its hearings, Ways and Means members concentrated on the combination of what had been mutually exclusive solutions to the health and financial problems of the elderly. Mills presided over this hectic process with confident but gracious assurance, asking questions persistently but encouraging from time to time comments from other members, especially from the senior Republican, Byrnes. The Byrnes benefit formula was slightly reduced; the payment for drugs used outside hospitals and nursing homes, for instance, was rejected on the grounds of its unpredictable and potentially high costs. After some consideration of financing the separate physicians' insurance through social security, the committee adopted Byrnes' financing suggestion of individual premium payments by elderly beneficiaries, with the remainder drawn from general revenues. But, although Byrnes had proposed that such premiums be scaled to social security benefits, the committee prescribed a uniform $3 per month contribution from each participant. The level of premium was itself a matter of extended discussion: HEW actuaries estimated medical insurance would cost about $5 per month, but Mills cautiously insisted that a $6 monthly payment would make certain that expenditures for medical benefits were balanced by contributions.

In its transformation into the "first layer" of the new "legislative cake," H.R. 1 was not radically altered. Levels of particular benefits were changed, reducing, among other things, the length of insured hospital care, and increasing the amount of the hospital deductible and coinsurance payment beneficiaries would have to pay. (Deductibles are the payments patients must make before their insurance takes over, and coinsurance contributions are the proportion of the remaining bill for which patients are responsible.) The continuing debate over these matters illustrated the divergent goals of those involved in reshaping Medicare. High deductibles but no limit on the number of insured hospital days were sought by those anxious to provide protection against chronic and catastrophic illness. Others insisted on coinsurance and deductibles so that patients would be given a stake in avoiding overuse of hospital facilities. But the most contested changes made in H.R. 1 involved the methods of paying hospital-based RAPP specialists (radiologists, anesthesiologists, pathologists, and physiatrists) and the level of increase in social security taxes required to pay for the hospitalization plan.

The Johnson administration recommended that the charges for services like radiology and anesthesiology be included in hospital bills unless hospitals requested some other form of payment. Mills, however, insisted that "no physician service, except those of interns and residents under approved teaching programs, would be paid" under H.R. 1, now Part A of the bill Mills had renumbered H.R. 6675. His provision required changes in the customary billing procedure of most hospitals, and became the subject of bitter disagreement. Such an arrangement, hospital officials quickly reminded the committee, would cause administrative difficulties and upset existing arrangements. But Mills stuck by his suggestion and easily won committee approval. More than any other issue, the method of paying these hospital specialists was to plague efforts in the Senate and conference committee to find a compromise version of the bill Mills steered through the Ways and Means Committee and the House.

Ways and Means also required more cautious financing of the hospital program than the administration suggested. Social Security taxes—and the wage base on which those taxes would be levied—were increased so as to accommodate even the most extraordinary increases in costs. The final committee report announced with some pride that their estimates of future hospital benefits reflected a "more conservative basis than recommended by the [1964 Social Security] Advisory Council and, in fact, more conservative than those used by the insurance industry in its estimates of proposals of this type." (Mills' penchant for "actuarial soundness" was justified by Medicare's costs during the first year of operation; in 1966 both hospital and physician charges more than doubled their past average rate of yearly increase, thus substantially inflating program costs beyond HEW's initial predictions.)

Throughout March, Mills called on committee members, HEW officials, and interest group representatives to lend their aid in drafting a combination bill. The advice of the Blue Cross and American Hospital Associations was taken frequently on technical questions about hospital benefits. HEW spokesmen were asked to discuss many details with directly interested professional groups and report back their findings. Blood bank organizations, for instance, were consulted on whether Medicare's insurance of blood costs would hamper voluntary blood-giving drives. Their fear that it would prompted the committee to require that Medicare beneficiaries pay for or replace the first three pints of blood used during hospitalization. Throughout, Mills left no doubt that he was first among equals —he acted as the conciliator, the negotiator, the manager of the bill, always willing to praise others, but guiding the "marking up" of H.R. 6675 through persuasion, entreaty, authoritative expertise, and control of the agenda.

The Medicare bill the committee reported to the House on March 29, 1965, included parts of the administration bill, the Byrnes benefit package, and the AMA suggestion of an expanded Kerr-Mills program. These features were incorporated into two amendments to the Social Security Act: Titles 18 and 19. Title 18's first section (Part A) included the hospital insurance program, the revised version of H.R. 1. Part B represented the modified Byrnes proposal of voluntary doctors' insurance. And Title 19 offered a liberalized Kerr-Mills program that, contrary to AMA intentions, was an addition to rather than a substitution for the other proposals.

On the final vote of the committee, the Republicans held their ranks, and H.R. 6675 was reported out on a straight party vote of 17–8. When the House met on April 8 to vote on what had become known as the Mills bill, they gave the Ways and Means chairman a standing ovation. In a masterly explanation of the complicated measure (now 296 pages long), Mills demonstrated the thoroughness with which his committee had done its work. Byrnes presented his alternative bill after Mills had finished, and a vote was taken on whether to recommit H.R. 6675 in favor of the Republican alternative. The motion to recommit was defeated by 45 votes; 63 Democrats defected to the Republican measure, and only ten Republicans voted with the Democratic majority. Once it was clear that H.R. 6675 would pass, party lines re-formed and the House sent the Mills bill to the Senate by an overwhelming margin of 315–115.

What had changed Mills from a Medicare obstructionist to an expansion-minded innovator? Critics speculated on whether the shift represented "rationality" or "rationalization," but none doubted Mills' central role in shaping the contents of the new legislative proposal. The puzzle includes two distinct issues: why did Mills seek to expand the administration's bill, and what explains the form of the expansion he helped to engineer?

By changing from opponent to manager, Mills assured himself control of the content of H.R. 1 at a time when it might have been pushed through the Congress despite him. By encouraging innovation and incorporating more generous benefits into the legislation, Mills undercut future claims that his committee had produced an "inadequate" bill. In both respects, Mills became what Tom Wicker of *The New York Times* termed the "architect of victory for medical care, rather than just another devoted but defeated supporter" of the Kerr-Mills welfare approach.* Mills' conception of himself as the active head of an autonomous, technically expert committee helps to explain his interest in shaping legislation he could no longer block, and his preoccupation with cautious financing of the social security system made him willing to combine benefit and financing arrangements that had been presented as alternatives. The use of general revenues and beneficiary premiums in the financing of physicians' services insurance was the committee's way of making certain the aged and the federal treasury would have to finance any benefit changes, not the social security trust funds. In an interview during the summer of 1965, Mills explained that inclusion of medical insurance would "build a fence around the Medicare program" and forestall subsequent demands for liberalization that "might be a burden on the economy and the social security program."

In sharp contrast to Mills' flexibility, HEW cautiously had settled

---

*"Medicare's Progress," *The New York Times*, March 25, 1965.

for proposing its familiar King-Anderson plan. In comparison to the committed Medicare advocates, Mills was the more astute in realizing how much the Johnson landslide of 1964 had changed the constraints and incentives facing the 89th Congress. President Johnson, busy with the demands of a massive set of executive proposals, was willing to settle for the hospitalization insurance which the election had insured. Liberal supporters of the Johnson administration were astounded by Ways and Means improvement of Medicare and befuddled by its causes. *The New Republic* captured the mood of this public at the time of the House vote, suggesting that the Mills bill could "only be discussed in superlatives":

fantastically enough, there was a tendency to expand [the administration's bill] in the House Committee. Republicans and the American Medical Association complained that Medicare "did not go far enough." Trying to kill the bill they offered an alternative—a voluntary insurance plan covering doctors' fees, drugs, and similar services. What did the House Ways and Means Committee do? It added [these features] to its own bill. Will this pass? We don't know, but some bill will pass.*

H.R. 6675 Passes the Senate, April–July

There was really no question that the expansion of Medicare would be sustained by the more liberal Senate and its Finance Committee. But the precise levels of benefits and form of administration were by no means certain. The Finance Committee chairman, Russell Long (D., La.), held extended hearings during April and May, and the committee took nearly another month amending the House-passed bill in executive sessions. Two issues stood out in these discussions: whether to accept the payment method for in-hospital specialists on which Mills had insisted on, and whether even more comprehensive benefits could be financed by varying the medical insurance premiums with the income of beneficiaries.

The first issue was taken up, with White House encouragement, by Senator Paul Douglas (D., Ill.). The question of specialist payment brought out in the open a dispute within the medical care industry. The American Hospital Association told the Finance Committee that permitting hospital specialists to charge patients

*"New Deal II," *The New Republic*, Vol. 152, No. 12 (March 20, 1965).

separately would both "tend to increase the overall cost of care to aged persons" and imperil the hospital as the "central institution in our health service system." HEW's general counsel, Alanson Willcox, prepared a list of supporting arguments which Wilbur Cohen supplied in defense of the Douglas amendment to pay RAPP specialists as specified in the original H.R. 1. "These specialists," Willcox pointed out, "normally enjoy a monopoly of hospital business," and yet they seek the "status of independent practitioners without the burden of competition to which other practitioners are subject."

The AMA responded with fury to Douglas' revisions. Defending the specialists, the AMA hailed Mills' payment plan as a way to break down the "corporate practice of medicine" which made many radiologists, anesthesiologists, pathologists, and physiatrists coerced "employees" of hospitals. "Medical care," the AMA reminded the Finance Committee, "is the responsibility of physicians, not hospitals." Apparently unconvinced, the senators approved the Douglas amendment in early June.

In mid-June the Finance Committee approved a plan to eliminate time limits on the use of hospitals and nursing homes. The supporters of this amendment were a mixed lot of pro- and anti-Medicare Senators, and it was clear the latter group thought this change might deadlock the entire bill. For those who wanted more adequate protection against financial catastrophe there was the subsequent realization that a well-intentioned mistake had been made. With the White House and HEW insisting on a reconsideration, the committee scrapped the amendment on June 23 by a vote of 10–7. In its place, it provided unlimited additional days of hospital care for which the patient would contribute $10 per day.

The Finance Committee also took up a variety of provisions within the Mills bill which administration spokesmen considered "important defects." The Medicare sponsor in the Senate, Clinton Anderson, argued that paying physicians their "usual and customary fees" (the Byrnes suggestion) would "significantly and unnecessarily inflate the cost of the program to the tax-payer and to the aged." The House bill had left the determination of what was a "reasonable charge" to the insurance companies, which would act as intermediaries for the medical insurance program, and Anderson saw no reason why these companies would save the government from an "open-ended payment" scheme. Medical spokesmen, however, were so critical of the overall Medicare legislation that fears of a physicians' boycott, and the absence of an obviously attractive alternative, persuaded Senate reformers not to raise further questions about the sensitive issue of what constituted reasonable charges.

The Senate, unlike the House, does not vote on social security bills under a closed rule. This meant further amendments and debate would take place on the Senate floor on the Finance Committee's somewhat altered version of the Mills bill. On July 6 debate was opened and the Senate quickly agreed to accept the committee recommendation to insure unlimited hospital care with $10 co-insurance payments after 60 days. Three days later, after heated discussion, the Senate finished with its amendments, and passed its version of Medicare by a vote of 68–21. On the crucial but unsuccessful vote to exclude Part A from the insurance program, 18 Republicans and 8 southern Democrats took the losing side. According to newspaper estimates, the expanded bill passed by the Senate increased the "price tag on Medicare" by $900 million. The conference committee was certain to have a number of financial and administrative differences to work out through compromise.

Medicare Comes Out of the Conference Committee, July 26, 1965

More than 500 differences were resolved in conference between the Senate and House versions of Medicare. Most of the changes were made through the standard bargaining methods of quid pro quo and splitting the difference. The most publicized decision was the rejection of the Douglas plan for paying RAPP specialists under the hospital insurance program. The bulk of the decisions were compromises between divergent benefit levels. The changes of duration and type of benefit involved either accepting one of the two congressional versions or combining differing provisions. The decisions on the five basic benefits in the hospital plan aptly illustrate these patterns of accommodation:

1. *Benefit duration.* House provided 60 days of hospital care after a deductible of $40. Senate provided unlimited duration but with $10 co-insurance payments for each day in excess of 60. *Conference* pro-

vided 60 days with the $40 House deductible, and an additional 30 days with the Senate's $10 co-insurance provision.

2. *Posthospital extended care (skilled nursing home)*. House provided 20 days of such care with 2 additional days for each unused hospital day, but a maximum of 100 days. Senate provided 100 days, but imposed a $5 a day co-insurance for each day in excess of 20. *Conference* adopted Senate version.

3. *Posthospital home-health visits*. House authorized 100 visits after hospitalization. Senate increased the number of visits to 175, and deleted requirements of hospitalization. *Conference* adopted House version.

4. *Outpatient diagnostic services*. House imposed a $20 deductible with this amount credited against an in-patient hospital deductible imposed at the same hospital within 20 days. Senate imposed a 20 per cent coinsurance on such services, removed the credit against the in-patient hospital deductible but allowed a credit for the deductible as an incurred expense under the voluntary supplementary program (for deductible and reimbursement purposes). *Conference* adopted Senate version.

5. *Psychiatric facilities*. House provided for 60 days of psychiatric hospital care with a 180-day lifetime limit in the voluntary supplementary program. Senate moved these services over into basic hospital insurance and increased the lifetime limit to 210 days. *Conference* accepted the Senate version but reduced the lifetime limit to 190 days.

None of these compromises satisfied the pro-Medicare pressure groups which had been anxious to make the law administratively less complicated. By late July, the conference committee had finished its report. On July 27, the House passed the revised bill by a margin of 307–116 and the Senate followed suit two days later with a 70–24 vote. On July 30, 1965, President Johnson signed the Medicare bill into Public Law 89–97, at the ceremony in Independence, Missouri, described at the beginning of this study.

1965 Outcome: Explanation and Issues

One of the most important lessons of Medicare's enactment is that the events surrounding its passage were atypical. The massive Democratic electoral victories in 1964 created a solid majority in Congress for the president's social welfare bills, including aid to education, Medicare, and the Economic Opportunity Act. To find the most recent precedent, we must go back almost thirty

years, to Franklin Roosevelt's New Deal Congresses. In the intervening years, we find a different pattern. Democratic majorities in
the Congress have not been uncommon, but normally the partisan
margins have been sufficiently close on many issues to give the
balance of power to minority groups within the party. Under these
circumstances, states' rights southern congressmen in coalition with
Republicans have often been successful in blocking or delaying bills
which entail the expansion of federal control.

The fragmentation of authority in the Congress compounds the
opportunities for minorities to block legislation; bills must be subjected to committees, subcommittees, procedural formalities, and
conference groups. To be sure, a solid majority support for a given
bill can ensure that it will emerge, more or less intact, as law, even
though it may pass under the jurisdiction of hostile congressmen
in the process. Ordinarily, however, it is difficult to create a committed majority. President Kennedy, in 1961, avoided a major
confrontation over Medicare because it was uncertain whether the
bill could pass a House vote and because he needed the support of
Ways and Means members for his other programs. Congressmen
must frequently make similar decisions; for example, many representatives who supported Medicare before 1965 were nonetheless
unwilling to launch a major drive to extract it from Ways and
Means. Like the president, they often needed the support of Medicare opponents for other legislation which they believed was more
important or had a better chance for successful enactment.

Within this context, backers of controversial legislation generally
adopt a strategy which looks to the gradual accretion of support.
They frame the issues so that opponents will find them difficult to
attack, then set out to accumulate the necessary votes. Particular
attention is given to crucial committee bottlenecks. The Executive
relies heavily on the influence of the House and Senate leadership
in this effort, and acts on the assumption that although it is seldom
possible to change the mind of a congressman on the merits of an
issue, it is sometimes possible to change his vote. Though the congressional leadership lacks formal means for enforcing party discipline, they have a variety of informal resources. Their personal
influence with the regional caucuses who selected Ways and Means
committeemen, for example, allowed them to deny assignments
to Medicare opponents and thereby to alter gradually the voting
margin on the committee.

By 1964, the use of this accretionist strategy by Medicare supporters seemed on the verge of success; and had the elections of that year resulted in the usual relatively close partisan margins in Congress, the Medicare Act of 1965 would have been much narrower in scope, and its passage would stand as a vindication of the incrementalist strategy. In fact, the 1964 elections returned a Congress in which many of the usual patterns of bargaining were irrelevant. The Medicare bill which finally became law must be analyzed according to the various responses to the highly unusual circumstances in that Congress.

In seeking answers as to why the legislative outcome differed so markedly from the administration's input, three separable issues are involved. Why did the traditional hospitalization insurance proposal pass as one part of the composite legislation? The congressional realignment after the elections of 1964 provides the ready answer. Why the legislation took the composite form it did is partly answerable in this way as well. The certainty that some Medicare bill would be enacted changed the incentives facing former Medicare opponents. Suggesting a physicians' insurance alternative offered an opportunity for Republicans to cut their losses in the face of certain Democratic victory and to counteract public identification of Republican opposition with intransigent AMA hostility to Medicare. Wilbur Mills' motives are fully comprehensible only in the context of congressional conventions, especially the relationship of the Ways and Means Committee to the House, and the committee's tradition of restrained, consensual bargaining among its partisan blocs. However, if the maintenance needs of the minority party and of Ways and Means members account for the Republican alternative bill and the committee's expansion of Medicare, the limits of that expansion require further explanation.

The context of the debate over government health insurance sharply limited the alternatives open to innovators. That long debate had focused on the aged as the problem group, social security or general revenues as financing mechanisms, and partial or comprehensive benefits for either all the aged or only the very poor among the aged. The character of more than a decade of dispute over health insurance programs for the aged explains the programmatic features of the combination that Wilbur Mills engineered, President Johnson took credit for, and the Republicans and American Medical Association inadvertently helped to ensure.

The finished product of 1965 was, to be sure, a model of un-intended consequences. The final legislative package incorporated features which no one had fully foreseen, and aligned supporters and opponents in ways which surprised many of the leading actors. Yet the eleventh-hour expansion of Medicare should not draw one's attention away from the constricting parameters for change. Were a European to reflect upon this episode of social policy making in America, his attention would be directed to the narrow range within which government health proposals operated. He would emphasize that no European nation restricted its health insurance programs to one age group; and he would point out that special health "as-sistance" programs, like that incorporated in Title 19, had been superseded in European countries for more than a generation. The European perspective is useful, if only to highlight those features of the 1965 Medicare legislation which were *not* changed.

Although the new law was broader than the King-Anderson bill in benefit structure, it did not provide payment for all medical expenses. P.L. 89–97 continued to reflect an "insurance" as opposed to a "prepayment" philosophy of medical care financing. The former assumes that paying substantial portions of any insured cost is sufficient; the problem to which such a program addresses itself is avoidance of unbudgetable financial strain. The latter view seeks to separate financing from medical considerations. Its advocates are not satisfied with programs which pay 40 per cent of the aged's expected medical expenses (one rough estimate of Medicare's effects); only full payment and the total removal of financial bar-riers to access to health services will satisfy them. In Medicare's range of deductibles, exclusions, and coinsurance provisions, the "insurance" approach was followed, illustrating the continuity be-tween the first Ewing proposals of 1952 of sixty days of hospital care and the much-expanded benefits of the 1965 legislation.

Nor were changes made in the group designated as beneficiaries under the insurance program. The administration had single-mindedly focused on the aged and the legislation provided that "every person who has attained the age of 65" was entitled to hospital benefits. Though this coverage represented an expansion over the limitation to social security eligibles in bills of the 1950's and early 1960's, the legislation provided that by 1968, the ben-eficiaries under Part A would be narrowed again to include only social security participants. The persistent efforts to provide Medicare benefits as a matter of "earned right" had prompted this focus on social security and, as a result, on the aged beneficiaries. The social security system was not the only way to convey a sense of entitlement (payroll taxes in the Truman plans were included for the same purpose), but the politics of more than a decade of incremental efforts had effectively undercut the broad coverage of the Truman proposals.

Title 19, establishing the medical assistance program popularly known as "Medicaid," made exception to the age restrictions. This bottom layer of the "legislative cake" provided comprehensive coverage for all those, regardless of age, who qualified for public assistance and for those whose medical expenses threatened to produce future indigency. As in the Kerr-Mills bill which it succeeded, financing was to be shared by federal government general revenues and state funds. The Medicaid program, too, owed much to the past debates, growing as it did out of the welfare, public assistance approach to social problems. Its attraction to the expansionists in 1965 did not rest on its charity features alone. In the eyes of Wilbur Mills, it was yet another means of "building a fence" around Medicare, by undercutting future demands to expand the social security insurance program to cover all low-income groups.

The voluntary insurance scheme for physicians' services, Part B of Title 18, represented a return to the breadth of benefits suggested in the Truman plans (although, unlike the Truman proposals, it was neither compulsory nor available to all age groups). Since the adoption of an accretionist strategy following the Truman health insurance defeats, coverage of physicians' costs had been largely dropped from proposals. Throughout the 1950's, reformers had focused on rising hospital costs and the role which the federal government should play in meeting those costs. Except for the Forand bills, proposals for health insurance between 1952 and 1964 fastidiously avoided the sensitive issue of covering doctors' care. Even when the election of 1964 eradicated the close congressional margin which had prompted the accretionist strategy in the first place, the administration continued to follow it. It was Wilbur Mills, and not the presidential advisors, who most fully appreciated the changed possibilities. Once again acting to build a fence around the program and ensure against later expansion of the social security program to include physicians' coverage, he pre-empted the Byrnes proposal with a general revenue-individual contribution payment scheme.

For a decade and more, the American Medical Association had been able to dictate many of the terms of debate, particularly on physicians' coverage. And although the 1964 election revealed how much the power of AMA opposition to block legislation depended on the make-up of Congress, the provisions for paying doctors under Part B of Medicare reflected the legislators' fears that the doctors would act on their repeated threats of non-cooperation in implementing Medicare. To enlist the support of the medical profession, the law avoided prescribing a fee schedule for physicians, and directed instead that the doctors of Medicare patients be paid their "usual and customary fee," providing that the fee was also "reasonable." Moreover, it was not required that the doctor directly charge the insurance company intermediaries who were to handle the government payments; he could bill the patient, who, after paying his debt, would be reimbursed by the insurance company. This left a doctor the option of charging the patient more than the government would be willing to reimburse. But sympathy with the doctors' distaste for government control, and fear that doctors would elect not to treat Medicare patients under more restrictive fee schedules, made "reasonable charges" appear a sensible standard of payment.

The eligibility requirements, benefits, and financing of the Medicare program represent a complex political outcome, a mixture of continuity and surprise not typical of the legislative histories of other social welfare measures. The long task of building support for a hospitalization program covering the aged had not prepared the Johnson administration for the unpredictable opportunities of 1965. Instead of the King-Anderson bills of the 1960's, HEW had the Mills bill to turn into an operational Medicare program by July, 1966. The politics of congressional bargaining had produced a considerably larger (and many felt a better) bill than the Johnson administration had proposed in the first weeks of 1965.

Epilogue

Since Medicare went into effect in July of 1966, the program has generated varied disputes in the political arena. Both the problems and the procedures for arbitrating them are markedly different, however, from those which had characterized Medicare disputes. Once Medicare was enacted, its publicity value dropped sharply. The press no longer had the drama of committee clashes or heated congressional debates to report. The broad alignment of opposing economic interests that had marked the earlier Medicare debate fell apart as the issue turned from whether the government would insure the aged against health expenses to how it would do so. Some physicians refused to cooperate, but the AMA's president, Dr. James Appel, was successful in directing his organization's energies away from threats of boycotts to consultations about the terms of medical service. Lobbyists representing hospitals, physicians, nurses, and nursing homes continually press their claims on the Social Security Administration, and through their trade journals keep members aware of the actual workings of the Medicare program. The aged, on the other hand, have lacked as effective a lobbying apparatus, and since the passage of Medicare, the voice of the aged consumer has become less distinct. Congressmen do pass the complaints of aged constituents on to the SSA, and for the hardships caused by the program's regulations for reimbursing physicians who directly billed their patients, there was ameliorative legislative action in 1967. In general, however, consumer problems are met on an individual basis, if at all.

The Medicare program has produced a combination of problem and fulfillment. The statistics on participation and utilization rates during the first year of operation seem to vindicate the social security approach:

of the approximately 19 million aged citizens, 93 per cent, or 17.7 million, were enrolled in the voluntary medical insurance program (Part B of Title 18).

one in five America's elderly had entered a hospital under the new law, and 12 million had used Part B services.

hospital expenses accounted for $2.5 billion of the $3.2 billion expended by the SSA for Medicare; Medicare reimbursed 80 per cent, or $600, of the average $750 hospital bill.°

Of the problems which Medicare administrators have confronted, the most serious has been the rapid increase in health care prices.

°"Current Data from the Medicare Program," Health Insurance Statistics, Department of Health, Education and Welfare, November 20, 1967.

The "customary and reasonable charge" standard has been difficult to define in practice, and there has been disagreement among doctors, government officials, and insurance intermediaries about the upper limit of "prevailing charges." Doctors feared that the insurance intermediaries would codify and freeze their definitions of reasonable charges, and their anticipation of a fixed fee schedule gave them every incentive to raise their fees. In the year between enactment of the Medicare law and its initial operation, the rate of increase in physicians' fees more than doubled.

Hospital prices have risen as well (by an unprecedented 21.9 per cent between July, 1966, and July, 1967), and HEW Secretary John Gardner reported in 1967 that much of the increase was prompted by the hospitals' re-examination of their costs and charges in anticipation of the Medicare program. The rapid and continuing increase in health care prices promises to remain a serious political problem, since it has implications not only for the program costs of Medicare, but for the average citizen who now pays higher medical prices.

This and other problems arising in connection with the Medicare program have received attention only after legislation was passed. The fragmentation of authority in American politics and the myriad opportunities for delaying legislative change require that promoters of controversial legislation seek broad agreement among a wide variety of groups on minimal change. As a consequence, attention is focused on appealing symbols and slogans: the desperation of the aged, the inadequacy of private insurance coverage, the fear of "creeping socialism." However crucial these concerns are for the legislative process, they prompt few answers (indeed, little discussion) about how to administer a program once enacted. It is not until programs are on the statute books that the problems of managing large-scale government innovations are directly confronted. A treatment of those problems, the resolution of which is often vital to the effectiveness of any program, would provide an appropriate subject for another case study.

SOURCES

This study rests upon varied sources: interviews, congressional hearings and debates, the personal files of government officials and pressure group spokesmen, newspapers, magazines, and published books and articles on health, medical care, welfare legislation, and American politics.

For the evolution of the Medicare issue, four books were most useful: Stanley Kelley's *Professional Public Relations and Political Power* (Baltimore: The Johns Hopkins Press, 1956); Herman and Anne Somers' broad account of the medical care industry up to 1960, *Doctors, Patients and Health Insurance* (Washington, D.C.: The Brookings Institution, 1961); Richard Harris's history of Medicare politics, *A Sacred Trust* (New York: The New American Library, 1966); and Eugene Feingold's *Medicare: Policy and Politics* (San Francisco: Chandler Publishing Company, 1966).

For the congressional responses to Medicare and executive and pressure group activities, a wider range of sources was employed. *The Congressional Quarterly* and the published Medicare hearings before the Ways and Means Committee (1958–1965) give basic descriptions of the treatment of bills within the Congress. The American Medical Association's weekly *AMA News* provides a useful index to doctors' responses to Medicare proposals. *The New York Times* and the *Wall Street Journal* were the main newspaper sources. Interviews were important, and I should like here to express my appreciation to: Dr. Ernest B. Howard, Assistant Executive Vice-President of the American Medical Association; Leo Brown, Director of Communications of the AMA; Mr. William Quealy, minority counsel, Ways and Means; Representatives Wilbur Mills and Al Ulman, members of the House Ways and Means Committee; Wilbur J. Cohen, Secretary of Health, Education and Welfare; Robert M. Ball, Commissioner of Social Security; Dr. William Stewart, Surgeon General of the Public Health Service; Ralph K. Huitt, Assistant Secretary for Legislation, HEW, and Robert Hills, Irwin Wolkstein, and Dean Costen of HEW. Particularly informative were interviews with reporters who covered Medicare developments, especially Arlen Large of the *Wall Street Journal* and John D. Morris of *The New York Times*. The generous assistance of many HEW officials during the summer of 1966 was valuable in the writing of the final section of this paper.

Three institutions have provided support for initial research and forums for criticism of earlier drafts: The Harvard University program on the Economics and Administration of Medical Care, the John F. Kennedy School of Government, and the Institute for Research on Poverty at the University of Wisconsin. Two colleagues provided valuable assistance in final revisions: my wife, Jan Schmidt Marmor, and A. D. Tillett of the University of Essex, England.

Further Reading

For students interested in pursuing this topic further, a useful guide to the differing legislative proposals since 1952 can be found in Margaret Greenfield's *Health Insurance for the Aged* (Berkeley: Institute of Governmental Affairs, 1966). The National Center for Health Statistics, the Public Health Service, and the *Social Security Bulletin* have published medical and financial profiles of the aged that are valuable and easily available. For comparisons with other social welfare legislation, two books are especially relevant: Frank J. Munger and Richard F. Fenno, *National Politics and Federal Aid to Education* (Syracuse: Syracuse University Press, 1962); and Gilbert Y. Steiner, *Social Insecurity: The Politics of Welfare* (Chicago: Rand McNally, 1966). Harry Eckstein's *The English Health Service* (Cambridge: Harvard University Press, 1958) can be read as a parallel analysis of social policy making abroad, and provides comparative illustration of the distinctively American pattern of medical politics.

Those interested in congressional responses to controversial social legislation in the 1960's should compare this case with the fate of federal aid to education bills in H. Douglas Price, "Race, Religion, and the Rules Committee: The Kennedy Aid-to-Education Bills," in Alan F. Westin (ed.), *The Uses of Power* (New York: Harcourt, Brace and World, 1962). The early administrative experience of the Medicare program is presented in Herman and Anne Somers' *Medicare and the Hospitals* (Washington, D.C.: The Brookings Institution, 1967). A good study of the Ways and Means Committee is John F. Manley, "The House Committee on Ways and Means: Conflict Management in a Congressional Committee," *The American Political Science Review*, Vol. LIX, No. 4 (December, 1965), pp. 927–939. For an authoritative description of the conventions of the House of Representatives, see Clem Miller, *Member of the House* (New York: Scribner's, 1962). For a discussion of congressional-executive relations, consult Nelson W. Polsby, *Congress and the Presidency* (Englewood Cliffs, N.J.: Prentice-Hall, 1964).

STUDY

2

The Presidency:
Americanizing the War in Vietnam

Eugene Eidenberg

In 1964 and 1965 presidential choices were made with respect to America's role in the war in Vietnam. During this period Lyndon B. Johnson faced difficult options on American involvement in Southeast Asia. A critical presidential decision of principle to "hold the line in Vietnam" was made early in 1964, and was subsequently implemented by a series of operational decisions. These decisions committed America to assume the major share of the fighting and to do whatever else was necessary to shore up the sagging military, political, and economic fortunes of the South Vietnamese.

Unexpected events can radically change the direction and pace of government policy making. Such "shocks to the system" were clearly evident with the sudden change of administrations (in Washington and Saigon) in November, 1963, and with the rapidly deteriorating situation inside South Vietnam during 1964. The need to decide, as well as the content of the decisions, was directly influenced by these external circumstances. More typically, the decision making process is incremental, because of the natural instinct of decision makers to attempt to retain links between their present actions and those taken in the recent past and to preserve their options for the future. Normally, action is taken on less than total information, and prudence requires that commitments (especially in areas involving war and peace) be made cautiously to allow for changes in circumstances which permit little or no control.

Decision making, which consists of choosing among a number of alternatives, involves a complex, highly uncertain process. Alternatives are not always clearly articulated, and it is rarely, if ever, immediately obvious which of the available alternatives is preferable. Powerful interests compete on all sides of controversial issues, and the merits of one alternative over another often are only marginally apparent. In the face of these uncertainties it is to be expected that the decisions presidents make tend to be incremental steps based on prior positions and actions and based on difficult assessments of where current decisions are likely to lead.

The complexity of the president's task is reflected in his multiple linkages with numerous constituencies. The policy choices relating to Vietnam were necessarily considered within the context of a host of other problems at home and abroad that competed for President Johnson's time and attention. The years 1964 and 1965 encompassed a presidential election, the extraordinary first session of the 89th Congress, and a series of crises—domestic and international—all of which conditioned the administration's effort to secure a base of support within the government and the country for the prosecution of a major military effort in Southeast Asia.

The picture that emerges is of a relatively lonely president making occasional basic decisions, often forced on him, and arrived at by filtering a continuous stream of events, public opinion polls, and congressional attitudes. These factors constantly suggested varying levels of support for decisions already made, or which might be made. The president did not, and could not, react alone to the events in Vietnam. He and his associates were watching the reactions of domestic groups and other governments (both allies and adversaries), and attempting to evaluate and project possible courses of action. Under Vietnam conditions which they interpreted as constituting an accelerating crisis, American leaders decided to engage in limited war in 1965 in order to decrease the chances of our involvement in major war in the near future.

Major American military involvement in Vietnam has become one of the most hotly debated issues in the United States. The controversy has divided significant elements of the president's own party and led to unusual challenges to his renomination; both developments contributed to Johnson's withdrawal from the race on March 31, 1968. Even as early as the end of 1965, the Gallup poll reported that one-fourth of the American people judged the United States to have made a mistake in sending troops in Vietnam. Two years later the figure was approaching one-half of the population, making the Vietnam conflict the most unpopular war in the nation's history.

President John F. Kennedy wrote, "The heart of the presidency is . . . informed, prudent, and resolute choice—and the secret of the presidential enterprise is to be found in an examination of the way presidential choices are made."* In this case study we attempt one such examination.

Some Themes in the Controversy

What were the views of those who prevailed in the Vietnam decisions and who opposed the deepening American commitment? What were the competing theories about the events in Vietnam out of which came the alternatives and the decisions?

In 1961 the State Department published a white paper defining the conflict in South Vietnam.† It characterized the guerrilla warfare techniques in use as originating in the teachings and writings of Mao Tse-tung and as having been employed earlier in Malaya, Greece, the Philippines, Cuba, and Laos. Its employment in Vietnam was unique, the white paper urged, because ". . . the country is divided and one-half provides a safe sanctuary from which subversion in the other half is directed and supported with both personnel and materiel."

Back in 1954, France had surrendered her colonial dominion over Vietnam after eight years of brutal war with nationalist forces (the Vietminh) led by Ho Chi Minh. The French garrison at Dien Bien Phu was crushed in the spring of 1954 by the nationalists, forcing the French to accept their defeat in Southeast Asia. The diplomatic consequences of the military situation were the Geneva agreements of 1954. Vietnam was divided at the 17th parallel, pending elections to unify the country scheduled for the summer of 1956. These elec-

*Theodore C. Sorensen, *Decision-Making in the White House* (New York: Columbia Paperback, 1963), Foreword by John F. Kennedy, p. xii.
†"A Threat to the Peace: North Vietnam's Effort to Conquer South Vietnam."

AREAS OF CONTROL AND INFLUENCE IN SOUTH VIETNAM, JANUARY 30, 1966

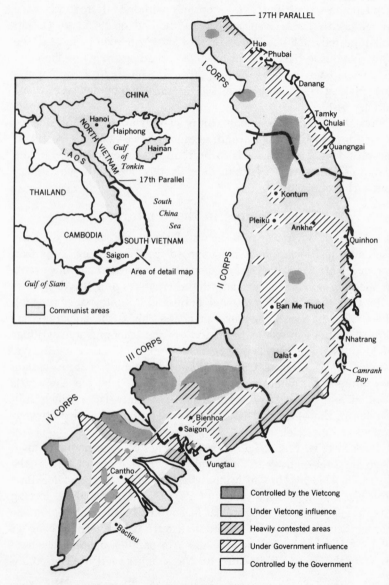

Controlled by the Vietcong

Under Vietcong influence

Heavily contested areas

Under Government influence

Controlled by the Government

© 1966 by the New York Times Company. Reprinted by permission.

tions were never held because the Premier of South Vietnam, Ngo Dinh Diem, with the support of the United States, refused to permit free elections in his country, arguing that Ho Chi Minh would not guarantee elections in the North.

From at least 1961 on, the official American view was that the guerrilla action in the South being mounted by the Viet Cong (South Vietnamese Communists) was aggression directed and controlled from North Vietnam. Later, the administration of Lyndon Johnson would contend that the line of control ultimately led to Communist China. Secretary of State Dean Rusk told a press conference in 1967, ". . . it is not very attractive to think of the world cut in two by Asian communism reaching out through Southeast Asia and Indonesia, which we know has been their objective, and that these hundreds of millions of people in the free nations of Asia should be under the deadly and constant pressure of the authorities in Peking. . . ."

Many opponents of the American role in Vietnam insist that a clear distinction must be drawn between the indigenous guerrillas of the South and the government of North Vietnam and, similarly, between North Vietnam and China. There is considerable evidence to suggest that the Viet Cong are an admixture of communists and nationalists who first mounted their insurgency against the French colonists and then against the repressive and authoritarian Diem regime which replaced French dominion. In addition, the long history of suspicion and conflict between the peoples of Vietnam and China reduces the likelihood that North Vietnam, even as a communist state, takes its orders from Peking. Furthermore, whatever the source of the hostilities, many have argued that the unfavorable political and military conditions in South Vietnam made unwise any extensive American military involvement.

The debate has not turned solely on the war's origins and support. A major element in the case for Americanizing the war concerns what Secretary of State Dean Rusk has called the "credibility of the pledged word of the United States." Under the Southeast Asia Treaty Organization (SEATO) protocols signed by the United States in 1954, each signatory agreed to recognize that aggression in the treaty area was a threat to the peace and safety of all signatories. This basic premise of collective security, and the American interpretation of its relevance in the Vietnam case, obliged the

United States to come to the military aid of South Vietnam upon its request. It is argued that to meet such a commitment wherever it arises, and no matter how uncomfortable its consequences, reduces the risks of open aggression in other, more dangerous circumstances. Secretary Rusk has urged repeatedly that if any adversary should suppose that our treaties are a bluff, or will be abandoned if the going gets tough, the result could be catastrophe for all mankind.

The opposing view is in part a direct attack on this interpretation of the obligation imposed on the signatories of the SEATO pact, and in part a pessimistic assessment of the possibilities of American success in South Vietnam. On the former point, John Foster Dulles, Secretary of State during the Eisenhower administration, told the Senate Committee on Foreign Relations in 1954 that the SEATO pact did not oblige the United States to put down a revolutionary movement that used subversive techniques, but rather was intended to deal with the more traditional threats to the peace posed by ordinary armed attack. The question here still turns on whether the events in Vietnam which ultimately led to large-scale American involvement were, in fact, revolutionary or were the result of overt aggression from the North.

But beyond the legal question of SEATO obligations there is dispute over a fundamental political judgment. Dissenters against American policy argue that South Vietnam is neither a nation-state in law or in the attitudes of its people, and that military and political stability cannot be achieved in a system that lacks even a minimum of support and allegiance of its citizens. In a report to the Senate back in 1953, Mike Mansfield (D., Mont.) said, "The basic problem which confronts all three governments [of the French Indochinese Empire], and particularly that of Vietnam, is to put down firm roots in their respective populations." Ten years later, President Kennedy reluctantly concluded that the political climate in South Vietnam had not improved. On September 2, 1963, he observed that while the United States would continue to assist the South in its fight against the guerrillas, ". . . the war [cannot] be won unless the people support the effort, and, in my opinion, in the last two months the government has gotten out of touch with the people. . . ."

The question of whether South Vietnam was either a legally or militarily defensible nation-state became secondary to the proposition—often called the "domino theory"—that on the protection of South Vietnam hinged the fate of all Southeast Asia and beyond. President Kennedy, again in September of 1963, indicated his belief in the correctness of the domino theory, "China is so large, looms so high just beyond the frontiers, that if South Vietnam went, it would not only give them an improved geographic position for a guerrilla assault on Malaya but would also give the impression that the wave of the future in Southeast Asia was China and the communists. So I believe it."

The debate on these and other points, all relating to the justification for the United States assuming the brunt of the war, intensified as American involvement deepened. While the Johnson administration sought to justify the war to critics who objected to the intensification of the fighting, it simultaneously sought to satisfy other critics that enough military pressure was being used to achieve victory. The administration insisted that its prosecution of the war in Vietnam represented a middle ground of restraint between unacceptable extremist alternatives. Secretary Rusk wrote: "I find no significant body of American opinion which would have us withdraw from Vietnam and abandon Southeast Asia to the fate which Asian communism has planned for it. Similarly, I find no serious opinion among us which wishes to transform this struggle into a general war."

The rhetoric surrounding the Vietnam issue had other dimensions. Efforts have been made to draw analogies between advocacy of withdrawal from Vietnam and appeasement of Adolf Hitler in the 1930's. The practice of finding historical parallels is not the province of the war's advocates alone. In 1966 a suggestion came from a French newspaper, *Les Temps Modernes*, that the communist world (e.g., the Soviet Union) prepare for a military blow against the United States Seventh Fleet, using as justification the proposition that American intervention in Vietnam without a Soviet response was appeasement in the pattern of the British at Munich. David Schoenbrun, an American correspondent who has reported from Vietnam, wrote in 1966:

I have never accepted the correlation between Munich and a settlement in Vietnam. Mao Tse-tung is not a Hitler, nor is Ho Chi Minh his servant. North Vietnam is not a powerful imperialist nation like Germany.*

*Theodore Draper, *The Abuse of Power* (New York: The Viking Press, 1966), p. 215.

As the American involvement in Vietnam deepened, domestic criticism intensified and broadened, and the rationale for American commitment similarly expanded, leading to an escalation of rhetoric and justification. The early rationale was keyed to the presence of American advisors and small numbers of American troops, and it held that the war had to be won by the efforts of the indigenous population, since protection of their freedom was ostensibly the central issue. The later rationale had to relate to the presence of more than 500,000 American troops in active combat and bearing the brunt of the military conduct of the war, and it therefore stressed the protection of America's vital national security. Complicating any evaluation of these rationales was the fact that the enlargement of the American involvement itself heightened American stakes in the war's outcome. Actions inescapably have their own momentum and consequences, and thus become new factors to be considered in determining the next action.

The International Environment

The climate of "world opinion" and the official posture of other governments comprise important parts of the context within which the American decision to commit its military resources has been made. Similarly, the United States role in Vietnam has had important influence on its relationships with other nations.

The Soviet-American relationship is of dominant concern because the threat of nuclear holocaust hangs over every major policy difference that develops between the two countries. The threat to improved Soviet-American relations has been apparent at every stage of the Vietnam situation. In 1966 (after the point of basic and operational decision), President Johnson publicly appealed to the Soviet Union to look beyond the Vietnam conflict because, as he put it, American goals in South Vietnam "do not threaten the vital interests of the Soviet Union or the territory of any of her friends." Of course the Soviets were under severe pressure within the communist world to maintain their commitments to North Vietnam.

In addition to affecting the critical American-Soviet relationship, American decisions on Vietnam have affected American relations with Western European allies. The United States has bilateral and collective security agreements with more than forty other nations. Anxiety and apprehension over the deepening American commitment to Vietnam have cost America the support of France, and have kept British support to a minimum while the latter continued her trade with North Vietnam. Within the American government, advocates of a policy more sensitive to the needs of Europe, such as Undersecretary of State George Ball, argued against the escalation of America's military commitment in Southeast Asia.

In Asia itself, the greatest fear has been aroused by the possibility that Communist China might enter the conflict, as she had done once before in Korea in the early 1950's. The commitment of several American administrations to South Vietnam has been matched by pledges of the Soviet Union and China to North Vietnam. Much of the non-communist world in Asia has counseled the United States to move with great caution to minimize the chances of Chinese intervention. The prospect of a general war in Asia, involving the armies of mainland China, has deeply troubled such governments as India, Pakistan, Japan, and Indonesia, all concerned with their own domestic and international problems. The only Asian nations with SEATO membership to provide substantial troop support to the United States in Vietnam have been Korea and Australia.

Although the United States has sought to internationalize its response to the North Vietnamese threat through the SEATO treaty, America has in fact been going it alone—and she has had to face both allied and enemy critical assessments of the dangers to world peace posed by the Americanization of the war in 1965. By the summer of 1966, James Reston wrote in *The New York Times*, following American bombing of the North Vietnamese capital of Hanoi and the port city of Haiphong, "There is now not a single major nation in the world that supports Mr. Johnson's latest adventure in Hanoi and Haiphong." On the other hand, the administration has long pointed to the support of many of the non-communist Asian leaders for America's basic commitment in Vietnam. Generally, international opinion has followed much the same course as that of the American population: the broad principles underlying the American commitment often attract majority support, but not the manner of keeping that commitment.

The United Nations

The United States sought to "internationalize" its presence in South Vietnam by employing the collective security concepts in the SEATO treaty (an attack on one member is an attack on all). But in the eyes of the world this has been solely an American effort. Unlike the Korean experience fifteen years earlier, the United States could not have secured the support of the UN for repulsing the aggression in Vietnam. The Soviet Union would not have absented itself from the proceedings of the Security Council as it did in 1950, thereby permitting General Assembly authorization for the UN effort. Moreover, the case for internationalizing the response in 1965 was less obvious than it was in 1950. In the Korean situation, armies marched across international boundaries. By contrast, the men and materiel that found their way across Vietnam's 17th parallel were smuggled and secreted into the South to aid not just regular military units, but also the guerrilla army of the National Liberation Front. In short, the line between invader and insurgent was cloudy at best (especially in the period described in this case study) and widespread political support within the UN for assuming the tasks the United States had set for itself in Vietnam was lacking.

As a consequence, support for the developing American policy was confined to private exchanges between the governments concerned, and the most clearly audible voices were those strenuously in opposition, including the UN's Secretary General, U Thant. American decision makers thus had to steel themselves to the rising pressures of negative world and domestic opinion. On March 31, 1968, President Johnson announced he would not seek re-election, and that he was substantially confining the range of American bombing in an effort to encourage negotiations to end the war. By May 10, United States and North Vietnamese diplomats were having their first formal contacts in Paris to negotiate a settlement to the war. The president's position on March 31 doubtless reflected in part his conclusion that he could not go on fighting a major war that did not have the substantial support of his constituents either at home or abroad.

Some Data on Vietnam

After the French surrendered control over Vietnam in 1954, Ngo Dinh Diem had the potential of being an effective non-communist leader capable of winning the allegiance and support of the people of South Vietnam. With the assistance of the United States, Diem tackled the herculean task of rebuilding a country torn by a decade of war, overwhelmed by an influx of nearly a million refugees from the North, and fragmented internally by various regional, language, and religious divisions. In addition, there was a "network of agents, guerrilla cadres, and caches of arms" left by the 150,000 communists who moved North following the settlement of 1954.

Apparently Diem made surprising progress against these heavy odds. By 1956, when the elections were to have been held, his efforts had led to some land reform, an increase in security at the province level, and a start on some health programs at the village level. A year later, two major changes in the South suggested there was trouble ahead. Diem's leadership had taken an authoritarian turn; he abolished municipal elections, ruled increasingly by decree, and fell under the unhealthy influence of his brother, Ngo Dinh Nhu, and Nhu's wife, Madame Nhu. Then at the end of 1957 the guerrilla war itself was begun against the regime in the South. The question that faced President Kennedy in 1961 was how to confront such a military threat in a developing nation that lacked political coherence and viability. That fundamental question remains one of the most bitterly unresolved issues of the entire Vietnam case.

Both Vietnams are heavily agrarian and rural in their economic structure, with rich alluvial deltas along the Red River in the North and the Mekong River in the South producing large quantities of rice. In fact, rice production in the South is normally sufficient to feed its population, whereas the North falls just short of meeting its own food needs. The industrial development of both countries is primitive by American standards, with the North having a more commercial and industrial tradition than the South.

South Vietnam's population of approximately 14 million is divided among 33 provinces. In 1964 the Army of the Republic of Vietnam (ARVN of South Vietnam) numbered slightly more than 200,000. An additional 200,000 men were mobilized into such units as the Civil Guard, Irregular Defense groups, and the Self-Defense Corps. The guerrillas of the NLF numbered somewhat less than 100,000 men, putting them numerically at a 4–1 disadvantage. North Vietnam is divided into 30 provinces and in 1964 had a standing army of approximately 300,000 trained and equipped troops. North Vietnam also has a home-guard militia of undetermined strength.

President Kennedy and Vietnam

When President Kennedy entered office in January, 1961, he was briefed on a series of communist military maneuvers which sought to clear out areas along the eastern border of Laos contiguous with Vietnam. He was informed of the CIA's estimate that the road improvement program from Laos into South Vietnam "was obviously preparatory to stepped-up military activity."* The larger communist strategy was seen in a resolution coming from the September, 1960, Communist Party Congress held in Hanoi, which endorsed what the CIA called "the stimulation and support of wars of national liberation." The Party Congress referred to the need, in its words, for a ". . . general struggle against the United States and Diem for the liberation of the South. . . ." Another related event stressed by the CIA was the December, 1960, Hanoi-announced formation of the National Liberation Front, which became the political arm of the military cadres fighting guerrilla actions in the South.

The "intelligence estimates," which formed one basis for American response and initiative, had reported a "pattern of infiltration from the North" as early as 1957, with "relatively small numbers of ethnic Southerners returning to their native provinces to encadre and direct the insurgent movement." By 1959 there was a quantum jump in the nature of insurgent attacks with a corresponding rise in infiltration, the rate reaching two to three thousand men per

*This reference to the CIA, and others throughout the chapter to other governmental officials, is, except where specified, taken from interviews the author conducted in September of 1967 with several key participants in the decisions.

year. By 1962, and especially in 1963, Intelligence reported the presence of "ethnic Northerners infiltrating the South to encadre and support the insurgency operations." By 1964 the CIA said that Northerners were being used as infantry replacements, and this was taken as further evidence of Hanoi's dominance over the events unfolding in the South. During 1962 and 1963 the CIA reported a fourfold increase in sabotage, terrorism, and harassments initiated by the Viet Cong and the North Vietnamese. The "incident level" moved from 400 per three-month period to over 1,600 in this period.

All during this period President Kennedy was wrestling with difficult options, which derived in large measure from the absence of a coherent strategy for meeting "the 'subterranean' technique of guerrilla warfare," as former Assistant Secretary of State Roger Hilsman describes it. After several trips to South Vietnam by top administration advisors, the "strategic hamlet" program became the focus of American policy. Its goal was to resettle the civilian population in a series of fortified hamlets in which they would be provided with necessary social services and be protected, militarily and politically, from the guerrillas. The promise of the program never materialized because of rampant corruption, failure to produce the promised social services, and the growing animosity of Vietnamese who were forced to move from traditional family and village sites. The program's failure came to be significant for the American decisions of 1964–1965. The growing instability in the South led to President Kennedy's public acknowledgment in the fall of 1963 that the government of Diem "had gotten out of touch with the people."

The character of the American role in Vietnam had changed, however, as early as 1962, with an increase in American troops in South Vietnam from several hundred to 12,000 "advisors." The decision was not unrelated to the president's meeting in Vienna with Nikita Khrushchev in June of 1961. "A few minutes after this meeting," James Reston of *The New York Times* reported, "President Kennedy told me that apparently Khrushchev had decided that 'anybody stupid enough to get involved in that situation [the Bay of Pigs] was immature, and anybody who didn't see it through was timid and therefore could be bullied.' "* Reston suggests that

*Washington Daily News, June 2, 1966.

Kennedy's decision to place 12,000 Americans in Vietnam was in part motivated by his desire to dispel the dangerously misleading image of himself which he believed Khrushchev held. If Reston's appraisal is true, it is ironical that President Kennedy made one of his first major moves in Southeast Asia less in response to a threat within that region than in reaction to America's relations with the Soviet Union. Though he did not want to precipitate a Soviet-American confrontation, the president was equally concerned that the Soviet leadership not misunderstand his capacity for firmness.

By November, 1963, an increasing American presence, coupled with Diem's growing intransigence and refusal to initiate political, social, and economic reforms in the South, provided the National Liberation Front and Hanoi with propaganda opportunities. But then, as one of the principal intelligence operators in the American government said, "We threw them [North Vietnam and NLF] a major curve ball with the overthrow of Diem, because they then had to fear a genuine coalition of anti-communist, pro-nationalist forces in the South that would have the allegiance of the people." Diem and his supporters were ousted from power on November 1. On November 2, Diem and his brother, Ngo Dinh Nhu, were murdered. A military junta led by General Duong Van Minh took control of the South after nearly eight years of Diem's leadership.

The nature and extent of America's role in Diem's overthrow have never been revealed in detail. Certainly the preceding quotation suggests that the removal of Diem from leadership was in part an American decision aimed at checking the political instability, corruption, and authoritarianism of the South Vietnamese government. The optimism of some in the administration that Diem's departure would create the conditions for a viable non-communist national coalition seems, with hindsight, to have been badly misplaced. Rather than establishing a climate within which the various groups such as the Buddhists, Catholics, and the military could unite, the coup d'état of November 1 released the terrible political and social pressures that had been boiling below the surface for eight long years. In the twelve months between Diem's fall and the end of 1964 there were ten major political upheavals within South Vietnam. Coups, counter-coups, and reorganization became the order of the day. It is hard to imagine a more chaotic political and social climate than that which gripped South Vietnam from the end of 1963 to 1965; in that same period major presidential decisions had to be made on America's commitment and role in Vietnam. Inevitably the instability within South Vietnam became a major issue itself in the administration's calculations.

The debate in Washington sought a military strategy that would maximize the chances for South Vietnamese political and civic stability. The strategic hamlet concept was deemed to have the least potential for damage to the social structure in the South. Many within the Defense Department were pressing, however, for a tactic of seeking and destroying the enemy, on the theory that political stability could only come after military security was assured. No firm commitment to a long-run American strategy had been made when John Kennedy was killed in Dallas, Texas, on November 22, 1963. In three weeks both South Vietnam and the United States underwent sudden changes in leadership.

Lyndon Johnson Becomes President

Lyndon Johnson became president at a moment when the conditions for high-level policy decisions on Vietnam were just being set in motion. The sudden changes in leadership in Saigon and Washington were soon followed by actions in Hanoi and within the Viet Cong leadership that would force a decision on the new administration. Hanoi became convinced that the instability in the South left the South Vietnamese vulnerable to a quick defeat, which could be brought about by stepping up its assistance to the Viet Cong.

The new president articulated a theme of policy continuity almost from the moment he returned to Washington from Texas. On Wednesday, November 27, he informed a joint session of Congress and the listening nation that its challenge was "not to hesitate, not to pause, not to turn about and linger over this evil moment, but to continue on our course so that we may fulfill the destiny that history has set for us." "This nation will keep its commitments," he vowed, "from South Vietnam to West Berlin."

The fact was that the American commitment resulted in different actions under different presidents. (At any time an observer could tell little about what specifics American policy was likely to produce. Specific policies of the moment took on long-term meaning only within the context of their direction over time. Vietnam policy was the result of a process, not the consequence of a single major choice.) It was soon to be clear to Johnson that the presence of 12,000 American "advisors" was not going to be adequate to meet the military challenge that was being posed.

The year 1964 was to bring a severe test for the president's decisional technique. The Johnson style of decision was highly personal and deliberate. Like most presidents, he was inclined to use the formal machinery of government only as a prelude to actual decision. William P. Bundy, Assistant Secretary of State for Far Eastern Affairs, remarked in an interview with the writer, "All the formal machinery contributes to the gestation process of decision, but most presidents concurrently are soliciting the counsel of those they have been close to all their lives, whether they have professional expertise or not."

The combination of long and successful careers in both Senate and Texas politics had left its mark on President Johnson. He was an acknowledged master at manipulating the instruments of personal power—private persuasion and exhortation—but appeared to have less facility for generating public support and sympathy for his policies. This difference in skills may have derived in part from the contrasting demands of presidential politics and of either congressional or Texas state politics. The rules of the game in the latter arenas placed a premium on the private exchange of information between relatively few power brokers who had achieved status. The requirements of the presidency, in an era of constant publicity and instant communications, were quite the reverse. Public education and persuasion to enlist the support of the nation in times of trial and crisis demanded other skills. The process of developing support for controversial policies begins with maintaining a general level of support for the personality and style of the president in the day-to-day conduct of the office, and this was Lyndon Johnson's persistent handicap.

The complexity of the issues a president must confront and the real limits on his power, no less than the personal style of the incumbent, shape presidential decision making in our time. In foreign affairs the president's growing responsibilities to decide the fate of mankind have been viewed by some as the most important development in modern American political history. It is true that Presidents Truman, Eisenhower, Kennedy, and Johnson have committed American troops to potential or actual wars without formal declarations by Congress, but the lesson of the modern presidency is not that its power is unlimited. Activist presidents, after all, have always found powerful resistance to their exercise of the power of the office. President Johnson is reported to have said, "The only power I've got is nuclear—and I can't use that."

The power of the presidency is really the special opportunities and advantages it affords for persuasion and bargaining. The office sits at the center of governmental activity; anyone with interest in the direction and pace of American policy on any subject will look to the presidency as the heart of the system. In the day-to-day affairs of state the advantages in bargaining situations go to the person with sufficient information on the issues at hand. The presidency, more than any other institution of government, has regular access to and control over the information that allows the process to function.

Years of experience in Congress had given President Johnson a preference for acting only when he had substantial information and support, or at least knew the extent of opposition to his goals. One consequence of this attitude toward decision making was that he became a cautious and deliberate man, or as one associate put it, to prefer to act "only when all his ducks were in a row." In addition, he relied on a limited number of people whose judgment he trusted and whose undivided loyalty was to serve him and the national interest. It is instructive to know something about these few trusted advisors and friends who had access to the president as he came to grips with the Vietnam issue.

The Men Around President Johnson

Secretary of State Dean Rusk came to his job in January, 1961, with considerable experience. He taught at Mills College in California, including a stint as dean of the faculty, served in the early 1950's as Assistant Secretary of State for Far Eastern Affairs, and was president of the Rockefeller Foundation for eight years (1952–1960). His role and stature in the administration of John Kennedy and Lyndon Johnson are somewhat clouded. His critics have been bitter and vociferous, and they have depicted him as reluctant to advocate new policy initiatives, and mulish in defense of those already adopted. Others who have worked with him describe a man of extraordinary intelligence, loyalty, and stamina, one who never oversimplified issues, but whose repeated public explanations of Vietnam policy sometimes obscured, for necessary and obvious reasons, its complexities. In his years as Johnson's Secretary of State, Dean Rusk has enjoyed the president's confidence and support, which assured him a major role in the decisions on Vietnam. In many ways Rusk and Johnson have similar origins—modest Southern backgrounds—which no doubt provide personal cement for an officially close relationship.

Robert McNamara, the Secretary of Defense during the time these decisions were made, came to the Pentagon after a meteoric and brilliant business career starting with the Harvard Business School and ending with the presidency of the Ford Motor Company at the time John Kennedy named him to the cabinet. McNamara contributed to the decisions on Vietnam a cool logic applied to evidence drawn from masses of data, which proved invaluable to a president who persistently sought sufficient information before acting. In addition, by the time Johnson had assumed the presidency, McNamara had achieved his legendary control over the rival branches of the armed services. He had helped create a military establishment allegedly capable of responding effectively to localized, "brushfire" wars, as they came to be called. Vietnam became the first test for that newly streamlined, flexible-response military capacity.

McGeorge Bundy was another man intimately involved in the Vietnam decisions. As the President's Special Assistant for National Security Affairs, he headed a staff in the White House responsible for keeping the president informed on international events in which national security was involved. Bundy was an enormously competent and successful assistant to President Kennedy and was one of the few White House staff members to continue under President Johnson. Before coming to the White House, Bundy had been educated at Yale, served on the faculty of government at Harvard, and had become that institution's youngest dean in its long history. His commitment was not to the personality in the White House, but to the institution and what it represented. Bundy knew perhaps better than any man the range of views held throughout the government on the Vietnam issue, and he tried to ensure that all these views and supporting material were brought to the president's attention. Bundy viewed his job as that of a "traffic cop . . . to make sure that the problems that require[d] presidential decision in fact got to the president. In the day-to-day context the president isn't always available . . . decisions are not all presidential . . . President Kennedy, for example, was constantly grabbing at loose ends of foreign policy matters to assert his control of the process."

Undersecretary of State George Ball, who also figured prominently in the Vietnam decisions under both Kennedy and Johnson, was an attorney with a reputation in the State Department for appreciating the limits on American power to accomplish policy goals. His view that the circumstances in Vietnam were not appropriate for American involvement led him to resist the deepening American commitment almost from the start. It was widely reported that Ball often was requested by Johnson to develop and present counter-arguments to official policy, a role which Ball could play in good conscience.

Bill D. Moyers, who played an important staff role on the Vietnam question, had come to the White House after having been deputy director of the Peace Corps under President Kennedy. A Texan, he had studied for the Baptist ministry before turning his considerable skills and intelligence to public affairs. He brought to LBJ's staff a variety of talents, most especially a personal loyalty and dedication. Moyers was to President Johnson what Theodore Sorensen had been to Kennedy: one of several equal special assistants who was just a little more equal than the others. His role in an issue such as Vietnam was largely to follow up White House decisions to see that the execution of policy was consistent with the president's goals. On almost every issue and in virtually every agency of government there is a liaison task that falls to someone on the White House staff. In the national security area McGeorge Bundy and Bill Moyers functioned as the points of contact for the president as, respectively, substantive expert and personal representative.

Maxwell Taylor, having been chairman of the Joint Chiefs of Staff and then ambassador to South Vietnam, had a special influence on Vietnam decision making. McGeorge Bundy described Taylor as "the most knowledgeable man in the government on the troop decisions of 1965." Taylor was of the view as early as 1961 that North Vietnam would have to pay some price for its share of "the damage being inflicted on its neighbors in the South." Taylor also was a principal architect (along with McNamara and others) of the concept of flexible response in military affairs. Taylor and Walt Rostow (who was to become McGeorge Bundy's successor in 1967) believed that American involvement in Vietnam would put an end to communist reliance on the tactic of a "war of national liberation."

Outside the official family of the administration, Mr. Clark Clifford was, in the words of a White House assistant, "a regular visitor and telephone conversationalist with the president on the entire range of issues and decisions that he faced during 1965." A long-time personal friend of President Johnson, he had also advised President Truman after World War II, and is widely credited with having recommended the whistle-stop campaign which helped elect Truman in 1948. Clifford was also something of a substantive expert on defense and national security questions, having helped draft the reorganization act during Truman's Administration which established the Defense Department. Clifford had also been consulted by President Kennedy off and on during his administration. His advice and counsel on Vietnam were so important to President Johnson that in 1967 he traveled as an emissary without portfolio to a number of world capitals to communicate the goals this country was seeking in Vietnam. During 1964–1965 he was in private law practice, though spending considerable time at the White House. In 1968 he became President Johnson's Secretary of Defense, replacing McNamara.

On Capitol Hill there were surprisingly few men, considering Johnson's long career in Congress, who had regular access to the president during 1964–1965 on the Vietnam issue. Other than peripheral contacts with Senate majority leader Mike Mansfield and J. William Fulbright, chairman of the Senate Foreign Relations Committee, the president's closest congressional relationship during this period was with Richard Russell, chairman of the Senate Committee on Armed Services. Russell had been one of Lyndon Johnson's mentors during his Senate days, and his closeness to LBJ was described as that of "a real 'come on the veranda and have a whiskey with the president, friend.'" In Russell the president had a man of towering reputation and skill, and of deep experience with questions of national security. Russell's general position was one of opposition to the growing American commitment in Vietnam, coupled with a consistently loyal attitude toward the president as a friend and as the commander-in-chief. In addition, Russell was committed to the position that if the United States had to be involved in a land war in Asia, it ought to use as much military power as necessary to achieve decisive victory. It is noteworthy that some of the most influential and powerful people around the president have been advocates of a much stronger military presence than has been authorized to date, since in the debate over American policy the publicity has gone almost entirely to those who have protested extensive involvement.

Finally, a number of others were credited with important parts in the Vietnam decisions of 1964–1965. The list should include Cyrus Vance, Deputy Secretary of Defense during this period, "... along with the entire second level of the national security personnel in the White House, at State, and in Defense." Specifically stressed to the writer was the late John McNaughton in the Defense Department, who was described as "McNamara's chief staff officer."

In sum, relatively few people had personal and regular contact with the president on the Vietnam issue. There were those, like Rusk, McNamara, Taylor, and Bundy, who held institutional positions requiring daily contact with the president on specific questions relating to Vietnam. Others, like Moyers and Russell, held official positions relevant to these decisions, but also had a highly personal entree to the White House. Finally, there was Clark Clifford, who held no official position in government, but whose years of friendship and experience brought special loyalty and policy objectivity to the process of advising the president.

Johnson's First Decisions

Barely three weeks in office, and with these advisors around or available to him, President Johnson announced on December 11, 1963, that he was sending Robert McNamara to Vietnam to assess the situation and to return with recommendations for action. On December 31, the president sent a New Year's greeting to the new South Vietnamese leader, General Minh. "The United States will continue," he stated, "to furnish you and your people with the fullest measure of support in this bitter fight. We shall maintain in Vietnam American personnel and material as needed to assist you in achieving victory." The message also expressed the hope that American personnel could be withdrawn as the South Vietnamese secured the countryside and reaffirmed Kennedy's position that "neutralization of South Vietnam is unacceptable."

Certainly this message to General Minh was not an irrevocable commitment to a major land war in Asia. From the start, however, the decisions on Vietnam were piecemeal and incremental. No one decision was responsible for the whole of United States policy; rather, all of them taken together provided the cumulative, consistent thrust of that policy. The New Year's message was in fact the first public confirmation of the president's view that the American commitment to Vietnam required maintaining the American presence in South Vietnam. As Assistant Secretary William Bundy said in an interview with the writer, "All during the early 1960's Kennedy could have said 'to hell with it,' and all through 1964 Johnson could have said 'to hell with it,' and both did not."

The administration's continuing belief in the validity of the domino theory was reflected in Defense Secretary McNamara's testimony before the House Armed Services Committee on January 27, 1964, fresh from his inspection trip to Vietnam. The situation in South Vietnam "continues grave," he judged, but "the survival of an independent government in South Vietnam is so important to the security of Southeast Asia and to the free world that I can conceive of no alternative other than to take all necessary measures with our capability to prevent a communist victory." Three days later, on January 30, the first in the succession of coups deposed the Minh military junta and replaced it with one led by Major General Nguyen Khanh. Two days later, President Johnson announced at a press conference in the White House theatre that General Khanh had given assurances of his intent to step up the pace of operations against the Viet Cong. Johnson reported he had told Khanh, "We shall continue to be available to carry the war to the enemy and to increase the confidence of the Vietnamese people in their government."

By the spring of 1964, however, the Viet Cong were in control of approximately 40 per cent of the villages of South Vietnam, while the government of South Vietnam controlled something over 30 per cent. These figures, contained in an American intelligence report, suggest one of the major reasons the administration was not willing seriously to consider a compromise settlement to the war early in 1964. French President Charles de Gaulle, seeking to restore French influence in the area that once was French Indo-China, recognized Red China in January of 1964 and called for a negotiated Vietnamese settlement based on a neutralization formula. Negotiations with the Viet Cong at a time of their maximum success were viewed as a direct threat to the new Khanh regime, and were apparently perceived by the president as a test of his ability to stand the pressure. It was later reported that the president told his ambassador to South Vietnam within days of Kennedy's assassination that he (Johnson) had no intention of being the first American president to lose a war. In any event, there was no question that the inability of the South Vietnamese army to secure the countryside, even with increased American military and economic assistance, heightened the pressure on Washington to assume more responsibility for South Vietnam's fate.

A Decision on Principle:
The Fork in the Road

On March 8, 1964, Secretary McNamara and General Taylor, the chairman of the Joint Chiefs of Staff, returned to Saigon for another personal inspection trip. The director of the Central Intelligence Agency, John McCone, had been dispatched several days earlier for another first-hand look also. These inspections reflected the administration's acknowledgment that the strategic hamlet program had been essentially destroyed and that South Vietnam's military position was declining rapidly. Terrorist attacks were multiplying, although their peak was still two years away; in early 1964 the rate of "incidents" was four times that of the year before. Hundreds of government troops were killed in bitter and disastrous fighting in the Mekong River Delta area of South Vietnam. Emboldened by this success, the Viet Cong launched a series of offensives which kept the South Vietnamese army off balance. In the words of an officer of the CIA, the Vietnamese situation was "deteriorating badly. The communists had real grounds for thinking they could topple the whole house of cards with a major effort, and it began in early 1964."

In a speech at the University of California at Los Angeles on February 21, the president mentioned the changing climate in South Vietnam, and he indirectly forewarned Hanoi of possible American action in carrying the war north to them. "The contest in which South Vietnam is now engaged," Johnson observed, "is first and foremost a contest to be won by the government of the people of that country for themselves. But those engaged in external direction and supply would do well to be reminded and to remember that this type of aggression is a deeply dangerous game." The press corps traveling with the president to Los Angeles were provided, as usual, with advance copies of the speech. Press Secretary Pierre Salinger briefed the press on the meaning and implications of the statement just quoted. The next morning several papers carried speculation, credited to "highly reliable sources," regarding possible American air raids against the North.

The use of American air power to cut the supply lines running from North Vietnam to the Viet Cong in the South was not a new possibility when the president spoke at UCLA. On June 28, 1961, Walt W. Rostow, an aide to President Kennedy, spoke at the United States Army Special Warfare School at Fort Bragg, North Carolina, on "Guerrilla Warfare in the Underdeveloped Areas." In that speech Rostow addressed himself to the matter of externally supplied aggression in which the supplier nation has "rights of sanctuary." He argued that externally supplied aggression was a "terrible burden . . . for any government in a society making its way toward modernization." He stressed, in a statement personally approved by President Kennedy, that "The sending of men and arms across international boundaries and the direction of guerrilla war outside a sovereign nation is aggression; and this is a fact which the whole international community must confront and whose consequent responsibilities it must accept. Without such international action those against whom aggression is mounted will be driven inevitably to seek out and engage the ultimate source of the aggression they confront." That statement in 1961 caused one high-level diplomat from an Eastern European nation to visit Rostow to confirm its meaning. Rostow made it clear that although Hanoi was indeed making such direct attacks, his statement was a prediction of possible American policy and not a description of current policy. In short, the United States was holding the option of using its air power to interdict the supply lines running from North Vietnam through Laos into South Vietnam.

When President Johnson re-raised that possibility in February, 1964, in his talk at Los Angeles, it caused the predictable speculation that the United States might "go north." Secretary of State Rusk promptly called a news conference to deny the validity of the speculation. Nonetheless, the speech was intended as a signal to Hanoi and was understood as such by those wise in the ways of diplomacy. President Johnson warned that this nation would not necessarily allow the principle of sanctuary to prevail under all circumstances. He deliberately did not specify what course the United States might embark upon, for he wanted to preserve his options in the face of the uncertain future, and he did not want to discuss details of military action before the fact.

Clues that the direction of administration policy was being fixed were provided by personnel changes in February. Roger Hilsman, Assistant Secretary of State for Far Eastern Affairs, submitted his resignation and was replaced by William P. Bundy, who moved over from a post in the Defense Department. (It was subsequently divulged that Hilsman's resignation may have been requested because of his growing disaffection with American policy in Vietnam.) Bundy's job in Defense as Assistant Secretary for International Security Affairs was filled by John McNaughton. Undersecretary of State Averell Harriman was made a roving ambassador, and a national security staff member in the White House, Michael Forrestal, resigned.

On March 15, following McNamara's return, the president presented his view on Vietnam on a television interview program conducted by reporters from the major networks. "Now we have had that problem for a long time," stated Johnson. "We are going to have it for some time in the future, we can see, but we are patient people, and we love freedom, and we want to help others preserve it, and we are going to try and evolve the most effective and efficient plans we can to continue to help them.... We must do everything we can, we must be responsible, we must stay there and help them, and this is what we are going to do." Two points in this statement merit comment. First, the president articulated a determination, independent of what specific action might be called for, to do what was necessary to stay in South Vietnam. Indeed, his comments suggest that no new operational decisions had yet been made, but that they would follow this basic decision of principle. Second, the evolutionary nature of American policy in Vietnam is reflected in these comments. As it was later put to the writer in an interview with one of the president's chief foreign policy advisors,

It was clear that unless there was a wholly unexpected shift in the internal coherence and capability of South Vietnam, they were going to lose. It was a clear and general view below the president that the United States ought to take steps to prevent this loss. . . . President Johnson made the strategic decision to hold in Vietnam early in 1964. He necessarily deferred the specifics of that strategic decision until, one, the election was over; two, the Gulf of Tonkin action had occurred; and, three, a more proximate nationally understood rationale for commitment could be generated.

There is no doubt that the president could have ended United States involvement in early 1964, at the cost of acknowledging that several hundred Americans had died for an unrealizable cause. But those with access to the president were arguing not for that option, but, instead, for continuing prosecution of a limited war against an elusive guerrilla army. Johnson's foreign policy team still believed that if more American troops were eventually required, it would not be to Americanize the war but rather to assist the South Vietnamese in deterring North Vietnamese escalation.

Agreement over the general point of staying in Vietnam was a necessary but not a sufficient condition for the specific presidential decisions that were to follow. That is why in the final analysis it is impossible to date with precision the president's decision that this nation was going to stay the course in Vietnam. It was not an operational decision, which once made was communicated in memo form to subordinates to execute. It was more a personal realization by the president that this country could not with impunity control events in Vietnam, nor predict with confidence when "the job would be done."

This watershed decision necessarily shaped subsequent operational decisions in a context which foreclosed continuous review of the basic commitment. The climate within the senior levels of the groups making foreign policy became one of awareness that debate on the question of America's presence had ended. This was one of the meanings of the Hilsman, Harriman, and Forrestal personnel shifts at the end of February. Hilsman later recalled that President Johnson's ". . . natural instinct was toward a military solution to the question of Vietnam, although hedging it with political qualifications." Hilsman was convinced that a political approach "was the wiser course." In between this basic decision of the president and the Americanizing of the war stood the presidential election of 1964, the Gulf of Tonkin events, and the administration's awareness that the popular understanding and support required for a major American military effort in Southeast Asia did not as yet exist.

The Presidential Campaign, 1964

The election campaign posed two specific problems for the president. First, what would be the most effective way to describe America's position in Vietnam? Second, how could the impending debate over American policy be framed so as not to mislead the North Vietnamese about the administration's firmness?

The first problem was resolved by reiterating the major theme of LBJ's first year in office—continuity. Virtually every action, decision, and speech the president made in the months after the assassination invoked the name of John Kennedy and spoke of present policy as a continuation of his predecessor's. With Vietnam, the president went back even further, citing the Eisenhower administration as the source of present American policy. The long-term direction of policy (the sum of actions over time) may or may not have been continuous and consistent; that is an issue best left to future historians. What the president failed to acknowledge was that conditions within Vietnam, the United Sates, and the world at large had not remained stable, and hence that American policy in 1964 was necessarily "different" from that of 1954.

During an April 4 press conference the president played down any partisan implications of the Vietnam issue, in part by suggesting that he was simply acting in line with previous policy. ". . . We are trying to do," Johnson urged, "what we have done for many years, that is, to aid the South Vietnamese in carrying forward, giving them advice and materials, and making that operation as efficient as possible, in order to preserve their freedom. . . . While we do have problems and serious ones, we do not think they are problems that should divide the country, or divide us according to political lines." On April 20 the president, addressing an Associated Press luncheon at the Waldorf Astoria Hotel in New York City, again sought to make clear to Hanoi the commitment of his administration, notwithstanding the confusions inherent in a political campaign. "This is an election year in the United States and in this year," Johnson warned, "let neither friend nor enemy abroad ever mistake growing discussion for growing dissension, or conflict over programs for conflict over principles, or political division for political paralysis."

The Republican candidate for president, Senator Barry Goldwater (R., Ariz.) chose to raise a question about the desirability of civilian control over nuclear weapons in the field—or, more specifically, whether North Atlantic Treaty Organization commanders should have authority to use tactical nuclear weapons without presidential authorization. On Vietnam, Senator Goldwater declared on March 4 that he believed in "carrying the war to North Vietnam—ten years ago we should have bombed North Vietnam, destroyed the only access they had to South Vietnam, with no risk to our lives." The day before he had speculated about the missed opportunity to use low-yield nuclear weapons in 1954 to remove the protective foliage covering the intricate supply routes to the South. The president and his fellow Democrats happily emphasized that Goldwater, depicted by them as a reckless adventurer, could not be trusted with responsibility for this nation's nuclear capacity.

Johnson's attempt to stake out a middle position was indicated in a speech on August 12 before the American Bar Association in New York City, "Some say we should withdraw from South Vietnam, that we have lost almost 200 lives there in the past four years and we should come home. Some others are eager to enlarge the conflict. They call upon us to supply American boys to do the job that Asian boys should do. They ask us to take reckless action which might risk the lives of millions and engulf much of Asia and certainly threaten the peace of much of the entire world. . . . The course we have chosen will require wisdom and endurance. . . . No one should think for a moment that we will be worn down, nor will we be driven out, and we will not be provoked to rashness."

The president's words had considerable evidence behind them when he spoke. At the end of 1963 there were approximately 14,000 American ground forces in Vietnam acting as advisors to the South Vietnamese Army. By the end of 1964 only 2,500 troops had been added to the total. Hence there was no reason to view Lyndon Johnson as anything other than the candidate who would contain the danger of spreading violence in Southeast Asia. The fact is that through the first half of the presidential campaign Vietnam was not a prominent issue. Public opinion polls showed that at the end of May, 1964, fully 60 per cent of the American people were not following events in Vietnam, and the attentive minority was evenly divided in its appraisal of how well the administration was doing. This poll was taken only five days after Secretary of State Rusk had said, referring to the choices in Vietnam, "A third choice would be to expand the war. This can be the result if the communists persist in their course of aggression." By the fall of 1964 the war issue had become the major focus of the campaign for the American people—in part because of anxieties aroused by Senator Goldwater's statements. On October 4 the Gallup poll reported, "The issue of war and peace . . . may be Senator Barry Goldwater's most vulnerable point—at least at the present. Much of the defection of those persons who classify themselves as Republicans (about 3 in 10) is due to a fear of Goldwater's foreign policies."

Although no president can afford to become the prisoner of the whims of public opinion, mid-campaign popular reaction to specific policies must engage his serious attention. Public opinion provides an outer limit on a president's freedom to act, but experience shows that a president can often form and lead public opinion in a direction favorable to his policies, especially in foreign affairs, where the issues tend to be less familiar to the citizenry and the president's position, in contrast to that of the Congress, is pre-eminent. The combination of Goldwater's statements and the pace of publicly visible events in Vietnam gave the president an enormous advantage that Goldwater could not overcome.

Events in early August gave the president another opportunity to enhance his support at home and to inform North Vietnam of America's determination to stay in South Vietnam. Two United States naval vessels were allegedly attacked in the Gulf of Tonkin off North Vietnam by North Vietnamese gunboats. These attacks triggered the first bombing raids by American war planes against the North as retaliation, and they led Congress to pass a resolution supporting Johnson's policies and granting him discretionary authority to use more military power.

In sum, the combination of presidential politics in 1964 and the events in Vietnam produced a series of cross-pressures on the president. In response, he attempted simultaneously to convince Hanoi that the United States could not be moved from Vietnam by force, and to persuade the American people that he was a prudent man, the obvious candidate for those who wanted no wider war in Southeast Asia.

This condition of severe cross-pressures stems from the presidency's multiple constituencies, both foreign and domestic. Lyndon Johnson's problem in 1964 was precisely that he had a domestic constituency to reassure and a foreign constituency that had to understand his will to "stay the course in Vietnam." The result of trying to make effective contact with both constituencies was, in the words of one observer, ". . . a confusing cacophony of hawklike cries and dovelike coos," which was largely responsible for the post-election charge of the war's critics that the president had betrayed his campaign pledges. Johnson's "credibility gap" became a very serious political and policy problem for the administration as more and more journalists remarked on the inexact relationship between his words and deeds. In Vietnam policy, it was alleged that Johnson had ridiculed Goldwater and then, after the election, had done precisely what Goldwater had been urging. Though some critics have accused Johnson of engaging in outright duplicity on Vietnam policy, the more likely explanation is that the president was trying to communicate to two quite different constituencies at the same time. The messages were almost certain to be ambiguous, contradictory, or confused, and to be heard and understood differently by different people.

The Gulf of Tonkin

On August 2, 1964, the American destroyer *Maddox* was attacked by several North Vietnamese gunboats as it stood off the islands of Hon Me and Hon Nghu in the Gulf of Tonkin

during South Vietnamese shelling of North Vietnam radar installations on the islands.* The president's judgment was that Hanoi had
to know that even in a political campaign America was united on
questions affecting its national interest. The president's response to
the attack, which was, according to a high-level State Department
official, "a copper-minted certainty and a surprise," was to issue
instructions to the Navy on August 3:

(1) to continue patrols in the Gulf of Tonkin off the coast of Vietnam;
(2) to double the force by adding an additional destroyer to the one already on patrol; (3) to provide a combat air patrol over the destroyers;
(4) to issue orders to the commanders of the combat aircraft and the
two destroyers to attack any force which attacks them in international
waters and to attack with the objective not only of driving off the force
but of destroying it.

Late the next evening, in a television broadcast the president told
the American people: "As president and commander-in-chief it is
my duty . . . to report that renewed hostile actions against United
States ships on the high seas in the Gulf of Tonkin have today
required me to order the military forces of the United States to
take action in reply." The action was a series of retaliatory air
strikes by carrier-based planes against gunboat ports and supporting
facilities in North Vietnam. The president emphasized that these
air strikes were limited and controlled responses to the "open
aggression on the high seas," because ". . . Americans know, although others appear to forget, the risks of spreading conflict. We
still seek no wider war."

Then the president reported a series of political steps calculated
to demonstrate a condition of unity and support that could not be
mistaken in Hanoi. He told the country, "I have today met with

*The circumstances surrounding the events in the Gulf of Tonkin in early
August, 1964, have been called into serious question. The Senate Foreign
Relations Committee is studying the background of the incidents to determine
the truth of the administration's description offered after the events. Of
necessity, the sequence of events described in this case follows the publicly
available description reported by the administration at the time. Senator J. W.
Fulbright, chairman of the Foreign Relations Committee and Wayne Morse
(D., Ore.) of the Committee have argued that at best the Gulf of Tonkin
incidents were the result of precipitous American response to uncertain and
poorly defined aggression; and at worst were the consequence of deliberate
provocation on the part of the American ships.

the leaders of both parties in the Congress of the United States and I have informed them that I shall immediately request the Congress to pass a resolution making it clear that our government is united in its determination to take all necessary measures in support of freedom and in defense of peace in Southeast Asia." Further, said Johnson, ". . . a few minutes ago I was able to reach Senator Goldwater and I am glad to say that he has expressed his support of the statement that I am making to you tonight."

President Johnson had been majority leader in the Senate when President Eisenhower had received congressional support for resolute action in the Middle East in 1957. He wanted such support for himself before August, 1964, but it was clear that the American people—and probably Congress—were not concerned enough about Vietnam to endorse action that would increase the chances of wider American involvement. The congressional view of Vietnam events in the years 1961–1964 was radically different from that after 1964. The Congress during the earlier period was nominally controlled by the Democrats, but in fact responded more positively to the views of its working majority—a loose coalition of Republicans and southern Democrats. During the 87th Congress (1961–1963) President Kennedy had submitted a substantial domestic legislative program which received a protracted and critical review from Congress. Not much visible policy attention was being paid to the Vietnam issues. It was clear that America was becoming involved in a peripheral way with a shooting war, but most members of Congress were not speaking out either favorably or unfavorably on that involvement.

It was during the political crisis in South Vietnam in November in 1963, when Diem was overthrown, that the depth of American involvement became a recurring question in House and Senate speeches. All during 1964 Vietnam was prominently debated both on the merits and as an issue of the presidential campaign. Then came the Gulf of Tonkin events, which represented the kind of crisis to which Congress often will respond. The administration was prepared to exploit the circumstances. Assistant Secretary William Bundy has since told the Senate Foreign Relations Committee that a general congressional resolution had been drafted weeks before the events in the Gulf, for introduction when the president felt it would be appropriate.

Since World War II, the president's responsibilities as chief diplomat and as commander-in-chief of the armed forces have become increasingly complex. The sheer volume of resources and power at the disposal of the United States has made this country pre-eminent among non-communist nations. At the same time international responsibilities have accumulated to strain the presidency's capacity for effective coordination and control of American policy. The constitutional system of checks and balances restricts a president's freedom to act, requiring him to share with Congress his general foreign policy purposes in order to maintain its support.

Senator J. W. Fulbright's view of the proper relationship between the Senate and the president in foreign policy was important in the context of events in August, 1964. As chairman of the Foreign Relations Committee, and as a fellow Democrat, Fullbright assumed the leadership for getting the Tonkin Resolution passed in the Senate. Before Vietnam, Fulbright was of the view that the presidency was unnecessarily restricted in its power to handle foreign policy responsibly because of "too niggardly a grant of power" from the Constitution. In 1965 his criticism of the changing American policy in Vietnam led him to reassess this view. Personally, Fulbright and Johnson had not been close during the years both men served in the Senate, but Fulbright felt that he understood the president. He told this author in an interview that he ". . . believed that we were in agreement on the basic nature and limits of our involvement in Vietnam. That is, if it came to it we would get out before assuming control of the fighting."

On August 5, the resolution went to Congress. On August 7, by a vote of 88–2 (Democratic Senators Wayne Morse of Oregon and Ernest Gruening of Alaska were opposed), the Senate adopted the resolution which, among other things, authorized the president ". . . to take all necessary measures to repel any armed attack against the armed forces of the United States and to prevent further aggression." The House of Representatives passed the same resolution without a dissenting vote, 416–0.

The tenor of Fulbright's views at the height of the Tonkin crisis are reflected in his answer to a question from Senator Daniel Brewster (D., Maryland) during Senate debate on the resolution:

BREWSTER: . . . my question is whether there is anything in the resolution which would authorize or recommend or approve the landing of large American armies in Vietnam or China.

FULBRIGHT: There is nothing in the resolution, as I read it, that contemplates it. I agree with the Senator that that is the last thing we would want to do. However, the language of the resolution would not prevent it. It would authorize whatever the commander-in-chief feels is necessary. It does not restrain the executive from doing it.

. . . Speaking for my own committee, everyone I have heard has said that the last thing we want to do is to become involved in a land war in Asia. . . .

The resolution, in the minds of top administration leaders, "was a message primarily aimed at Hanoi during our political season. We were not sure what Hanoi's reading of our response to the attacks had been, and we didn't know how she would interpret our election. We needed to make clear to Hanoi that we could and would respond again if attacked." The president himself indicated that the Tonkin Resolution was at least in part directed to Hanoi when he said on September 17, "Our seasons of debate have been miscalculated as seasons of distraction and diversion and division. There must be no such miscalculation in 1964."

If at one level the resolution was directed to the president's foreign constituency (Hanoi), at another the administration was receiving (in its view) unlimited political authority to prosecute the war, while simultaneously uniting the country behind LBJ's leadership. A White House aide close to the president on foreign policy matters reported in an interview, "From the standpoint of the president the gut issue on Vietnam went to the Congress with the Gulf of Tonkin resolution. We now had the support to do whatever necessary to prevent the collapse of South Vietnam." There has been an intense dispute over what was intended by, claimed for, and done with the Tonkin Resolution. The furor and divisiveness that were to follow the decisions to bomb the north and to increase the troop levels in Vietnam in 1965 resulted mostly from differing interpretations about what was said and meant during the late summer and fall of 1964. Many Senators have since agreed that the resolution was a limited endorsement for limited action, yet administration spokesmen have gone so far as to say that it was tantamount to a declaration of war. Perhaps the only two Senators who appreciated this latter "sense" of the Tonkin Resolution at the time were Morse and Gruening. Senator Morse said during the Senate debate on the resolution, "Senators who vote for it will live to regret it."*

Prelude to Decision, 1965

The 1964 elections gave the Democrats a dominance over the federal government's executive and legislative branches unequaled since Roosevelt's second term in 1936. The 89th Congress of 1965–1966 was to be asked to enact extensive social welfare legislation critical to Johnson's Great Society program. Blue-ribbon task forces were at work early in 1964 developing bills for the new Congress and after the latter convened, the White House unleashed a dizzying flow of messages and legislative requests. The new Democratic majority in the House changed that body's rules to facilitate consideration of legislation, and through it all the president kept in close personal touch with his gargantuan program.

The financial cost of maintaining the American presence in Vietnam through all of 1964 and into the second half of 1965 was small enough to preclude argument that America could not afford at the same time to fund billions of dollars worth of new and expanded domestic programs. By January of 1965 the war effort was costing approximately $2 million per day, including both military and technical assistance. Furthermore, the landslide election victory for the president disposed Congress to follow his wishes in both international and domestic policies in an uncharacteristically uncritical way. The 1965 congressional session enacted the first elementary and secondary education program, the long-sought-after Medicare bill, "war on poverty" measures, and the Voting Rights Act.

Notwithstanding all this legislative activity, the president's time was being increasingly directed to the conduct of foreign relations. One presidential aide mentioned in an interview with the writer that it took "a long time for the president to develop his personal priorities so that he was regularly spending more time on foreign rather than domestic policy." The aide stressed that it was not a matter of the president not being "comfortable" with questions of

---

*It was Morse's position that the American air strikes against North Vietnam constituted a serious escalation of the war in violation of international law.

foreign policy, as many people have suggested, but rather that it derived from his years of legislative experience and leadership. Congress, after all, traditionally exercises more influence in the domestic than in the international sphere. Whatever the president's own predilections, the unending international disruptions during his first two years in office compelled his increasing attention to foreign policy matters. In addition to Vietnam, there was, in 1964–1965, rioting in Panama, which resulted in negotiations for a new treaty on the control of the Panama Canal Zone; debate on the issue of the multi-lateral control of nuclear weapon systems in the North Atlantic alliance; bloody fighting in Cyprus between Greek and Turkish nationals and a specter of war between those two nations; and the civil war in the Dominican Republic and eventual American involvement there.

By the summer and fall of 1965 Vietnam had come to take the lion's share of the president's time, and his honeymoon with Congress had ended. The conduct of American foreign policy in 1965, especially in the Dominican problem during the spring, created a crisis of confidence on Capitol Hill to which the administration's handling of the specific issues in Southeast Asia was not immune. The fork in the road in Senator Fulbright's thinking about Vietnam came directly from the Dominican experience. The United States had sent the Marines into the Dominican Republic in April, 1965, during an abortive revolution against the regime of Donald Reid Cabral, ostensibly to protect American lives and to prevent a takeover of the Dominican Republic by a communist element. The facts regarding the threat to American lives and the seriousness of the communist threat (the administration had lists of fifty to seventy names of communist conspirators) were then—and still remain—very much in dispute. It is clear that American troops stayed in the Dominican Republic until the counter-revolutionary forces had assumed control of the situation. As a result, Fulbright's confidence in the president's prudence and commitment to the limited use of American military power was destroyed.

The 1965 Decisions

As previously discussed, the decisions on Vietnam in 1965 were conditioned by earlier commitments and events. First, a basic "decision of principle" had been made by the president that this nation would do what it could to stabilize the military and political situation in South Vietnam. Indeed, according to the administration, this was what the American commitment was all about. In doing so, however, the United States government found itself struggling against the forces of militarism, corruption, and chaos that have torn at South Vietnam all during this war. The American dilemma has been to justify massive support for a government and social system that had neither the superficial trappings of democracy nor the more fundamental characteristics of a viable nation-state. Second, the president had received the almost unanimous support of the Congress for the committing of substantial resources in Vietnam. Third, Lyndon Johnson had won an overwhelming personal and political victory in the election of 1964. Fourth, military and political conditions in South Vietnam were deteriorating at an accelerating pace. Of these four factors, the firm administration commitment to "hold" in South Vietnam until some military and political stability could be created, and the internal conditions of Vietnam itself, were the considerations most important to the decisions to be made in 1965.

Debate focused on the deteriorating political and military trends in South Vietnam, and these did not suggest a clear and persuasive line of action for the administration. The disputes over what specific actions to take in providing military assistance to South Vietnam should be understood as a normal condition in any highly stressful decisional situation. When the stakes are high, and outcomes of action uncertain, there is a predictable reserve against plunging into a radical course of action. The merits and counter-arguments are heard and reheard as the president seeks a course that will produce desired results in a situation over which he does not have complete information or control. One White House staff assistant said: "At the time of decision, the president has to make a 100 per cent action commitment on 51 per cent of the information. Unfortunately, there is rarely any middle ground between 'yes' and 'no.'"

The president himself saw the issues in Vietnam rather starkly and heroically. Though specific actions may have been the products of incomplete information, Lyndon Johnson saw South Vietnam near total collapse and was prepared to do what he could to prevent it. However, the widely shared decision to stay in Vietnam did not mean that the people who helped make the decision shared any notions of what it meant operationally. One national security advisor to the president stated: "No one, including the president, knew what it would take to hold in Vietnam. The hard fact is that the government was not asking what the implications of holding in Vietnam were. Long-range planning is very difficult in the heat of the day-to-day situation."

Altogether, the 1965 decisions were the operational consequences of the antecedent choice to hold made in 1964; and they were narrowly defined incremental changes in response to the administration's view of events taking place in Vietnam itself. Several forces restricted the president's freedom to quickly escalate or de-escalate American involvement.

First was the unprecedented election victory which could be viewed simply as a defeat for Goldwater's escalation policies and a victory for the announced Johnson policy of restricted American military involvement. But LBJ's landslide election could also be read as furnishing high support for any course the president decided was in the nation's best interest. By the end of January, 1965, there was a general feeling in the nation (Gallup reported a ratio of 4–1) that South Vietnam was losing to the Viet Cong; that American influence ought to be used to find peace through negotiations if possible (Gallup reported 8 out of 10 favored this course); but that if the issue came to either being pushed out of the country or forced into military crisis, opinion was 4–3 in favor of sending American troops to prevent the loss. In short, the president could count on majority backing should stronger action be required.

A substantial limit on rapid escalation, however, was the prospect of so losing control of events that general or possibly nuclear war might result. Two prior presidents (Eisenhower and Kennedy) had carefully attempted to delimit American actions in Vietnam in order to avoid a Soviet-American confrontation. Since the advent of nuclear weapons, all presidents have shouldered the awesome obligation of keeping a ready defense while also stabilizing international tensions sufficiently to prevent recourse to a nuclear strike. As suggested earlier, in Vietnam the president had to see that American action did not suddenly become so threatening or provocative to China or Russia that one or both would become directly involved. Indeed, the cataclysmic risks inherent in primary reliance on the nation's nuclear capacity was a major reason for America's development of the flexible response capability first made operational in the Vietnam situation. No doubt there was strong feeling within the military and in the administration that this capability ought to be given a chance to cope with events in Southeast Asia.

Finally, an important factor militating against precipitous American action was the general predisposition to avoid any decisions that might eliminate too many future options. Calvin Coolidge's observation is relevant, if a little dated. He was fond of saying that when a problem came down the road he would jump in a ditch, and "nine times out of ten it will pass you by." Lyndon Johnson's style may not have been to jump in the ditch, but certainly by temperament he resisted extreme action in any direction on the theory that it would unnecessarily lose friends and foreclose future alternatives.

The Bombing Decision

If early 1964 saw a deterioration in South Vietnam, by the end of the year the situation was reaching critical proportions. The administration, knowing that a continued American "holding operation" was inadequate, searched for alternatives. A high-ranking intelligence official observed: "There was a major mounting of more military threats than the South Vietnamese army could handle —there was a rupture in the delicate equilibrium between threats and capability to respond. By early 1965, South Vietnam was perilously close to defeat—not a defeat of the sort the French suffered at Dien Bien Phu in 1954—but a Waterloo defeat of attrition and collapse. The will to resist was increasingly reduced. The South Vietnamese army was being whipsawed by more threats than it could meet."

Then at 2:00 A.M. Sunday, February 7, 1965, Saigon time, the Viet Cong attacked American and South Vietnamese installations in the Pleiku area in central South Vietnam, killing 7 and wounding 109 Americans. In addition, sixteen American helicopters and six American fixed-wing planes were damaged or destroyed by mortar fire. The United States retaliated by launching air strikes from three aircraft carriers, the *Ranger*, the *Hancock*, and the *Coral Sea*, steaming about 100 miles off the South Vietnamese shore, against the barracks and staging areas in southern North Vietnam. The president announced that American dependents of civilian and military personnel were being withdrawn from Vietnam.

In rethinking the choices for extending the American commitment in Vietnam, the president's inner circle of national security advisors felt that ". . . the retaliatory bombing tactic—and eventually the continuous bombing of military targets in the North—was less of an Americanization of the war and [was] a step less likely to get us irreconcilably involved than was the commitment of large numbers of troops." The administration was still not seriously thinking about American troops taking over the war, although that alternative was being discussed more frequently. There remained the hope that air power would coerce Hanoi to cease their infiltration of the South, and perhaps would even bring them to the negotiating table.

The judgment that tactical bombing against the supply routes running from the North into the South would effectively reduce the flow of men and materials was very controversial. Studies on the effect of Allied bombing on German industrial production during World War II show that bombing can have the unintended result of raising the enemy's morale while only marginally affecting his production capacity. In Vietnam, the tactical bombing of supply routes involved as targets not production plants, but trails, bridges, columns of trucks, and streams of people on foot and on bicycles carrying supplies and weapons on their backs. American critics argued that no bombing strategy could be effective against such targets, and that the attempted disruption of the supply routes simply solidified morale in the North and made America's conduct of the war a target for negative world opinion.

Nevertheless the administration saw the issue differently. The Central Intelligence Agency was reporting the movement of North Vietnamese regular troops into the South over the trails and roads that had been in preparation for over a year. Walt Rostow, in an interview with this author, dated the start of the decisional process as follows: "The time of decision came for the president when in the latter half of 1964, Hanoi helped support a radical increase in Viet Cong main forces; switched over to heavy weaponry; opened the Laos trails; and used them to introduce regular North Vietnamese forces."

Despite Rostow's assertions, debate over the activity from the North during this period has been considerable. The State Department's white paper, "Aggression from the North: The Record of North Vietnam's Campaign to Conquer South Vietnam" (published in February, 1965) reported only 5,000 regular North Vietnamese troops in the South. Taken by itself, that datum does not suggest why the South Vietnamese were in such precarious condition. However, the intelligence community, evaluating the events at Pleiku and the increased movement of men and materiel from the North, concluded that the North Vietnamese government was moving "to finish South Vietnam off. The immediate impetus for a decision was the recognition that either we fished or cut bait—or South Vietnam was lost."

On February 11 and 24, further retaliatory strikes by American and South Vietnamese aircraft were undertaken. On February 25, Secretary Rusk emphasized in a news conference this nation's view on responsibility for military activity in the South: "North Vietnam . . . has directed and supplied the essential military personnel and arms . . . aimed at the overthrow of the government of South Vietnam. . . . The evidence of North Vietnam's direct responsibility for this aggression has been repeatedly presented. . . ." On February 28, American and South Vietnamese officials announced that President Johnson had decided to open continuous limited air strikes against North Vietnam in order to stem the flow of men and arms to the South and to "bring about a negotiated settlement." The bombing decisions had been made.

The United States government neither announced nor acknowledged that any major shift in its policy had occurred. During a March 13 news conference the president observed, ". . . the incidents have changed, in some instances the equipment has changed, in some instances the tactics and perhaps the strategy in a decision or two have changed . . . [but] our policy is still the same. . . ." Clearly, however, whether the bombing decision was labeled a change of tactics or something more, it sharply affected the world's and our own view of what American policy was. It marked a turning point in the line of American policy that had been building for at least five years, and it signified an increase in the scale of the war's violence. The bombing decisions meant to those in the Johnson administration who participated in them that "we had once and for all cast our lot in favor of major action." For the president's national security team, "the war began in February of 1965."

It is significant that the commitment to bombing was essentially an operational decision reached in the crisis context of how to save the South. There is no indication, either in the published record or from the interviews conducted for this study, that the decision makers were seriously estimating the costs of staying in Vietnam. The assumption was that we would stay and that somehow the cost would be worth the payoff once our goals were achieved: the viability of South Vietnam as a nation-state, the return of North Vietnamese to their homeland, and the suppression of the Viet Cong insurgency. But how the United States government viewed the commitment of North Vietnam was never made clear. How long were the North Vietnamese prepared to supply the South at the expense of heavier and heavier bombing? How much manpower would the North devote to the war in the South? Were the North's leaders prepared to match the United States at every stage of the war's intensification? The United States believed the North was prepared for a long war of attrition, but if we demonstrated that we would stay in Vietnam as long as necessary, then the North's will to endure would ultimately be broken.

The Troop Decisions

The bombing had no depressing effect on North Vietnam's determination to prosecute the war. Hanoi rejected an American offer to negotiate, calling it a trick, and the first three months of 1965 saw a sharp increase in sabotage and terrorism incidents. The American position, Secretary Rusk indicated, was that negotiations would begin only when Hanoi showed that it was ". . . prepared to stop doing what it is doing and what it knows it is doing against its neighbor." Six months earlier the United States had refused an attempt, organized by the Secretary General of the United Nations, U Thant, to set a meeting with Hanoi in Burma, on the grounds that such talks would destroy the morale of the South Vietnamese government.

In short, the North Vietnamese were not prepared to admit the American assertion that they had troops in the South and were therefore helping to prolong the war, and the United States would not permit negotiations to start as long as they felt South Vietnam's military and political situation was not as strong as it should be. The confluence of these factors eliminated chances for serious talks between the two sides for three-and-one-half years.

The relationship between the political instability in Saigon and the deteriorating military situation, even after United States bombing was begun, is difficult to uncover. The decision makers in Washington acted on the intelligence estimates of the time: "[T]he continuing whipsawing of the South's forces was a prime contributor to the political instability in the South, not the other way around." Another commentator, Theodore Draper, wrote: "The crisis in 1965 in South Vietnam was far more intimately related to South Vietnamese disintegration than to North Vietnamese infiltration. . . . In effect the South Vietnamese crisis of 1965 was essentially a reprise of the 1963 crisis, not a totally new phenomenon as argued by the State Department."* Whatever its sources, the political disintegration in the South stimulated the Viet Cong and Hanoi to increase their pressure for the final victory that increasingly seemed within their grasp. It is at this point that the presence of North Vietnamese regular troops in the South became more apparent; Assistant Secretary William Bundy reported that by the spring of 1965 intelligence disclosed that four regular North Vietnamese army regiments were in the South.

In May, the CIA's leading Vietnam authority returned to Washington and reported to McGeorge Bundy in the White House, ". . . the atmosphere of defeat in South Vietnam is palpable. Unless there is a major increase in the size of the army in the field there will be a complete military collapse in the South." The CIA estimate was verified and given urgency by the military chiefs, who were growing alarmed over the deepening military crisis. The decision for the president was rapidly becoming a question, as Walt Rostow described it to this author, ". . . of whether to pull out 25,000 troops or do what was necessary to prevent the disintegration of South Vietnam that was coming from the expansion of the North's effort through regiment-sized units being moved South."

McGeorge Bundy received a series of CIA estimates in the spring of 1965 assessing the consequences for all of Asia if the United States withdrew from Vietnam. These "reaction estimates" argued

*Draper, op. cit., p. 85.

forcefully that a United States withdrawal would leave China as the only world power with influence in Southeast Asia, and would seriously threaten United States strategic interests. Secretary of Defense McNamara had articulated these concerns in a speech in March, 1964, after his return from a visit to South Vietnam. "Its location [Southeast Asia] across East-West air and sea lanes flanks the Indian subcontinent on one side and Australia, New Zealand, and the Philippines on the other; and dominates the gateway between the Pacific and Indian oceans. In Communist hands, this area would pose a most serious threat to the security of the United States and the family of free world nations to which we belong." The estimates also took a careful look at the fate of other Southeast-Asian nations (Thailand, Cambodia, Laos, Malaysia, to name only four) should Hanoi be allowed to demonstrate that a "war of national liberation" could succeed. An intelligence officer intimately involved in the Vietnam issue said: ". . . at root in Vietnam is a test case of the invincibility of wars of national liberation supported externally, but conducted as an internal insurgency operation. . . . In fact this was one of the ways the issue was put to the president when he was considering American responses on the issue." Finally, the estimates stressed the maintenance of the American commitment as a test of its pledge and obligation and of its military strength and flexibility. As Walt Rostow said at a later date in an interview, "American interest in South Vietnam in large part stems from a serious threat to the credibility of our commitment. We made one, started to follow through on it, and then had to decide to go all the way or back down. The meaning of our deterrent capability is at stake."

Again, the estimates were based on evaluations of the costs of getting out, with no questions asked about the costs of staying in. Why those critical questions were not asked leads one to the basic views on Vietnam of the president and the administration's other leading spokesmen. Writing in *The New York Times* in May of 1968, Eliot Fremont-Smith argues that President Johnson took a "poorly calculated and incoherently justified step" (in Americanizing the war), which was brought on in part by his dated cold-war view of international relations. The president and his advisors paid insufficient attention to the costs of staying because they were convinced we had to stay, no matter what the cost. In this view, after all, nothing less than the protection of South Vietnam from external oppression, the containment of Communist China, and the defeat of the tactics of wars of national liberation were at stake.

The president characteristically took his time in reaching a final decision on the question of American troops. "When the president takes a problem," one of his aides said, "he will walk around it for a long time. He conducts a series of discussions; will talk about it with old friends; wait until he has a feel for every facet . . . it is a process that takes a long time." It is probable that the "decisions" to use troops were made in a technical sense in the spring of 1965, although they were not announced until midsummer. The "walking around" also allowed time in which to develop support for an emerging but not yet completely visible policy.

One sign of the growing American commitment in Southeast Asia was the president's May 4 request for a $700 million supplemental appropriation to cover military expenditures, "especially in Vietnam," for fiscal 1965. (At the end of 1964 approximately 25,000 American troops were in Vietnam; by March, 1965, that number had reached 35,000 and by June, 1965, there were nearly 75,000. From the end of 1963 to mid-1965—eighteen months—American forces had grown threefold.) President Johnson told a gathering in the East Room of the White House, comprised of members of the House and Senate Appropriations, Foreign Relations, and Armed Services committees, "This is in no way a routine appropriation. For each member of Congress who supports this request is voting to continue our effort to try to halt communist aggression . . . This is the firm and irrevocable commitment of our people and our nation, whatever the risk and whatever the cost." Three days after submitting his request, Johnson received and signed the measure, which had been passed by the House, 408–7, and by the Senate 88–3.

A commitment as extensive as 75,000 troops and several billion dollars annually, it was soon seen, was inadequate to reverse the deteriorating situation in Saigon. "By June," William Bundy recalled, "it was clear to all the president's senior advisors that we would have to up the level of American troops. . . . This is the fork in the road when we crossed into another kind of commitment." In late June: "A serious policy review was begun. Planning papers and policy review papers were prepared in the State and Defense Departments to be added to the reaction estimates being circulated from the CIA at the highest levels of the government." In early July, McNamara returned to Vietnam for a very intensive first-hand look, accompanied by Henry Cabot Lodge, Jr., who had just accepted assignment to his second tour as ambassador to South Vietnam, replacing Maxwell Taylor. At a July 9 press conference, Johnson indicated that the McNamara trip was likely to be a prelude to an increase in American forces. "We have lost in the neighborhood of some 300 men in the period since I have been president. We expect that it will get worse before it gets better. . . . Our manpower needs there are increasing, and will continue to do so. . . . Whatever is required I am sure will be supplied."

On July 13, the president stated that American military commanders in Vietnam had been given authority "to use American forces . . . in the ways which [they] consider most effective to resist the communist aggression. . . . [T]hey will be available for more active combat missions when the Vietnamese government and General Westmoreland agree that such active missions are needed." These words confirmed that the American presence was about to change from support for the South Vietnamese Army to assumption of the offensive in the ground war. And, Johnson forewarned, ". . . it is quite possible that new and serious decisions will be necessary in the near future."

Upon McNamara's return in late July the president entered a week of "intensive consultation with his senior foreign policy team." William Bundy said, of this week, "we looked very much down the pike, much more than had been the case to this point in our involvement in Vietnam. For the first time we began to have some planning for financial and manpower needs. The immediate choice was to double our force levels . . . with an idea that we would have to go to 200,000 . . . but the president meant to look at each stage prior to execution . . . we envisaged the possibility of future decisions expanding the scope of our involvement."

On July 28, in a televised press conference, the president announced the results of his intensive week of consultations. He reviewed the history of the war and described his conviction that America's presence in Vietnam was important not only to protect South Vietnam but also to save all of non-communist Asia from ". . . the grasping ambition of Asian communism." He mentioned the mounting military pressure on South Vietnam and then gravely announced: "I have asked the commanding general, General West-moreland, what more he needs to meet this mounting aggression. He has told me. We will meet his needs. . . . I have today ordered to Vietnam . . . certain . . . forces which will raise our fighting strength from 75,000 to 125,000 men almost immediately. Additional forces will be needed later, and they will be sent as requested."

Such momentous decisions obviously were not made lightly. For in Americanizing the war, the Johnson administration not only accepted the less than predictable costs of a major land war in Asia on difficult terrain against an elusive enemy, but it also bet that Soviet and Chinese involvement would remain at acceptable levels. The effects of its policies on the triangular relationships between the United States, the Soviet Union, and Communist China re-mained a paramount American concern. As with the bombing decisions, it was mandatory that the American course of action should avoid provoking a direct confrontation with Russia or China. In addition, the United States had to be sensitive to the delicate relations among the communist nations Russia, China, and North Vietnam.

Secretary of State Rusk gave the administration's 1965 view regarding the relationship between North Vietnam and China. He told the Senate Foreign Relations Committee that China was the source of the doctrine for the war in South Vietnam, whereas Hanoi was simply the instrument of that doctrine (the war of national liberation). To others, however, the matter was not that simple. Russia has been the major supplier of heavy weapons for the North Vietnamese, carefully protecting its interest in Southeast Asia lest China become the only communist power influential with the na-tions of Indochina. For its part, China had been careful to maintain its contribution to the effort in fear of having North Vietnam (a traditional enemy of the Chinese) permanently look to the Soviet Union for aid. American policy frequently has been criticized for its failure to exploit these traditional and modern rivalries.

American policy also risked closing the gap between Russia and China, which had been growing with their ideological, political, and economic disputes. Americanizing the war minimized America's capacity to exploit the rift between the two world communist powers, and threatened to reverse its growing rapprochement with Russia, a development kindled by the Nuclear Test Ban Treaty of 1963.

Johnson's 1964 decision to hold the line in Vietnam thus gave birth to a second round of implementing decisions. In February, 1965, the bombing started with a highly selective list of targets approved personally by the president. Through the spring and summer there were small increases in troop levels, but the decision to Americanize the war on July 28 meant that force levels would be maintained at whatever strength was necessary to deny South Vietnam to the North in the short run, and to secure the South militarily for the long run.

Some General Lessons

The Options. Judged by hindsight, the bombing and troop decisions of 1965 followed with a qualified inevitability the fundamental decision "to hold" made earlier. Once the latter decision was made, the tactical (and even strategic) military decisions depended not on the policy initiatives of American decision makers, but rather on the uncertain capacity of the South Vietnamese to withstand the mounting military, terrorist, and political pressure from North Vietnam and from the Viet Cong in the South. When was that basic decision to hold made? Some of the president's foreign policy aides place the date as early 1964, others as later that year when the crisis developed in the South. In a recent book, Tom Wicker, a political analyst on *The New York Times*, says that Johnson made the decision 48 hours after assuming the presidency. "I am not going to lose Vietnam," the president is reported to have said. "I am not going to be the president who saw Southeast Asia go the way China went." Once this goal was defined, all subsequent problems were perceived only in the narrowed context of alternatives that would most efficiently achieve it. It was not until March, 1968, when the president de-escalated the bombing of the North and withdrew from the campaign for re-election, that there was any sign that the basic premise of America's effort was being questioned or altered. In the intervening three-and-one-half years American policy was a continuous effort to achieve for the South Vietnamese a goal they were increasingly unable to achieve for themselves, and perhaps one that had never been within their reach.

The direction of American policy on Vietnam was supported by virtually every senior national security advisor to the president. As viewed by the administration, the operational choices facing the president in 1964 were: (1) to maintain present levels of American involvement with military advisors; (2) to move toward a withdrawal of American forces; (3) to move toward a limited and graduated response that would permit North Vietnam to pull back before the war reached unacceptable proportions; and (4) to hit North Vietnam and the Viet Cong very hard with one or more overwhelming military strikes. The men around the president saw options 1 and 2 as identical in their consequences (a surrender of the South to the North), and never seriously considered them. Option 4 was held to involve excessive risk of a general war. This left the limited and graduated response strategy (option 3) as the choice of all the senior advisors at the time the decisions were being made.

The tragedy in the events that have followed the exercise of that option is that it was adopted precisely because it was thought to minimize the chances of a large-scale or prolonged war. Either no one close to the president considered the implications of the graduated response should North Vietnam and the Viet Cong refuse to yield, or American intelligence about North Vietnam's capacity and will to resist was badly in error. From 1965 on, the decisions to add targets to the bombing list, or to increase the troop commitments became "simply of a tactical sort . . . ," to use the words of a high State Department official. Under different circumstances, and perhaps with different leadership, the alternatives in Vietnam might have been more varied and the choices made among them could have led to a peaceful settlement of the dispute. However, once Johnson made that decision of principle, subsequent American policy in Vietnam was made all but inevitable.

Another close participant said of the mid-1965 troop decisions, ". . . these were a series of incremental decisions that seemed justified at the time. We all faced the tough question of trying to assess the cost/benefit ratio of withdrawing or going on at each stage, and the conclusion was that no matter what the cost might be now, it would not be as expensive as allowing it to go." A member of the CIA with expert knowledge of the Vietnam question said: "There can be argument over whether American involvement is right had we known what the cost would be, but I'd be very surprised if anybody could have said at any point prior to 1967 what these costs would in fact be." Perhaps it was faulty intelligence or the difficulty in fighting guerrilla wars or an outdated "cold-war" ideology that persuaded America that it was critical to fight a war it could not win. Whatever the reason, by now it is clear to all observers that the cost of "staying the course" in Vietnam far exceeded any estimates that were available to the decision makers when they made the choice to continue the war.

The United States expected that its show of force and determination would persuade North Vietnam to seek a negotiated settlement to the war. The American misunderstanding is made evident by the gap between the original conception of what would constitute a sufficient show of force and determination and what has actually been required. In 1965 the administration was talking about forces as great as 200,000 men; by early 1968 American troops in the field had passed the 500,000 mark. In 1965, restricted but continuous bombing of "military" targets in the North to slow the infiltration of men and materiel was begun; in 1967–1968 the North Vietnamese capital of Hanoi and the port city of Haiphong had become regular targets for the American air force. In 1965, American troops were committed to "buying time" for the South Vietnamese to develop a viable nation politically, socially, and economically; in early 1968, the North Vietnamese and the Viet Cong mounted attacks against the major cities of the South which demonstrated that the military security for the population centers of the South still had not been achieved.

The nagging difficulty with America's Vietnam policy is the administration's recognition that "there can be no such thing as a purely military solution to the war in Vietnam," while at the same time its military policy made more elusive the political conditions necessary for a solution. A basic contradiction of American policy has perhaps doomed it to failure from the start. On the one hand, the need to secure the allegiance of the Vietnamese by instituting social and economic reform in the South has been emphasized. It was always assumed that at some point the South Vietnamese would have to bear the burden of their own defense, which could be achieved only if the civilian population supported the government. However, the military policy of searching out and destroying the enemy and his support facilities (more often than not, the villages and hamlets of the countryside) ultimately had to alienate many thousands of innocent civilians who were brutalized, uprooted, and harassed by government and American forces naturally suspicious of potential enemies among the civilian populace, as well as by marauding Viet Cong forces. Moreover, allowing for the quagmire of South Vietnamese politics, American efforts to coerce or other-wise bring about reform of the South Vietnamese government were feeble and ineffective.

   Decision Making. America's involvement in a major land war in Vietnam came, as George Ball wrote, despite the ad-ministration's strong predilection to avoid such an entanglement. "It was the result of a process, not a single decision," an observation which takes on added meaning if we consider McGeorge Bundy's contrast of America's policy on the Cuban missile crisis of 1962 and on Vietnam. "The Cuban situation," urges Bundy, "was in re-sponse to privately held information over which we had complete control. Secondly, Cuba 1962 concentrated the processes of govern-ment so that every decision was made by the president and every-one knew it . . . there was a focusing of the process. Vietnam was the product of slowly-building pressures, both external and internal to American government and to the real situation in Southeast Asia. The issues of Vietnam in 1965 didn't ripen according to any grand strategic plan." Bundy makes an important point, but it should not obscure the judgment that Johnson's faith that his poli-cies would bring Hanoi to the bargaining table was a version of a "grand strategic plan."

Once the choice was made to "stay the course" in Vietnam, subsequent choices were confined to tactics and means in a strategic commitment not seriously open to review. That same commitment led the administration to focus on short-run operational concerns at the expense of long-range planning. It also foreclosed options which were not to be made available again until three frustrating years of inconclusive fighting had passed and American public opinion had become increasingly disenchanted with the war. When in 1968 Johnson announced he would not run again, he became the victim of his earlier neglect to consider fully the implications and costs of an indeterminate and deepening American involvement in Vietnam.

The typically incremental nature of governmental decision making also has to be considered in attempting to comprehend American policy in Vietnam. The scale and character of America's military presence in 1964 and in 1968 provide stark contrast, but the current stage was reached by successive steps, each of which seemed at the time a reasonable extension of the previous level of activity and an appropriate response to changing events. Johnson was particularly committed to incremental policy making prior to his election in 1964 in his own right, because he was anxious to establish links of continuity to the policies of John F. Kennedy.

The evolution of Johnson's policy on Vietnam took place in an official environment strongly supporting that policy. Among those who had the president's ear there were few dissenting views, and many of them, with the conspicuous exception of Undersecretary of State George Ball, took the direction of urging even greater military efforts. It was LBJ's style to rely heavily, on Vietnam policy and other matters, on the judgment of a small number of personally trusted advisors, rather than, as Eisenhower did, on the National Security Council. In this, Johnson was more like Kennedy, who disliked, in McGeorge Bundy's words, "scheduled decision making," and who preferred to work with "small ad hoc groups formed to meet special problems."

Presidents vary in how they structure receipt of the information and advice they desperately need, but none can escape the ultimate responsibility for decision making thrust on them by the modern American system of government. "The buck stops here," stated the motto on Truman's presidential desk. As President Kennedy observed, ". . . the president must finally choose . . . he bears the burden . . . the advisors may move on to new advice." Also, the personal views of the presidential incumbent, as distinguished from the organization of his decision making process, may at times have decisive effects. Tom Wicker has argued that Johnson's hard-line, cold war attitudes on international communism and his newness in the presidential office led him to narrow his options too early and too inflexibly, i.e., his commitment to "stay the course" in Vietnam was overly explicit and premature. Others have urged that had John Kennedy lived, he would have extricated the United States from its enlarging commitment in Vietnam.

Since history cannot be rerun, no definitive responses to these assertions can be had. The Vietnam involvement, however, was predicated on a view of America's role in resisting communist aggression which was by no means peculiar to President Johnson and the men around him. Indeed, even today the growing disillusionment of the American public is caused less by our involvement in Vietnam than by its inconclusiveness and indefiniteness. Furthermore, the intent of the Johnson policy, however poorly it worked out in practice, was to avoid involvement in a major war, which was and remains a goal widely shared by Americans. It is one thing, therefore, to suggest that Vietnam policy under Johnson was flawed by important miscalculations and misperceptions, but quite another to argue that the policy defects derived from Johnson's personal attitudes or that the policy undoubtedly would have been changed for the better had John Kennedy not been assassinated.

The Senate and Foreign Policy. The Vietnam issue provoked a continuing debate on the role of the Congress, more specifically the Senate, in foreign policy decision making. J. W. Fulbright, chairman of the Senate Foreign Relations Committee, came to challenge both the substance of Vietnam policy and communication between executive and legislature on that policy. The dispute tapped basic attitudes on the legislature's role in foreign policy.

A member of the executive branch expressed one view: "Historically, the Senate has only two choices about its role in the making of foreign policy. (1) It can have the role of the junior partner making an important although secondary contribution. The Vandenberg Committee [Senate Foreign Relations Committee during the 1940's], when that committee was coherent and well run, comes to mind. (2) Another alternative is the situation we are witnessing today. A Foreign Relations Committee that is divided. . . . Fulbright has very little clout with his colleagues . . . with the chairman presenting a raucous negative voice." Another executive branch spokesman said: "The legislative role in foreign policy making is limited to the special role of the Senate and that has been modified by the conditions and requirements of the cold war. Anyway, the president can't really involve the Senate with Mansfield [Majority Leader Mike Mansfield] being lukewarm to the effort and Fulbright being hostile and not having control of his committee."

Many senators, for their part, are saying that this administration will never again be able to get a resolution of the Gulf of Tonkin type passed. In June, 1967, the fifty senators briefed by the State Department on the deepening Middle East crisis were unanimously opposed to unilateral United States military involvement. (This may well represent a mislearned lesson from Vietnam, because of the significant differences in American obligations to and interests in the Middle East as compared to Vietnam.)

In the final analysis, the Senate's role is confined by its limited information and by the ad hoc nature of policy making generally. As Fulbright himself put it: "It was and is very difficult to do anything about the procedures of the president." Fulbright had always been aware, as an associate of his said, that "the nature of executive consultation with the legislature on foreign policy amounts really to nothing more than briefings. The 'executive sessions' of the Foreign Relations Committee don't amount to a hell of a lot, just a good public relations job that there is real and substantial consultation going on." The senator felt he was presiding over a committee which had less and less effect in its jurisdiction and that the erosion of the Senate's role in making foreign policy, a trend evident since 1940, was becoming dangerous. Fulbright, in an interview, recalled the bombing decisions of February, 1965, as a case in point. "The president called the congressional leadership to the White House and had the Director of the CIA, the Secretary of Defense, etc. all demonstrate to us the reasons why the only course of action open was to bomb. This was the 'consultation' of the president with Congress on that important decision. Mike Mansfield and I were the only ones at the meeting to demur on the bombing . . . the president just did not give a damn."

The deterioration of personal relations between Johnson and Fulbright illuminates the tenuousness of legislative-executive relations in the foreign policy area. One presidential assistant said: "The problem of Fulbright is not that the president began to take actions that flaunted the chairman's views so much as Fulbright decided unilaterally to leave the team and take his differences of opinion to the public forum. That is not the way the game is played. The president and his administration can tolerate differences of opinion but within a structure of dissent that is quietly approached."

Senator Fulbright's response to this view suggests the profoundly different institutional approaches of the two men to their mutual problems: "When President Johnson was Majority Leader in the Senate, all Democratic chairmen were in a sense on 'his team,' but after he moved to the White House different relations necessarily resulted between Senate chairmen and the President. I suppose that the President desired and expected to retain the influence he had as Majority Leader and combine it with that of the presidency, but this is rather an unusual thing to do. In a sense I suppose one might say that I 'left the team,' but I believe it is more accurate to say that I remained a Senator and naturally continue to have a responsibility to the Senate and to my constituents somewhat different from that accruing to a member of the President's Administration."*

Fulbright recognizes that before the Senate can play a more significant role in foreign policy, "there will have to be major changes in the attitudes, not only of the executive, but in the Senate. The Senate has for several years accepted the premise of Presidential prerogative in this area. I do not believe that [it] was the intention of the Founding Fathers, nor is it in the interest of the country to have the influence of the Senate overwhelmed by the executive. I believe that senators can make a worthwhile contribution in the development of wiser policies. I feel the country would benefit if the executive regarded the Senate as a partner rather than a rubber stamp."

Conclusion

We have investigated here the scope, character, and effect of presidential decision making. We have examined decisions over a two-year period on a significant issue about events over which the president had limited control, and in a context of unbelievable complexity and demands on one man and one office. Much may be learned by reconstructing important decisions, both as to how they are made and how they influence and are influenced by events. The president of the United States must confront the powerful forces of Congress, public opinion, advisors of strong will and talent, and foreign governments in making his decisions. All limit his freedom to act, but they also preserve the presidency as a fundamentally democratic political institution checked and

*From a letter to the author from Senator Fulbright.

balanced in the interest of the society. The debate on the correctness of the Vietnam course America embarked on in 1965 continues, and can be expected to engage political historians for generations. Beyond that debate the Vietnam case helps reveal both the strengths and the weaknesses of the presidency as a decision making institution. Since in our time the national and world consequences of presidential decisions are without parallel, that subject merits continuing and close attention.

Sources

The most important source of information for this case study came from a series of interviews conducted in September, 1967, in Washington, D.C. and New York City. Though much of the interview material could not be attributed to particular sources, I want to take this opportunity to thank the following who gave so generously of their time and information relating to the decisions described in this chapter: McGeorge Bundy, President of the Ford Foundation; William P. Bundy, Assistant Secretary of State for Far Eastern Affairs; Walt W. Rostow, Special Assistant to the President; Senator J. William Fulbright, Chairman of the Senate Committee on Foreign Relations; Senator Everett M. Dirksen, Senate Minority Leader; John Roche, of the White House Staff; and eight other individuals in both the executive and legislative branches of government who wish to remain anonymous.

All quotations attributed to presidential statements made either in formal speeches or at press conferences came from, *Public Papers of the Presidents, Containing the Public Messages, Speeches, and Statements of the President of the United States,* John F. Kennedy, 1963, and Lyndon B. Johnson, 1963–1964, Vol. 1 and Vol. 2; 1965, Vol. 1 and Vol. 2; U.S. Government Printing Office, Washington, D.C., 1964, 1965, and 1966.

Background Information Relating to Southeast Asia and Vietnam (Revised Edition), Printed for the use of the Committee on Foreign Relations, Committee on Foreign Relations, United States Senate, U.S. Government Printing Office, Washington, D.C., 1965.

The Congressional Record, August, 1964, U.S. Government Printing Office, Washington, D.C.

State Department Bulletin, U.S. Government Printing Office, Washington, D.C., 1962, 1965, 1966.

Further Reading

The following is a highly selected list of recommended readings on the Vietnam issue:

Books

Draper, Theodore. *Abuse of Power.* New York: Viking Press, 1967.

Fall, Bernard B. *The Two Vietnams: A Political and Military Analysis.* Rev. ed., New York: Praeger, 1964.

Fulbright, J. William. *The Vietnam Hearings.* New York: Vintage Books, 1966.

Goodwin, Richard N. *Triumph or Tragedy: Reflections on Vietnam.* New York: Vintage Books, 1966.

Halberstam, David. *The Making of a Quagmire.* New York: Random House, 1965.

Hilsman, Roger. *To Move a Nation.* New York: Doubleday, 1967.

Raskin, Marcus G., and Fall, Bernard B. *The Vietnam Reader: Articles and Documents on American Foreign Policy and the Vietnam Crisis.* New York: Vintage Books, 1965.

Shaplen, Robert. *The Lost Revolution.* New York: Harper and Row, 1965.

Articles

Carver, George A. "The Faceless Viet Cong," *Foreign Affairs,* April 1966, pp. 347–372.

Fall, Bernard B. "Vietnam in the Balance," *Foreign Affairs,* October 1966, pp. 1–18.

Lacouture, Jean. "Vietnam: The Lessons of War," *The New York Review of Books,* June 23, 1966, pp. 3–5.

The following is a selected list of studies of the presidency in action on a variety of issues at different times in recent history:

Abel, Elie. *Missile Crisis.* New York: Lippincott, 1966.

Koenig, Louis W. "Foreign Aid to Spain and Yugoslavia: Harry Truman Does His Duty," *The Uses of Power.* Alan F. Westin (ed.), New York: Harcourt, Brace and World, 1962.

——. "Kennedy and Steel: The Great Price Dispute," *The Centers of Power.* Alan F. Westin (ed.), New York: Harcourt, Brace and World, 1964.

McConnell, Grant. *Steel and the Presidency.* New York: W. W. Norton, 1963.

Neustadt, Richard E. *Presidential Power.* New York: John Wiley and Sons, 1960.

Snyder, Richard C., and Glenn D. Paige. "The United States Decision to Resist Aggression in Korea: The Application of an Analytical Scheme," *Foreign Policy Decision-making*, Snyder, Bruck, and Sapin (eds.), Glencoe, Ill.: The Free Press, 1962.

Wicker, Tom. *JFK and LBJ: The Influence of Personality Upon Politics*. New York: William Morrow and Co., 1968.

The Bureaucracy:
Antipoverty and the Community Action Program

Richard Blumenthal

In Durham, North Carolina, the Community Action program meant one thing to Mrs. Ann Atwater and quite another to Mayor Wensell Grabarek—and the difference between them reflected the upheaval provoked by this component of the war on poverty in hundreds of American communities. "I came to the conclusion in my childhood," said Mrs. Atwater, a large indomitable woman who once went on welfare to support her two children, "that there were flaws somewhere in society. But I didn't know what to do until Operation Breakthrough came along. I didn't know what my rights are and how to get things. The reason that the people who *run* things in this town are so set against Breakthrough is it's been such a good bulldozer for the poor." The people who run things—or *ran* things, as they might regretfully insist—do not exactly welcome Mrs. Atwater's awakening. "These antipoverty people come in from the outside and stir up poor and impressionable folks to hatred and distrust," says Mayor Grabarek, a thin but well-appointed public accountant. "It just alienates the moderate white folks to have these people come marching into our city council meetings. It's the federal government challenging local government—the whole thing's designed to bypass or challenge local authorities."

The Durham Example: Marching on the City Council

The Mayor and Mrs. Atwater might have turned into the best of enemies even without Operation Breakthrough. But the federal-funded local agency sparked the "confrontation" and set in motion much larger forces of social change. This strange little corporation won support at first from both the local government and the poor. But it spawned new institutions and attitudes among the poor that ended up challenging not only the local government but the entire local Establishment. Though some local officials served on its governing board, it was set up independently of the local government. It encouraged the poor to wrest benefits from the so-called "power structure," such as more jobs from businessmen, better housing from the landlords and public Housing Authority, and more welfare assistance from the City Council and bureaucrats. Above all, it insisted that the poor organize and speak for themselves, largely through local neighborhood councils set up by Breakthrough.

This was Durham's Community Action, one sample of a federal program hailed by Sargent Shriver, former director of the Office of Economic Opportunity (OEO), as "the business corporation of the new social revolution," and as the "boldest of OEO's inventions." Some agencies differed from Durham in immediate goals and methods, targeting schooling instead of housing, or using legal services instead of neighborhood councils. Others cooperated more closely with elements of the Establishment, even of the city government, which might be sympathetic to their cause. But Durham illustrates the dynamic of revolution at work in almost all of them, for over 80 per cent of these local corporations worked independently of local governments.

In Durham, the first spark was supplied very largely by a lanky, soft-spoken Negro named Howard Fuller, who had joined Operation Breakthrough in 1965 after working for an Urban League project in Chicago "tryin' to get employers to accept token black faces." Fuller and five students began organizing neighborhood councils throughout the southeast section, a Negro area of shanty-town slums called "Hayti." When the summer ended and the students returned to school, he worked out in the streets alone, often more than sixteen hours a day, seven days a week—moving from house to house, making friends, "telling black folks how to get together." The first months were frustrating. People would promise to attend meetings and then not show up; occasionally they turned him away from their doors. But Fuller gradually succeeded in gaining members for the council.

Once organized, the councils decided to make their first fight on housing. In one neighborhood after another, slum-dwellers, by calling out the housing inspector, began challenging slumlords to repair substandard buildings. When one realtor bought forty dilapidated shacks and immediately raised the rent several dollars a month, the Edgemont council proved that the houses failed to meet the local code—showing inspectors the unpainted, rat-infested hallways, the unscreened windows, and cracked floors. Taking on the public housing authorities as well, the councils pressed for pre-eviction hearings, changes in rules for women with illegitimate children, and for an end to unannounced visits by janitors checking for male visitors in apartments belonging to women on welfare.

Since victories through use of the Establishment's institutions produced only marginal improvements in housing conditions, the councils moved the battle from the courts and bureaucracies to the streets. Their most spectacular campaign, nearly ending in a riot during the summer of 1967, involved the Public Housing Authority's plan to build a new development in the southwest district, at Bacon Street, where all but one of the public projects were already located. The Breakthrough councils first galvanized their members to deluge the city government with letters and petitions, protesting the segregation of Negroes in the worst section of town. When the city government flatly refused to rezone, they launched a series of marches on the city council.

On several successive nights they met in St. Joseph's Church for rallies and then paraded, two and three hundred strong, down Pettigrew Street, along the railroad tracks that divide the Negro and white sections, past Operation Breakthrough headquarters, past jeering white youths and nervous policemen and a battalion of national guardsmen, into City Hall. Filling the galleries, they told the embarrassed councilmen that there would be "long, hot summers" if their requests for better housing and more jobs were ignored. Fuller narrowly averted violence twice—first when a beer can hit one of the marchers in the face, and the two sides surged toward each other; and then, on the second night, when some of the marchers overturned garbage cans and broke windows as they turned home.

Local newspapers filled their front pages throughout the week with warnings of "Another Newark Threatened Here." And the Establishment gave righteous vent to all the fears and frustrations that had quietly accumulated during Breakthrough's earlier challenges. City councilmen attacked Fuller, as well as other Operation Breakthrough staff, for participation in the meetings and marches. Representative James Gardner, a Republican congressman from the adjoining Fourth District in North Carolina, learned that Operation Breakthrough cars had been used to transport marchers to St. Joseph's Church, and he demanded that Sargent Shriver investigate the Community Action agency. "Breakthrough has just gone too far, much too far," said Carvie Oldham, director of the local public housing agency, shortly afterward. "None of our tenants were dissatisfied until the poverty program looked for things to challenge."

Denunciations, such as those of Mayor Grabarek, streaming from local Establishments throughout the country, have moved Congress to revoke the autonomy of these corporations. While extending Community Action in 1967 for another two years, Congress amended the act to require that all local agencies funded by OEO be controlled by local governments. The administration justified the change as a necessary concession to southern Democrats, whose votes were needed to thwart Republican attempts to dismantle the Office of Economic Opportunity and drastically cut antipoverty funds. But the administration itself shed few tears over the new provision: the corporations had long since turned the entire program into a political albatross.

The fact remains that for two years the federal government financed a revolution—aiming like all revolutions at a fundamental redistribution of power—against local governments and against itself. How did it decide to begin this program? How well did it anticipate the results? Who was involved in originating Community Action and what did they think they were creating? The decision to begin Community Action was more important than the decision to dilute the program, and more revealing of how the government goes about engineering social change.

This judgment, and the Durham events that provoked them,

provide an appropriate backdrop to a close inquiry into the origins of this innovative policy and administrative procedure. We will first examine the men who developed the policy and their views of the problem of poverty.

The "Guerrillas"

The men who came forward with the idea of Community Action called themselves "guerrillas." They lived, as one of them later put it, "off the countryside of the government and foundations," meeting quietly during the early '60's to argue about the problems of engineering "revolutionary change." Gradually, they recruited new rebels, enlarging their circle to include men of widely different background and viewpoint: academics and politicians as well as bureaucrats and foundation executives. Whatever their differences, they all had made a diagnosis of poverty that suggested the need for institutional change—a dramatic, powerful intervention that would shake up the prevailing system. There was nothing subversive in their activity—not a single Communist or New Lefter in the lot. In fact, they drew most of their members from two highly respectable programs initiated in the late '50's and early '60's, the Ford Foundation's Gray Areas project and the President's Committee on Juvenile Delinquency.

Their leader was David Hackett, director of the JD Committee, though, like most good rebel generals, he was only first among equals. Hackett had received a rather limited mandate from the executive order creating the Committee in May, 1961: to coordinate the agencies of government treating juvenile delinquency and to demonstrate improved methods of crime prevention. But he and his staff had purposely exceeded this mandate by attacking the larger subject of poverty and its effects. They argued that the relationship between poverty and crime was too intimate to deal with delinquency in isolation, and they created corporations, public and private, to bring together local institutions on policy boards and thus plan comprehensive programs to alleviate poverty.

Hackett succeeded in throwing the federal government's weight into this new area, despite grumblings from many federal departments and local officials, because he was firmly supported by his patron, the attorney general. "The Committee worked," as Hackett later recalled, "because of Robert Kennedy and the power he exercised and the power he was able to wield." Hackett was a political and social intimate of both Kennedys. He had roomed with the attorney general in prep school, and he had served the president as a principal lieutenant in organizing the 1960 campaign. Though hardly an idea man himself, the square-jawed former hockey star excelled at recruiting original thinkers, persuading them to join the administration, and then sitting them around a table to knock heads. The Kennedys admired his matter-of-fact, down-to-earth style. He batted around ideas as he had once shot hockey pucks, never holding onto them for detached or deep speculation, but outpacing many other Kennedy aides in shrewdness, dexterity, and guts. Before directing the JD Committee, he had been Robert Kennedy's special assistant and political trouble-shooter in the Justice Department.

Even with the attorney general's backing, however, Hackett never would have succeeded in launching his Community Action prototypes had it not been for his confidential partnership with Paul N. Ylvisaker, director of the Ford Foundation's Public Affairs Program. In the early '50's Ylvisaker had convinced the Foundation that it should help fight poverty as a counterweight to the urban renewal program. The government, he contended, was overstressing "bricks and mortar" renewal of buildings, parks, and roads, and was slighting the need for "human renewal," for educating and training the people who would use these facilities. Although very different in personality—Ylvisaker was an intense, almost mystical man of Lutheran upbringing—he and Hackett became close friends, and they pooled their resources on a common strategy and division of labor.

The two key elements in this strategy were planning and consensus. Both Hackett and Ylvisaker insisted that communities formulate precise, detailed diagnoses of poverty problems and prepare blueprints for new social services and organizations. Since each could tap only a small amount of money—$4 million a year from Ford and $10 million a year from the JD Committee—they demanded that local leaders win support, financial as well as moral, from all local groups with resources to contribute. And they adopted nearly identical guidelines for the corporations, numbering seventeen throughout the country, which they compelled local leaders to set up.

They required, as one observer has remarked, that each agency be a "kind of halfway house between the private and public sectors of the community, having political muscle without being excessively political, and enjoying support from influential citizens without being the creature of a Yankee Protestant élite." Though the relationship between the Ford Foundation and the JD Committee cannot be fully documented, "the opinion of all the principal actors clearly indicates that . . . the Ford Foundation played the entrepreneurial role of creating the type of new civic agency which could do in the big cities what the President's Committee wanted done, with Ford receiving in return an enormous federal multiplication of the seed money it invested."

During this period, from 1961 to 1964, Hackett began "brainstorming" the government for men interested in the problems of poverty. Inviting them to meetings without the sanction of their superiors, he encouraged them to think well beyond existing programs, to scorn the conventional wisdom. One of the most active in the group was Fred Hayes, an iconoclastic young technocrat who was then assistant commissioner of program planning for urban renewal at the Housing and Home Finance Agency. Another was Richard Boone, hard-boiled and occasionally abrasive, who spread his influence over a variety of urban and education programs from his Special Projects Office in the White House. Boone concentrated on the JD Committee, while collecting ideas for other programs. Sanford Kravitz, a third guerrilla, served as program coordinator of the JD Committee; the gentle academic thus learned to deal with tight-fisted mayors and wily ward bosses, as well as with blue-blood civic leaders. Richard Cloward, a professor at the Columbia School of Social Work, had been instrumental in setting up Mobilization for Youth, a JD Committee project in New York. With Lloyd Ohlin, then a JD Committee staff member, Cloward had written *Delinquency and Opportunity*, a book published in 1960 that provided much of the intellectual framework of the JD Committee and, later, of OEO.

A Structural View of Poverty

Gathering ideas during the early '60's, these men developed assumptions that denied the most cherished doctrines of the social welfare profession. Much of their analysis is now so well-accepted that their original language sounds hackneyed and repetitive: the "powerlessness" of the poor, their need for "identity," the "cycle" of "escape" and rebellion. But at the time their theories altered the entire intellectual framework of antipoverty efforts.

The social workers saw poverty as a problem of individual psychosis—a problem caused by particular shock in childhood or some special mental handicap or deficiency. They believed that each individual would require a particular mixture of treatment and advice to regain "motivation." The opportunities were plentiful, but each man would have to select the ones that suited him. Only by curing individual pathologies, case by case, could social workers eliminate the poverty of groups.

The proponents of community action saw the cause of poverty in "structural barriers" thrown up by the system and its institutions, not in personal traumas, and they analyzed the psychological effects in groups, not individuals. Delinquent subcultures, argued Ohlin and Cloward in *Delinquency and Opportunity*, resulted from "the discrepancy between culturally induced aspirations and the possibilities of achieving them by legitimate means." A delinquent, in other words, reacted to the gap between what he was told to want and what in fact he could achieve, to the wide gulf between what society was supposed to be and what it really was. On the one hand, the middle-class work ethic and ideology assured him that anyone could work hard and succeed. On the other, he found very tangible barriers that put him at a competitive disadvantage to others. A slum environment crippled him educationally; court convictions and prisons gave him the stigma of criminality; racial discrimination closed doors to jobs and promotions. His failure meant that he must either reject himself, asserting his own incompetence, or reject the middle-class ideals.

No wonder that his so-called "psychoses," the responses to this dilemma, often alternated, as psychologist Kenneth Clark wrote, between "self-depreciation and curious compensatory grandiosity and posturing."* The older poor, particularly among Negroes, generally chose the first course, accepting the harsh social verdict that they were inferior human beings. But most of the young poor spit this "colonial" identity back in the face of the white middle class, choosing to defy authority rather than emasculate themselves. Their

*Harlem Youth Opportunities Unlimited, Inc., *Youth in the Ghetto* (New York: Harlem Youth Opportunities Unlimited, Inc., 1964), page 11.

defiance was often blind and irrational because they knew no other way.

In explaining why institutions were not more responsive to the needs and desires of the poor, the guerrillas went beyond the argument (later endorsed by the Budget Bureau) that powerholders were hamstrung by bureaucratic rigidities and lack of coordination. They admitted that "inefficiency" (the bugaboo of all bureaucrats) was perhaps one fault of local agencies, but they contended that "bureaucracy as the instrument of power" tended naturally to "reflect the interests of the dominant social classes." (More efficient bureaucracy, in other words, might be even more unresponsive to the poor.)

People in the dominant middle class were just as self-interested as anybody else in society; they naturally resented paying higher taxes so that schools in the slums could be improved and poor children could compete more successfully with their own offspring. Moreover, institutions might discriminate against the lower class simply as a result of the pervasiveness of middle-class norms. The insistence that the poor show sufficient "need" to qualify for welfare assistance established a humiliating donor-donee relationship between recipient and case-worker. The welfare worker shared the middle-class addiction to *professional* standards; he considered himself a professional doing things *for* the poor, rather than a fellow human being working *with* them. The guerrillas never developed this notion of middle-class biases into a full-blown theory of class conflict, but they recognized that institutional change could never be achieved without provoking friction. They all realized, as Fred Hayes put it, that shaking up the system would "challenge some very well-entrenched interests."

Three Views of Community Action

Although they agreed very generally on this analysis, the guerrillas differed quite sharply among themselves about specific issues. How serious was this class bias? Who should take the lead in changing institutions to eliminate it, and by what means? The diverse views fell into roughly three separate groups of opinion, each offering a different vision of what community action would mean to the poor.

The first group, led by Ylvisaker and Hackett, believed that federal officials could stimulate reform from the top down, i.e., by manipulating the local power structures from power bases outside the communities. They contended that institutional change would depend on "outside brokers," like themselves, arm-twisting local agencies into adoption of new policies with promises of grants. They regarded themselves as catalysts, as practitioners of what Ylvisaker called the "social application of the art of jujitsu, of exerting smaller forces at points of maximum leverage to capture larger forces otherwise working against us." Though they believed that the "awakening of self-respect" among the poor had to be a critical goal—that poverty, as Ylvisaker said, could not be solved by mere "gobs of giving"—they did not envision participation of the poor in policy making.* Ghetto dwellers might be consulted as a source of information, but they would not develop or administer the program. Neither the Ford Foundation nor the JD Committee had included the poor on the policy boards of local corporations.

The two other groups, however, implicitly denied that the impetus for reform must come from outside the community and from the top down. They urged, instead, much more significant involvement of the poor within the community.

One group, led by Richard Boone, promoted a notion of "bureaucratic infiltrators" in the belief that hiring the poor to run programs was the most effective way of changing local institutions. Beginning on a note of antiprofessionalism, Boone criticized a "social work system choking on its own insistence on special educational formula as the rite of entry into full certification." The poor man should take over many of the jobs now performed by professionals. Uncorrupted by middle-class biases, he would regard his friends and neighbors as comrades, not as clients or cases. The "infiltrators," in short, had what Boone called a "hidden agenda," the hope that the poor who became employees might quietly rise up the bureaucratic ladder in sufficient numbers to influence policy from within.

Boone, an inveterate staff member himself, believed that real power in organizations belonged to bureaucracies rather than governing boards. Members of the governing boards of antipoverty agencies, comparable to directors of companies, could only set down

---

*Paul Ylvisaker, "Community Action: A Response to Some Unfinished Business." Address to the Citizens Conference on Community Planning, Jan. 11, 1963, Indianapolis, Indiana.

general policy guidelines; they would always rely on the staff to implement their decision and the latter would thus determine real policy. In emergencies (scandals or splits in the bureaucracy) the governing boards might exercise some power, but representatives of the poor elevated to the boards would probably be outvoted in these instances anyway. Restricting representation of the poor to governing boards would permit the Establishment to deny poor people an effective voice and to claim the poor's support for board programs. The representatives of the poor, though called "indigenous leaders," would have no real constituency or accountability. Many of them, experience showed, would gradually acquire the interests and outlook of the Establishment. If they dared demonstrate independence and courage, their election to such boards would be open to challenge.

Cloward headed the third group within the guerrillas which believed in "community organizers" and rejected Boone's call for infiltration of Establishment institutions by the poor. The best administrator, they insisted, would be no better than a faintly uppity Establishment puppet because bureaucracies were inevitably pawns of the power structure. Professional staffs were too diverse and well entrenched for any small group of infiltrators to rattle, much less reshape. The poor would never command the skills needed to take over enough key positions to gain power.

Instead of catering to Establishment organizations, the proponents of community organizers advocated creating new and separate institutions that would enable the poor to express dissent and challenge local officials. They based their strategy on a nonbureaucratic view of power that took conflict between interest groups as the main battleground. They argued that the present poor lacked the kinds of associations which other minority groups had formed in the past to gain power. Fraternal and religious bodies or political machines, said Richard Cloward, had often provided a "base from which to convert ethnic solidarity into the political force required to overcome class inequality." Today, however, such grass roots organizations would be strangled by apathy among poor people, a result of the new culture of poverty, and by cutthroat competition from larger political oligopolists, the main contenders in a new, closed market of political influence. The federal government must take the initiative in nurturing groups that would represent the poor; it must finance community organizing as a kind of political antitrust measure.

The government must help the poor in the concealed conflict in the courts, as well, where landlords and employers hire high-priced legal talent to run roughshod over the rights of tenants and workers. Here, legal services provided by the Community Action agencies could defend the interests of the slum-dweller—persuade him, in fact, that he had interests to defend—and prevent the system from working in favor of the middle and upper classes.

Cloward and the community organizers attacked three elements of the Hackett-Ylvisaker approach: the service orientation, the stress on consensus and coalitions, and the insistence on planning. They agreed that the poor must acquire new skills, but they argued that the unskilled must also acquire new power. Unless the poor gained a more effective voice in the system, services would only perpetuate the donor-donee relationship. Consensus embalmed in a community-wide structure would only further insulate these services. In a broad-based coalition, local agencies could afford to ignore most dissent or anesthetize it with a dose of token representation or public relations. They could buy off dissident leadership with executive positions, high pay, and low power; they could stimulate testimonials of gratitude and support by threatening to cut off funds. Instead of forcing the reactionary agencies to keep pace with the best ones, consensus would drag the best down to a lowest common denominator. Planning, as practiced by such coalitions, would place a premium on systems of analysis that the poor were not equipped to understand or criticize effectively. The planner's tools—phasing and assigning priorities, cost accounting, long-range blueprints—would discourage participation by the poor.

A Basic Disagreement

Most of the guerrillas believed there was a basic unanimity, that "differences were of degree," as Fred Hayes contends, "not basic theory." No doubt many of the proponents assimilated ideas out of a general mix. Richard Boone spoke of the need for organization and for creating new institutions. David Hackett stressed participation through employment, and also talked of "organizing block groups of community groups" to initiate a "dialogue" between the poor and the power structure. But unanimity was an illusion: the differences of degree were so great that the guerrillas' revolutionary visions were contradictory and, in many ways, incompatible.

The critical division was the question of conflict versus consensus. On one side stood the Hackett-Ylvisaker "power brokers," who saw community action as a means of nurturing more effective cooperation and more lasting alliances between the most progressive elements of the Establishment and the poor. On the other side were the Cloward community organizers, who valued disruption and conflict almost as ends in themselves. They believed that confrontation with the Establishment would promote the psychological health of the poor, as a form of catharsis or self-expression, whether or not it produced better schools or more jobs.

Theoretically, there was no reason why bringing pressure to bear from outside the community (top down) should be incompatible with organizing the poor within the community (bottom up). In practice, however, the class conflict fueled by the community organizers would be likely to explode the delicate coalitions planned by the power brokers. The demands of the poor for immediate material improvements would collide with the plans of Washington technocrats for long-range programs and social investment. Torn between the two would be the bureaucratic infiltrators, poor men elevated to the corridors of power by the benevolent bureaucrats, still sympathetic to the needs of their ghetto neighbors but newly sensitive to the wishes of the Washington brokers. The infiltrators would be compelled to choose for themselves between consensus (leading, it was hoped, to services) or conflict (leading to increased power).

The issue of conflict versus consensus thus inescapably raised the question of power. Should the poor gain power indirectly by improving their economic capability, making use of improved agencies and services, and leaving their fight for the moment to benevolent but uncontrolled outsiders? Or should they demand immediate power by organizing within the community to express their grievances, though this frontal assault on the status quo might cause the Establishment to cut off services?

The power brokers, urging the first course, assumed that the poor would never gain real power without jobs, skills, and income; they wanted to reallocate power in favor of one social minority under the guise of "neutral" uplift programs that seemed to benefit the whole society. The community organizers assumed that the poor would remain psychological paupers, despairing and destructive, unless they gained some significant voice in this system of jobs and income. Better, then, to fight for power first and expose the hypocrisy of a power structure that wanted to educate the natives but permanently colonialize them. Such a battle would at least help rebuild the shattered identity of the minority group, an identity which the poor desperately needed to make genuine progress.

The basic disagreement remained mostly subterranean, only occasionally flashing out in discussions. The guerrillas easily dimissed the bursts of friction as misunderstandings or differences in degree. They were united, after all, on the urgency of convincing the government to accept their concept and of avoiding squabbling among themselves. In explaining their views to the Budget Bureau, they naturally stressed the points on which they agreed, rather than those on which they differed. Few of them argued *against* the ideas of others so much as they argued *for* their own.

President Kennedy Gives the Go-Ahead

Although the idea of community action eventually became the main weapon in the war on poverty, it played no part in the original decision to fight that war. The decision to launch an antipoverty program and the decision to include community action were made separately by different people, at different times, for somewhat different reasons. The antipoverty decision was made by President Kennedy, who heeded the urgings of his Council of Economic Advisors (CEA) that the country would be afflicted permanently with a new kind of *structural* poverty unless the federal government attacked the problem. The community action decision was made by the Budget Bureau, which sought a new administrative device to coordinate the attack on poverty and to decentralize some of the decision making, giving it to the communities. Both decisions were ratified eventually by President Johnson, who vigorously molded the program to his own personality. Prodding the president and bickering among themselves, the executive departments intervened in attempts to help shape the program as it slowly took form.

Within the CEA staff, the most active supporter of the *structuralist* idea was Robert Lampman, a former professor of economics at the University of Minnesota. Joining the Council in 1962, Lampman began studying the nation's income distribution. In widely circulated memoranda during the summer of 1963, he showed that past or pending administration measures, such as the investment tax credit of 1962 and the projected massive tax cut, would do little to help the poor. He attacked the "aggregatist" argument that poverty was a matter of joblessness, and that the entire labor force could be employed if total demand (spending on goods and services) were matched with the country's total capacity (its stock of labor and capital). Even if fiscal policy could manipulate demand to create a job for every unemployed person, he argued, there would still be poor people. For the poor—to reverse what Fitzgerald said about the rich—were different from you and me. They were somehow disabled as economic agents, as breadwinners, and as income earners, bereft of the skills—sometimes even of the ability to acquire skills—needed to produce and earn in modern society.

Lampman, referring to his argument as "no nonsense from anybody liberalism," set out a statistical profile of these 31 million people, comprising one-fifth of the nation's population.[*] There were nine million poor families—one-fifth non-white, one-fourth fatherless, one-third headed by persons over 65. High rates of employment and gross national product increases of about 2 per cent yearly had reduced the proportion of poor in the population from 26 to 19 per cent between 1947 and 1957. But, even assuming full employment and a 2.5 per cent GNP growth rate, about 15 per cent (31.3 million people) would still be poor in 1970. (With a 3.5 per cent growth rate, the poverty estimate was 11.7 per cent.) State and national public assistance programs, though already costing $15 billion, furnished less than one-fourth of the poor with any income. Many cash support programs, such as unemployment insurance

[*]Robert Lampman, "Interpretive Summary of 1962 Annual Report," Memorandum to Members of the Council of Economic Advisers, Dec. 23, 1961. Also: Robert Lampman and David A. Nichols, "Post War Poverty Trends," Aug. 5, 1963, and Robert Lampman, "An Offensive Against Poverty," June 10, 1963. These three memoranda, among the most important that Lampman sent to the members, included many of these statistics. The figures on poverty in 1964, apart from the projections, were first published in *Economic Report of the President, 1964* (Washington, D.C.: U.S. Government Printing Office, 1964), pages 56, 57.

or old age and disability insurance, provided more money to non-indigent persons than to the poor.

Despite efforts of journalists and politicians to spread some of this information to the public, there was little awareness, much less alarm, about poverty in 1963. The written material included John K. Galbraith's *The Affluent Society*, Michael Harrington's *The Other America*, Henry Caudill's *Night Comes to the Cumberlands*, Dwight Macdonald's *New Yorker* article "The Invisible Poor," and, earlier, the hearings conducted by Senators Paul Douglas and Eugene McCarthy in the Joint Economic Committee. Yet Walter Heller of the CEA found only a studied indifference when he proselytized antipoverty efforts among unions and the daily press.

Although Lampman continued his barrage of memoranda to the White House, President Kennedy's closest advisors were divided. None was really against the notion of fighting poverty, but many believed that it would lack political appeal and hence should be delayed until after the 1964 campaign. Theodore Sorensen, special counsel to the president, Charles Schultze, assistant director of the Budget Bureau, and Wilbur Cohen, assistant secretary of Health, Education and Welfare, warmly supported the program. But others, including Meyer Feldman, deputy special counsel to the president, and Willard Wirtz, secretary of Labor, were more cautious. President Kennedy himself worried about the timing of the measure. He was sensitive to warnings of a white back-lash, and he acknowledged that the "middle class might feel threatened" if the government appeared to care only about the plight of the poor.

But the president had believed for some time that an antipoverty program would be necessary, and necessary now, not later. He had been deeply moved by his experience in West Virginia during the 1960 primary and he had called, later in the same year, for a war on poverty. Since then, he had read Harrington's book—Lampman found a dog-eared copy Kennedy had borrowed in an Oval Room bookcase the day after the assassination—as well as the Macdonald piece.

In June, Kennedy gave Heller a tentative go ahead, and in August told the CEA chairman that he definitely wanted a program. But it was not until mid-November, a few days before his death, that he decided to make the antipoverty program a major legislative recommendation. One of the important factors in this mid-November decision, according to his aides, was a story by Pulitzer prize winner, Homer Bigart, in *The New York Times*, appearing on October 20, 1963. The piece described deprivation in eastern Kentucky, where unemployed coal miners and subsistence farmers faced "another winter of idleness and grinding poverty." Kennedy asked Sorensen to mimeograph the article and send it to the entire Cabinet. He then called in Franklin D. Roosevelt, Jr., of the Commerce Department, to prepare a special emergency program for the region while Heller began assembling a full-scale, nationwide program.

From CEA to BOB

Anticipating Kennedy's "go-ahead," Heller assembled a task force in early June of 1963 to begin mapping out overall strategy. Since Lampman was returning to academic life, Heller chose another CEA staff member with experience in this area, William Capron, to lead the group. Capron, a personable and forceful economist, relied heavily on Lampman's co-worker, Burton Weisbrod, who had helped write the original memoranda on poverty and income distribution. These CEA economists naturally focused on the individuals as economic agents. Since poverty almost by definition meant low incomes, the relevant question was: what can be done for, or to, individuals that will raise their productive capacity and enable them to get work and earn more money?

The task force thus arrived at the theme of "investment in human development," a theme that would minimize "handouts" (cash assistance) and maximize self-help (training and initiative). The strategy would emphasize the prevention of poverty, particularly among the young, rather than "rehabilitation" or "amelioration." It would consist of a comprehensive program of services in education, job counseling, and training, courses in health, and home management designed to attack the web of poverty at every side. As Heller summed it up on November 5 in his most important memorandum, the program should "concentrate on relatively few groups and areas where problems are most severe and solutions most feasible." A coordinated and comprehensive attack in a few areas would be more effective than a "shotgun" approach.

The November 5 memorandum marked a major turning point,

because it shifted responsibility from the CEA to the Bureau of the Budget (BOB) and led to the first consideration of community action. Heller sent the memorandum to all the departments, requesting that each submit specific proposals for the program to the BOB during the week of November 15. But Budget Bureau officials, disappointed that the departments' suggestions were little more than a rehash of old, obsolete proposals, solicited new suggestions from David Hackett and others on the JD Committee.

The key man among these BOB officials was William Cannon, the brash but brilliant assistant chief of the Legislative Reference Division. Cannon took charge of hammering out the general outlines of the legislation, and, from the very beginning, he "touched base with all kinds of people with all kinds of ideas" in order to get something new. He sought a "countervailing force to the old line agencies," he recalls, "to make something click." It was Cannon who invited Hackett to submit the JD Committee memorandum, though Heller had not included the JD Committee in his November 5 memorandum. With the Hackett proposal in hand, he saw his role as being a neutral negotiator among the disputing departments and bureaucrats: "My job was to be an honest broker. . . . I was wired into more people in the government than anyone else, and I was trying to make peace."

For all his claims to "benevolent" neutrality, Cannon himself had very definite ideas about what the new program should be. After studying political science at the University of Chicago and working for four years in the Navy Department, he had returned to Chicago to head the university's development program, a job that put him, as he later said, "up to my neck in the problems of the community." As a political scientist—and he always insisted with an ironical smile that his first love remained political science—he believed that the United States desperately needed new institutions at every level to initiate and direct social change. He felt, as he admitted quite frankly, that bureaucratic administration was a "bloody bore." But he considered "creative bureaucracy" the key to good government, and he believed no antipoverty program could be successful without institutional reform.

Cannon's views reflected a general concern in the Budget Bureau with administrative efficiency. As they surveyed agencies responsible for fighting poverty, these BOB technocrats were appalled by the paucity of comprehensive planning, the fragmentation of authority, and the bureaucratic small-mindedness that pervaded the welfare establishment. The federal effort, consisting of more than forty programs in housing, education, and health, had grown into a huge, gangling adolescent, whose right hand barely knew of the left's existence, much less what it was doing. Equally unschooled and uncoordinated were the local departments, operating as petty fiefdoms, insulated and entrenched, beyond the direct control of elected officials. The crazy-quilt pattern of authority in local governments negated clear and rational lines of command, and made unlikely any cooperation between officials of different departments, though they might be dealing with the same families in the same places. The bureaucratic milieu, in federal as well as local programs, quickly killed originality and idealism. Systems of promotion and fringe benefits rewarded those who played by the rules of the game and did not question their superiors or the conventional wisdom.

Budget Bureau officials complained that the federal departments ignored these administrative problems in their replies to Heller's memorandum. "All they did was pull out old ideas which had been knocking around," Capron said recently, "and put them in a package." Though their proposals numbered in the hundreds, most consisted of recommendations defeated by Congress previously or pending at that time. The Department of Health, Education and Welfare (HEW) concentrated on programs for adults and the elderly—Medicare and vocational rehabilitation—and suggested relatively few programs for young people. The Labor Department, more sensitive to Heller's emphasis on "poverty prevention" among young people, stressed "educational investment" programs, but urged job-creating and job-training efforts above all, and also included suggestions for improvement in existing income maintenance programs.

In effect, each department was jockeying for position, attempting to gain control over the antipoverty effort (or at least win more funds) by selling programs which only it could administer. The Budget Bureau granted them the courtesy of a "thank you" and not much more. Cannon and other BOB officials were convinced that this "old line approach," relying on individual departments to run programs without overall coordination, would only aggravate the "fragmentation" of the federal effort.

Despairing of the departments, Cannon telephoned Hackett and asked him to elaborate on a preliminary memorandum that the JD Committee director had prepared earlier in the month. "The initiative came from Cannon," Hackett recalls. "We got an extra push because he knew of us." What attracted Cannon to Hackett's proposals, contained in November 6 and December 21 memoranda, was the emphasis on planning, demonstration, and testing before spending any large amounts of money; and on the role of local agencies in coordinating the various fragments of the local attack. Hackett proposed that a Cabinet committee organize various task forces (divided into urban and rural sections) to study the problem of poverty for a full year before recommending any legislation. During this time, he suggested, the federal government should fund demonstration community action projects to "keep the study recommendations before the public," and to show the "value of comprehensive approaches" and the need for a "new concern for the poor."

In the proposal for "development corporations" that Cannon presented to top-ranking officials at the BOB and CEA in mid-December, he incorporated, almost verbatim, the most important recommendations of Hackett's memoranda. He suggested that the federal government set up programs of demonstration and testing in no more than ten areas, five urban and five rural. Relying on local action and self-help, these development corporations would spend an entire year tooling up and planning for their "undertaking comprehensive programs of research, demonstration, and testing." They would receive "substantial amounts of federal assistance" once the president approved their plans—up to $10 million per year for each area—and the bill would allow the president to waive restrictions in existing legislation that required matching grants from the local governments. This demonstration program would last up to four or five years. During this time, the government might sprinkle seed money to a few other communities "in the way of stimulating planning and coordination," but "not of the scope or range that would be . . . within the ten demonstration areas."

Cannon thus wanted to map out the terrain and reconnoiter the enemies' strength, as well as test his own weapons, before launching a major war. As Charles Schultze remarked to BOB director Kermit Gordon, Cannon seemed to have two objectives: concentrating funds in certain target areas and creating mechanisms to pull together, "on a demonstration basis at first," the large number of diverse existing and proposed federal programs. Cannon purposely avoided defining the structure of these development corporations, but he did imply that they would be controlled by local governments, "responsible to" and under the "aegis" or "supervision" of local executives. The local governments themselves, he recommended in one memo, should apply for the grants and set up the corporations. At the federal level, a council on poverty composed of all department heads and chaired by a presidential appointee would decide (subject to presidential ratification) whether to approve or disapprove applications. Though this council would also be responsible for "expediting and solving major problems," the day-to-day "ordinary administration" of programs would be assigned to the departments.

Cannon's plan for local corporations won immediate praise from his superiors in the Budget Bureau and was accepted in December. "Cannon has hit on a good scheme," Schultze reported to Gordon. Schultze made only a comparatively minor suggestion that a "federal czar" might be appointed in each of the ten development areas to open doors to the Washington decision makers and "knock heads together when necessary in order to get cooperation" from local agencies. Gordon, apparently, was equally pleased with the community corporation idea, for he pasted up Cannon's proposals in a memo called "An Attack on Poverty" and in late December, 1963, sent them, word for word, to President Johnson and the departments as the first official BOB outline of the new federal program.

President Johnson Says "Move!"

When Walter Heller approached Lyndon Johnson two days after President Kennedy's assassination to tell him of the proposed war on poverty, the new chief executive replied: "That's my kind of program. It will help people. I want you to move full speed ahead." Johnson thus dispelled Heller's fear that he might scuttle the program or require a prolonged period of convincing (as Kennedy had) before supporting it. But Johnson also showed, just as spontaneously, that he would not be content with rubber-stamping the proposals of the CEA or BOB. This was not going to be a Walter Heller or Kermit Gordon program, nor even a John F. Kennedy program. It was going to be, clearly and dramatically, a Lyndon Johnson program—the cornerstone of Johnson's Great Society—and Lyndon Johnson was going to have it in time for his 1964 presidential campaign.

Johnson began "riding herd" on the program almost as soon as Gordon distributed his "Attack on Poverty" memo suggesting development corporations in late December, and his influence bore heavily throughout the following two months. During this same period, the departments recovered from the wounds they had suffered in November with the BOB's rejection of their first proposals and returned to do battle. Now that the president was in the ring, they recognized, they stood a fighting chance again.

There was plenty of room for influence from both sides, the president and the departments, because the community corporation idea was by no means clear in the memoranda or even in the minds of BOB and CEA officials. In fact, the idea had raised as many questions as it had answered. First, regarding the size and scope of the recommendations: How much money should be spent? Should it be targeted at a limited number of areas or spread more thinly throughout the country?

Second, concerning the specific services to be provided: What programs should be included as *components* of Community Action (the program became known by this name or simply CAP during this period)? Should other *single-purpose* programs not channeled through Community Action be contained in the antipoverty legislation? (Unlike the component programs, which would be adjuncts of local agencies and a general, comprehensive attack, single-purpose or categorical programs would aim at specific, limited problems—retarded reading, for example—and would be controlled by the federal departments.)

Third, regarding the administration of CAP: What should be the structure of local agencies and of the federal coordinating unit? How much responsibility for day-to-day operation of the program should be left to the departments?

Finally, how should the federal and local levels be related?

In the size and scope suggested, President Johnson and his advisors were disappointed with Cannon's recommendation that funds be concentrated in a few target areas and support planning and demonstration. They wanted to set up agencies in as many places as possible, spend far more than the $100 million proposed by

Cannon, and move "full speed ahead" to a full-scale operation by 1964. "We wanted to learn from our failures," recalls Hackett. "What we said was: 'Go stage by stage, don't rush into the legisla-tion.' But Johnson just said, 'Go.' The word came down to move." The president was more concerned with the votes of the non-poor than those of the poor; he wanted to make the program as visible as possible. Plans and tests did not make very good election-mill grist. Many congressmen, notably Edith Green (D., Ore.) were already exasperated by the JD Committee, which had used its funds to stimulate planning and demonstration, instead of directly attacking the problems of crime with action projects. Negro leaders, weary of words and promises, would surely take the federal pro-gram as another sign of "tokenism" unless it appeared real and definite.

The new president wanted not only to win the presidency in 1964 but to win it in his own right, and he hoped the poverty program would be the first pillar in the Johnson administration. He believed deeply that this was, indeed, his kind of program, and he wanted to stamp it as truly his own. The target area-planning-demonstration approach, drawn from the Kennedy wing of the JD Committee, had been nurtured by David Hackett for Attorney General Robert Kennedy and, ultimately, for President Kennedy himself, as a first step toward a possible antipoverty pro-gram. So Johnson's aversion to using it was not simply a matter of political calculation; he felt instinctively (and perhaps somewhat resentfully) that he must not allow the ideas of aides of the dead president to dominate his administration. He had endured the pro-longed post-assassination worship of Kennedy, and it had increased his desire to prove that he could do as well in the office. Indeed, he believed that although he lacked much of Kennedy's style, he would go down in history as an even greater president, because in the end he would deliver the goods.

And yet, though he wanted the program to be large and impres-sive, Johnson also wanted it to be frugal. The outlay suggested by the Budget Bureau for Community Action—beginning with Gordon's $100 million and ranging up to estimates of $500 million—would mock the president's promises of a vast "War on Poverty." No one would believe that the suffering of one-fifth of the nation could be erased, or even eased, with such a paltry sum. No such program would be taken seriously, the president's advisors believed, unless it totaled more than $1 billion. But the president, at this same time, was waging a vigorous economy drive, urging departments to tighten their belts, raging against waste and inefficiency, shutting off lights in the White House when aides left them on at night. Every additional dollar allocated to fighting poverty would mean a dangerous (and politically embarrassing) increase in the deficit, belying his promises of a "rock-bottom" budget and opening him to Republican charges of fiscal deception and extravagance.

Legerdemain

Johnson's advisors soon hit on an obvious solution. Why not take a few single-purpose programs then pending before Congress—programs like job-training or loans to small businesses, for which spending had already been budgeted—and lump them together in the new, expanded antipoverty package? This legerdemain would not only increase the apparent size of the program at no extra cost, but would also broaden its appeal. Particular interest groups with a direct stake in one of the single-purpose programs would throw their support behind the entire package.

Neither the President nor his advisors saw any possible objection to including such programs from the standpoint of Community Action. In their view, Community Action itself was simply a means of channeling services into areas. They were sympathetic with the BOB's concern about administrative efficiency and coordination, but they were most enthusiastic about the theme of human investment, about helping the poor to help themselves by raising productivity. They saw the approach as original and creative because it aimed at providing training to the young, rather than doling money to the adult. What did it matter if some of the services which helped break the cycle of poverty were channeled by the departments directly, outside the structure of Community Action?

Why, they asked, did the structure of the Community Action agencies matter at all? The White House was satisfied with the BOB's explanation that local governments should set up agencies in accordance with the particular problems and needs of the areas. This open-ended reliance on local initiative pleased the White House. It would leave decisions to men who best understood the situation and, by assigning them some of the credit and some of the blame, it would increase their stake in the program. It would also upstage the Republicans, always complaining of the burgeoning federal bureaucracy and the need for decentralization. And, because it would bypass the state governments, it would undercut overlapping state programs and deprive Republican governors of any credit. Community Action programs would be in safe hands, controlled directly by the local executive and supervised by Washington officials.

The White House certainly never thought that the poor themselves would have any part in developing or administering the program. The president, according to his closest aides, apparently believed that the local governments themselves would operate the Community Action programs, rather than rely on separate corporations. Johnson continued in this misunderstanding until shortly after the legislation was passed.

Departmental Infighting

The departments and agencies shared many of the president's opinions of Community Action, as well as many of his misconceptions, though they arrived at both out of somewhat different motives and interests. They agreed immediately with the White House in opposing Cannon's approach of planning and demonstration in a limited number of target areas. Public visibility mattered less to them than it did to the president, but they were interested in gaining action programs—the bigger the better—because they wanted to augment their power and appropriations. Like poor cousins with a rich uncle, they paused in their usual bickering long enough to band together against a newcomer. This newcomer, they feared, might have eyes bigger than his stomach. The requirement of a year of planning "would result in the submission of not very meaningful pieces of paper," the Housing and Home Finance Agency disdainfully commented. "What do we know about poverty," asked the Labor Department (somewhat less serenely), "that would lead us to suppose that the first step to getting rid of it is to have poverty-stricken communities prepare plans?"

The departments unanimously and loudly opposed making Community Action the only program in the legislation; most were extremely critical of the idea, and some demanded that it be dropped altogether. "Community Action is a middle-class conception of how to solve a middle-class problem," wrote Assistant Secretary of Labor Daniel Patrick Moynihan on behalf of his department. "If we just put up $50 million for it, we will end up having employed $50 million worth of middle-class planners." If CAP is accepted, he said in another memo, "it is certain beyond any doubt that not one single poor person will ever get a penny of the money."

Health, Education and Welfare contended that no new program or expenditure was necessary to improve coordination—a goal endorsed in principle by all the departments—because HEW itself had been authorized in 1956 to make grants for research and demonstration projects experimenting with coordination. The annual appropriation for such projects averaged less than $1 million, though $5 million had been authorized—a fact that HEW tactfully avoided mentioning. And even $5 million, remarked one BOB official, would "make a molehill out of what is really a mountainous problem." The opposition of HEW was so strong during early December that one BOB official recommended to Gordon that the Cabinet should meet to determine "whether the president is serious about developing a new program."

The other departments were more hospitable to Community Action, but each nonetheless raised polite objections. Secretary of Agriculture Orville Freeman advised the BOB that in many rural areas local leadership might be "weak or indifferent" and, therefore, "unequal to the task" of planning an attack on poverty. Secretary Luther Hodges said gravely that the Commerce Department's experience with the Area Redevelopment Act suggested that "there will be many cases where minority groups would be denied representation on local Community Action committees, unless steps are taken to assure their participation." Only the Housing and Home Finance Agency supported the concept outright. "Intense involvement and participation by the local communities are essential to the success of the program," wrote HHFA Administrator Robert Weaver.

In their initial effort to destroy or at least modify Community Action, many departments raised remarkably penetrating questions about the operation of these proposed corporations: What would they do? Who would control them? Where would they flourish? But the federal agencies never expanded their questions into a systematic critique or analysis. They took random shots, sniper-style, and when they saw their shots missing, they turned with heightened interest to other questions. First, how would shares of the component programs, administered by Community Action agencies, be divided among the departments? Second, which single-purpose programs, if any, would be thrown into the total package? Third, who would exercise control at the federal level—what kind of new agency or which existing department—and how would this coordinator relate to existing departments and agencies?

They returned, in short, to squabbling among themselves. The Labor Department again urged job-creating and job-training programs, an extension of minimum wage coverage to services and agriculture, and beefing up of unemployment insurance and measures to aid the migrant farmer. Labor officials warned that Community Action work-and-training programs might overlap their Manpower Development and Training Act (though only a handful of recipients had qualified for training under MDTA courses); they therefore argued for a separate employment section in the new antipoverty bill. HEW officials claimed, on the contrary, that they should receive all but $40 million of the CAP money for their own programs, principally in education and health. The remaining $50 million, they generously suggested, should go to Labor for summer work projects. Labor officials, not at all grateful, complained that summer work projects would duplicate or detract support from the then pending Youth Employment bill (approved by the Senate in 1963 but still before the House).

Agriculture officials urged, meanwhile, that they should receive half of the CAP money for the rural poor, since nearly half of the impoverished families lived in rural areas. Curiously oblivious to opposition in both the White House and BOB to income-maintenance projects, they recommended for top priority a program of grants to subsistence farmers, arguing that most of these farmers were too old to absorb the training needed for jobs in the cities. They failed to explain, however, why the federal government should subsidize the most inefficient farmers, when there were already surpluses of agricultural products and the government was attempting to create incentives for modernization with other programs. After a pointed hint from the BOB, the Agriculture Department withdrew from competition with the Big Two (Labor and HEW) and scaled down its demands to match those of the Commerce Department.

Commerce officials wanted to expand the coverage of the Area

Redevelopment Administration, which provided loans and technical assistance to entrepreneurs among the poor, from the 1,000 counties it then served to the entire country. Agriculture officials urged that they should receive at least as much as Commerce, since there were surely as many farmer entrepreneurs as business entrepreneurs among the nation's poor. The Interior Department, though officially included in these deliberations, remained oddly aloof; it said it wanted money to improve conditions on Indian reservations, but did not say how much and offered no specific programs.

On the issue of control at the federal level, the departmental infighting was somewhat milder, but no less menacing to the BOB's proposals. When its first recommendation—a council of Cabinet members chaired by a non-Cabinet presidential appointee—provoked bitter opposition, the Budget Bureau decided to defer the whole decision to the White House. The BOB suggested an alternative— the appointment of an assistant secretary in HEW to oversee the program—but declined to state its preference. HEW, not surprisingly, favored this second suggestion, but proposed a third in the hope of satisfying the other departments while retaining "final authority" for itself. It suggested an interdepartmental committee, chaired by the secretary of HEW, including all the heads of other agencies. Both Labor and HEW believed that "basic responsibility," as Labor put it, "should be assigned to a Cabinet officer."

But the other departments and agencies feared their interests would be trampled on if one of the Big Two took control. They believed they would have much greater bargaining power in the council of equals initially suggested by the BOB, where no department would have more than one vote, and final authority would rest with a non-Cabinet member. Under HEW's proposal, they warned, a subtle hierarchy of influence would prevail. The HHFA, smallest of the agencies, urged that each department retain responsibility for funding its own programs.

Though they disagreed on who the coordinator should be, all the departments wanted to limit his authority. They agreed with the Labor Department that the wording of the assignment should "emphasize the initiation of programs and their monitoring, rather than their administration." The coordinator would exercise final approval or disapproval over applications from local Community Action agencies; the departments would continue with administration, which meant the day-to-day setting and implementing of policy in the service programs' components.

The BOB's Outlines, January, 1964

The criticisms thrown up by the White House and the departments clearly altered the approach that emerged from the Budget Bureau in late January. In the "Outlines" and "Specifications" prepared during January, the BOB dropped the words "demonstration" and "testing" almost entirely, and it deleted the provision for a planning period. Throughout, the BOB substituted the rhetoric of the battlefield for the more moderate terminology of corporate experiment. Striking at the "main front" of poverty, the program would use "weapons directly aimed at improving human motivation and performance." There would still be corporations, but their initial objective was changed from reconnaissance and intelligence to open attack. No longer would they be established as advanced positions in a limited number of target areas; the anti-poverty "main front" would be a vast beachhead, stretching across the country and mobilizing the resources of all communities. A "building block" technique would free many communities from the task of formulating any kind of long-range strategy before funding. Communities could submit "preliminary plans," relating proposals for particular services to general goals. The plans did not have to be extremely comprehensive or detailed, nor did the communities have to implement the services comprehensively. Community Action programs, like building blocks, could be "placed into effect by stages." Communities needed only to show, at each stage, that the new services would not "impede eventual development" of a more comprehensive program.

The shift from reconnaissance to battle, and the extension of the battlefield across the country, required a much larger commitment of human and material resources. In the January outlines, BOB officials raised cost estimates of the Community Action proposal from $100 million to $500 million. They suggested that another $500 million already budgeted for other programs be earmarked for Community Action, but without merging the programs themselves with the antipoverty package. The antipoverty legislation would waive certain restrictive rules in these programs—such as the requirement for matching funds from states—and a large measure of control would be shifted from the departments to the federal Community Action coordinator and local agencies. Half of the funds authorized for HEW's special education projects, the BOB officials took as an example, could be channeled through Community Action. With this adroit alternative, the BOB stalled the departments and presidential advisors who wanted to include specific, single-purpose programs. They kept Community Action through February as the only title in the bill, though their victory was short-lived.

As for dividing the $500 million in Community Action funds among various components, the BOB arrived at a rough allocation in January and succeeded in defending it all the way through Congress. Though the federal budget contained only a general request for $500 million, the BOB designated some $50 million for the development and administration of local programs; $275 million for direct assistance to communities for special services such as summer work projects, health examinations, and rehabilitation for the handicapped; and $175 million to the departments for existing and new programs. Out of this last item—money which could be used only in conjunction with approved Community Action projects —it decided to give $40 million to HEW for community work and training, maternal and child care, and other welfare programs; $35 million to Labor for job counseling and training services (especially for Selective Service rejectees), MDTA projects, and migrant labor services; $40 million to the Agriculture Department for loans, grants, and technical assistance to marginal family farmers and for improvement of housing and community facilities. Also, for smaller programs: some $20 million for Area Redevelopment Administration loans to small businesses; $20 million to the HHFA for experimental rent subsidies; $15 million to the Department of Interior's Bureau of Indian Affairs; and $5 million to the VISTA program.

Unresolved Questions and Differing Perspectives

The BOB's January outlines left unresolved some important questions. It maintained icy neutrality on the issue of the federal coordinator, saying only that applications should be approved by a single unit in accordance with rules and regulations issued by the president. It remained vague on the structure and operation of the local corporations. Community Action areas, it recommended, should be "reasonably compact, contiguous, and manageable," with a "concentration of residents who are poor." The second issue it thought best to leave to the communities or the implementers, who would be most knowledgeable in this area and make best use of the flexibility.

The first question produced an angry row in the president's office on January 23 between various department secretaries and assistant secretaries, and ultimately led the president to appoint Sargent Shriver to head the antipoverty task force. Shriver, the president reportedly believed, was the only man available with sufficient prestige to prevent the departments from tearing the program apart in their fight for control. As director of the Peace Corps, the Kennedy brother-in-law had garnered praise and respect throughout the country (and throughout the political spectrum), gathering an impressive reserve of power in dealing with Congress and the departments.

These questions, though hotly debated, were not the most important ones remaining unanswered. Beneath the apparent consensus within the executive branch, there persisted fundamental differences about the objectives and methods of the new program— differences that were easily obfuscated by the sword-waving rhetoric of "all-out continuous wars" and "main fronts," and easily ignored by boasts of maximum flexibility for local initiative.

The Budget Bureau had lost its bid for an approach of planning and demonstration and of a limited number of target areas. Because it still believed that the most important goal of Community Action was to make institutions work together more efficiently, the BOB continued to oppose including single-purpose programs. The White House had dictated an "opposite" approach of action programs to be spread throughout many areas of the country. But the president and his advisors would not be satisfied unless the program produced politically marketable results; this was the main reason for their decision against the BOB on the issue of single-purpose programs. The departments had not received as much money as they had requested for their Community Action components. But they continued to see the new program as a prize of power and appropriations—a prize that would be divided among the great and small according to the aggressiveness and appetite of each.

The CEA would be eager to please the president with statistics showing the wondrous benefits of the program in raising incomes and improving standards of living for the poor. But the goal it considered most important—the prevention of poverty, particularly among children—would be the least measurable of all and would not produce results until the children grew up to become income-earners themselves. The CEA and the president would continue to be most concerned with the aggregate picture. Poverty might be a very pressing problem, indicating a *structural* weakness in the economy, but the prosperity of most people (most voters) depended on sound rates of aggregate spending, employment, and growth. And if the goals of the "structural-oriented" antipoverty effort ever collided with the aggregate-oriented goals of the rest of the economy—if antipoverty spending should lead to inflation—the administration knew which ship to abandon.

These differences did not prevent the men in the executive branch from viewing the program within a common framework of beliefs and restraints, an unspoken and perhaps unconscious collection of rules and assumptions that allowed them to understand (even if they did not share) each other's objectives. They took for granted the fact that they had differences. Accustomed to working in a system of divided power and continual bargaining, they were well versed in the risks and rewards of ruthless bureaucratic infighting. They had fought much like this in early years on every new program, on every new appropriation for old programs. It was the Washington way of life.

What united these men was at least as strong as what divided them. They viewed the program from the common perspective of men in power, dependent on popular acceptance and approval. As public servants, they were working longer hours for lower pay than their counterparts in private enterprise; but the ethic of self-sacrifice, combined with the possibilities of power, were substantial compensations. They viewed their function as doing things *for* people—whether providing services or money or leadership—and thus helping people to help themselves. They valued efficiency and stability and respected certain measures of effectiveness, principally statistical. The Washington milieu had trained them to guard power jealously and regard it as a precious commodity, easy to bestow but very difficult to recover.

Their objectives, though different, were not necessarily incompatible. Prosperity on an aggregate level could not alone solve the problems of poverty, but it was very likely to make structural weaknesses easier to deal with by sustaining general health and vigor in the economy. An improvement in institutional efficiency, though perhaps less politically attractive than other possible aims, might still increase the program's political influence. Even the struggle among the departments, however divisive and unpleasant, might raise questions and lower marginal costs as the profit motive often does in private enterprise. The differences between the president and his advisors, the departments and the CEA and BOB, blended eventually into semi-consensus. The official participants differed about the size of the pie and the relative division of slices, but they did not disagree on its flavor or shape.

There was no consensus, by contrast, between these men, taken as a group, and the men who had originally worked out the Community Action idea. The goals of the original proponents in many respects were fundamentally incompatible with those of federal officials. "The most important thing uniting the proponent group," as Fred Hayes put it, "was a lack of faith in existing institutions." The guerrillas all believed that power must be redistributed, in some measure and by some method, from the Establishment to the poor. Because they wanted, in this sense, to make a revolution, they believed that "disruption to a certain extent was an indication that Community Action was working well."

The last thing in the world that the federal establishment wanted was revolution or disruption or a fundamental redistribution of power. These federal officials wanted those who held power presently to change their ways perhaps, but certainly not to relinquish the reins. The whole idea was to get all these agencies, local officials, and civic leaders working together more smoothly, with more money and energy. Why squander resources on continued dissension? Why, particularly, on dissension with the poor? These men were trying to do something for the disadvantaged—raise their economic capacity with improved services—not wire them into the already overloaded political circuits. The federal government was not in the business of providing confidence-boosting therapy to people who might feel, *en masse*, that they were "powerless" or incompetent. This was a hard-nosed economic program designed to help people help themselves, no soft-headed psychological venture into the vast unknown of identity, ego, and class.

The Budget Bureau perhaps supported the methods of the Hackett-Ylvisaker camp: outside agents using the leverage of grants to alter the practices of local institutions. But they were not out to alter class biases in such local agencies, and any involvement of the poor, whether in running the program or joining "cause-oriented" groups, probably would promote conflict and further undermine administrative efficiency. Strain and conflict, protest and complaint, pickets and petitions—these consequences of the involvement of the poor would be even more unwelcome at the White House. The resentful, frightened cries of local politicians would mean fuel for the Republicans and nay votes in Congress.

Several men in the federal establishment and among the guerrillas saw shadowy outlines of these differences. Cannon understood Hackett's views well enough to observe: "Dave was overwhelmed with a sense of the problem of social change and movement." He recalls of Cloward's ideas: "I never really could figure out what the hell it meant. They seemed out to change the system. I wasn't. I wanted a federal program that would coordinate other federal programs." Daniel Patrick Moynihan understood the potential danger in these unarticulated theoretical distinctions, and buttonholed a number of officials at the Budget Bureau, including Charles Schultze, attempting to warn them of potential pitfalls. "What they think of CAP is exactly the opposite of what you think of CAP," he told them at one meeting, "and you're going to have all kinds of disagreement and conflict." But the officials, Moynihan recalls, "didn't seem to listen." Their own views "had a very strong hold on their minds."

The Moynihans and Cannons, though they sensed the seriousness of these differences, never wrote them down in a systematic critique or analysis. Hackett, Hayes, and others believed that maximum flexibility should be left to the future implementers who would have to rule on applications for grants from local communities. "The definition of Community Action was purposely not spelled out," Hayes recalls. "At the time it was enacted, we did not want to have a lot of statutory restrictions. . . . We wanted it open and we left it that way." This was not the time for minutely detailed rules.

It would be absolutely vital, because of these intentionally unresolved differences, to have a strong federal unit that could set a clear and consistent policy once the applications began arriving. Though the rules might be postponed, Hackett argued, there would need to be a "structure in which debate and argument could go on between the communities and the federal government as well as between the departments, and then be resolved." The unit must be independent of the departments, responsible only for coordinating all the various agencies and funds, without the burden of directly operating a program.

The issue of the federal unit, along with the rest of these troublesome questions, was passed on to the task force which the president appointed in February to formulate the final legislation. Sargent Shriver inherited, of course, not only the questions enumerated in this section, but also those of the guerrillas, the three distinct views of Community Action discussed earlier. Few of the men in the federal establishment saw even the shadows of this first set of differences, and certainly never systematically discussed them during the decision to make Community Action the centerpiece of the antipoverty package. Not that the guerrillas conspired to conceal their views from the BOB, the CEA, or the president and his advisors; indeed, Cloward, Hackett, and others sincerely endeavored to explain the concept as fully as they understood it. "We were just listening," recalls one BOB official, "for different things."

The Task Force Decides

The Shriver task force took less than a week to overrule the Budget Bureau by agreeing to include single-purpose components. By late February, 1964, it settled the makeup of the federal unit, the wording of the legislation, the division of funds among departments, and the strategy for securing congressional approval. But it ignored, almost entirely, the important differences that still divided the various groups, and failed to define the idea of Community Action more clearly. This failing reflected, more than anything, the interests and personalities of the most influential task force members. The lower echelons divided into an intricate set of committees, composed of permanent staff loaned by the departments, semipermanent volunteers from private life, and temporary consultants from everywhere. Membership in most cases was informal, Adam Yarmolinsky recalls, "never a black and white thing." Never, that is, except for the two most important members: Sargent Shriver, the director, and Yarmolinsky, his assistant.

Fresh from his stupendous success with the Peace Corps, Shriver impressed his aides with his "receptivity to new ideas," his "amazing drive," and his willingness to give them great leeway and responsibility. But he did not appear interested, much less inspired, by the idea of Community Action. Various officials introduced him to the concept at a meeting on February 2, the day after his appointment was announced. "After Heller and Schultze and I all tried to explain it that Sunday night," recalls William Capron of the CEA staff, "he said he didn't see how something like that would work. From the very first he saw this as one big headache."

Shriver challenged the assumption that cities would be able to set up their own Community Action agencies. "Where you need the money worst," he told Capron and others, "you'll have the worst plans." He appeared to understand Community Action only vaguely. "He kept thinking of the program as rigidly structured," recalls one official, "with greater controls to eliminating the pork barrel." Leaving the substance of the program to his aides, he turned to the role he knew best, that of super-salesman. He was politically invincible, bright and dynamic, suave and polished, honest and articulate. And sell he did, to big business and big labor, to mayors as well as congressmen; all heard from Shriver and lined up behind the program.

The man responsible for directing the work of the committees and recommending decisions to Shriver was Adam Yarmolinsky, short, wiry-haired, and slump-shouldered, who had earlier been a writer and foundation executive and, most recently, special assistant to Defense Secretary McNamara. Though completely the opposite of Shriver in appearance and background—intellectual energy flashed from his raven-like eyes—Yarmolinsky shared Shriver's skepticism about Community Action. He understood the concept completely, but he believed that the main cause of poverty was structural unemployment, which should be treated by government expenditure directly on job training and job creation. Community Action seemed vague and intangible, at best only a method of organization. The departments' many proposals, by contrast, were definite and specific, aimed at precise and familiar objectives.

With the departments denouncing Community Action on one side, and Shriver and Yarmolinsky doubting it on the other, the task force quickly abandoned the Budget Bureau's initial decision to exclude single-purpose programs. At the task force's first official meeting on February 4, Secretary of Labor Wirtz attacked the defenders of the idea—principally Heller, Schultze, and Capron—for caring "all about the troops" and nothing about the "ammunition." The consensus of the meeting was that single-purpose programs would be added and Community Action cut back. Within the week, Shriver transferred to the antipoverty bill Labor's Youth Employment bill (then pending before Congress and later written into the Job Corps and Neighborhood Youth Corps of Title II); HEW's Community Work and Training proposals (providing work for persons on relief); and the Agriculture Department's proposal for rural grants and loans. In his first report to the president, he reduced spending on Community Action from $500 million to $300 million, raising the other allocations to $400 million for youth programs, $50 million for rural grants and loans, and $50 million for adult work and training programs.

Neither the components nor spending projections changed much after this first week. The task force added during the next six weeks a loan program for small businesses (funded by the Small Business Administration and therefore not requiring any new appropriations), and the National Service Corps (the Domestic Peace Corps proposal, eventually called VISTA). The final version of the bill requested $962.5 million, instead of $850 million, and the allocation for Labor Department job training programs was raised to $150 million.

The remaining major issue—organization at the federal level—was not settled so quickly or easily. Shriver wanted to create an independent agency—later called the Office of Economic Opportunity—headed by a director appointed by the president. He prevailed over HEW officials, who wanted their own secretary to take the role, by persuading the rest of the departments to support his plan. But he needed to call on the president to win his next two battles. First, he fought the Labor officials for the Job Corps, arguing that without some concrete, visible program to operate, the federal unit would be trampled by the departments and forgotten by the public. "He latched on to the Job Corps," one task force member recalls, because "it was clear, and he thought it would catch on like the Peace Corps." Next he outfought the BOB and CEA to win a place in the Executive Office, contending that the fledgling federal unit would founder unless it had the direct, personal backing of the president. The Budget Bureau countered that the Executive Office, originally created to provide staff services to the president, should not be open to agencies directly operating programs.

Shriver's victories undercut the objectives of both the Budget Bureau and the original guerrillas. Single-purpose programs—the Job Corps, youth employment, work-training, and work-study—moved to the forefront of the bill in Title I, and squeezed Community Action into Title II.

Drafting the Legislation

After these battles, the actual writing of Title II came as an anticlimax. The drafters were intent on leaving the provisions as flexible as possible for the future implementers. Many of those who helped write the Title—Cannon, Boone, Hayes, and Hackett— had been involved at previous stages. The actual drafters—principally Harold Horowitz, associate general counsel at HEW, and Norbert Schlei, assistant attorney general—believed there was an "underlying consensus" on the idea. "There was a whole line of development from the Ford Foundation to the President's Task Force Committee," says Yarmolinsky, "and we figured they knew what they were talking about."

They barely discussed the provision which subsequently caused the most controversy, the requirement that Community Action plans be "developed and conducted with the maximum feasible participation of the residents of areas and members of groups" affected. Apparently, none of the drafters foresaw the uses to which civil rights groups would put these words. (In response to later demands, Congress amended the legislation in 1966 to give the poor one-third of the seats on the local policy-making boards.)

The member of the task force most responsible for the inclusion of the provision, though not its exact language, was Richard Boone. Officials at HEW wrote a pre-task force version that required Community Action organizations to include representatives of neighborhood groups, but their aim was merely to prevent discrimination against Negroes in the South. Boone urged at the very first meeting that the task force take a much broader view of "involvement." "When you get a plan in an urban area," he told the others, "it may be just a plan among organizations . . . it may not *involve* the poor." As Boone repeated again and again the word "involvement," Yarmolinsky finally turned to him in exasperation, "How many times are you going to go on saying that?" Boone, unruffled, replied: "Until you put it in the legislation."

Still, there remains a touch of ominous mystery to the origin of the words "maximum" and "participation." Yarmolinsky attributes them to Boone, but Boone says "no, Norbert Schlei used them first." Schlei says his "only recollection is that (they) are in a rough, initial draft produced by Harold Horowitz." Moynihan, on the other hand, notes that "some suspicion points to Frank Mankiewicz," though "there is no proof."

The meaning of the words, in any case, was no clearer than their authorship. Boone and others wrote memoranda to the task force explaining the need for "involvement and support of those groups which can reflect the needs and aspirations of the poor." But members of the task force who noticed the phrase—and few of them did—usually continued to think it a "safety clause" designed for the old HEW purpose of preventing segregation in southern programs. "Nobody listened much," recalls James Sundquist, then assistant secretary of Agriculture and drafter of Title III. "If you have a program for somebody, you want him to participate, you want the maximum number of people to be affected. It seemed very obvious, very innocuous." It was framed very generally, many task force members believed, to avoid southern opposition in Congress. The objective of the drafters, says Yarmolinsky, was never to "get the poor to think of themselves as a political force. This didn't occur to us and it didn't occur to any of the highly professional politicians we consulted."

The rest of Title II, as Fred Hayes notes, was likewise "very, very general." The definition of Community Action, in fact, was circular. A Community Action program designed to eliminate poverty was "one which mobilizes and utilizes" resources by providing "services, assistance, and other activities . . . of sufficient variety, size, and scope to give promise of progress toward the elimination of poverty. . . ." The definition of the geographical areas set virtually no limits in size or character on the prospective region to be served.

The description of the Community Action organization furnished only clues, at best, as to structure and function. Charged with "conducting, administering, or coordinating" the program, the agency could be either public or private nonprofit as long as it was "broadly representative of the community." At every point, the drafters left the future director broad discretion to "prescribe such additional criteria as he might deem appropriate."

Heeding the wishes of the White House, they avoided any reference to planning and dealt only with action aspects. Yet even here they left loopholes. They wrote the bill to allow spending in limited amounts on "research, training, and demonstration" and to imply that Community Action agencies would be forced, after a "limited period of funding, to present a comprehensive strategy."

The official explanation of the legislation prepared by the task force for Congress similarly avoided precise definitions, as well as any discussion of institutional change or transfer of power. The crucial "lesson" of past experience, the summary observed, was that solutions must be comprehensive and that communities must be left "wide discretion." It mentioned at various points that the Community Action organizations would have to be "broadly representative" and "provide a means whereby the residents of the program areas will have a voice." But it did not weave these scattered references into a systematic defense of the need for participation or involvement of the poor. Indeed, it did not use either of these words.

The task force gave Congress no hint of the vast differences in objectives that still divided the groups involved in assembling the Community Action program. The reason was partly that they wanted to impress congressmen with their enthusiastic unanimity, but mainly that they remained unaware of the dividing issues. It was certainly not that they feared congressional disapproval. The task force members were frankly oblivious to the opinions of congressmen, for they were confident that the legislation would pass. Although it is customary for officials in the executive branch working on a major bill to consult senior members of committees and/or their staffs during the drafting, the writers of Title II observed that at least four committees in each house could claim jurisdiction over Community Action. Neither knowing nor greatly caring which would finally win, they decided simply to consult none of them. President Johnson, following the assassination, was speeding through measures that had been stalled months and years under President Kennedy. And the President had tagged the war on poverty "must" legislation. This was, after all, his kind of program.

Congressional Action

On August 2, 1964, barely one week before the antipoverty bill was passed by the House, Phil Landrum (D., Ga.), the manager of the bill, was asked by a freshman colleague for an explanation of the Community Action Title. Landrum reached in his desk, and tossed across a copy of the *Congressional Presentation*. "That pretty much says it," he told the congressman. "Of course you know"—he leaned forward now—"this bill was written over there." And he pointed out his window toward the White House and the federal departments, shimmering in the noonday sun.

To Landrum, as to many of his colleagues, the phrase "over there" summed up the differences in duty, thinking, and perspective between the legislature and the executive. The faint trace of suspicion, skepticism, and resentment reflected a broader division in power and function. Congress, a separate branch of government, had a creative role to play in clarifying and improving the antipoverty program, in rendering the work of anonymous bureaucrats responsive to the vaguely sensed will of the people. By this view, then, Congress might have foreseen the political implications of Community Action; the legislative process might have brought to light the differences in viewpoint within the executive on the role of the poor, institutional change, and the objectives of Community Action.

The fact is, however, that the objectives of Community Action were never resolved on the Hill. The theory of CAP was explored only superficially, and the "maximum feasible participation" clause was ignored entirely. On these parts of the measure, Congress did not go beyond the simple summary contained in the *Presentation*. Most legislators not on the committee which dealt with the bill— Education and Labor in the House, and Public Works and Labor in the Senate—had only the vaguest notion of what CAP would mean in practice; and even many members of these committees now admit that they did not comprehend the type of activity Community Action would entail. "Without reflecting on the intent and quality of the other members," says Congressman Landrum, "I don't think they realized what it would do." The best informed members of the committee, estimates Congressman Charles Goodell (R., N.Y.), the ranking Republican on Education and Labor, "understood about 50 or 60 per cent" of the Community Action Title.

The major question in the House was the "aid to parochial schools" issue. Congressmen from big-city, Catholic constituencies, like Roman Pucinski (D., Ill.) and Hugh Carey (D., N.Y.), objected to the requirement that all education programs be administered by public agencies, which meant, as Attorney General Kennedy acknowledged, a prohibition on aid to parochial schools. After a bitter fight, carried out mostly behind the closed doors of the Democratic caucus, the House Education and Labor Committee finally agreed to allow aid to private schools for special remedial education programs and other noncurricular activities open to all children in the neighborhood. The compromise barred "general aid" to any school, public or private.

Both the House and the Senate were worried about the broad discretion and power of the new antipoverty director. The Republicans warned shrilly of the "poverty czar" and his "dictatorial" authority. The Democrats, too, worried about writing the director a blank check on funding, so they wrote an entirely new section entitled "Allotments to States." This provision set forth an intricate system for dividing antipoverty money based on the number of public-assistance recipients and the average annual number of unemployed and of children in poor families, within each state.

The Senate was particularly worried about the potential power of the director to bypass state governments in funding local Community Action organizations. Southern Democrats suspected the whole program was designed merely to promote integration and help Negroes. Some Republicans deemed it a devious ploy to hoodwink state legislatures, dominated by rural Republicans, and to channel federal aid to the Democratic big cities. Rallying to the common banner of states' rights, conservatives of both parties in both houses wrote in the "Governor's Veto." This provision gave the governor authority to veto any contract between the federal government and any agency in his state, public or private, under the Job Corps or Community Action programs. The administration consented to the amendment as the price of southern Democratic support, despite warnings that it would destroy Title II of the 1964 Civil Rights Act.

The House committee struggled with several of the issues that had concerned the president, his advisors, and the departments. Edith Green (D., Ore.) raised the question of planning versus action. Angry with the JD Committee for failing to produce any concrete results, she and others persuaded the committee to remove any phrases that seemed to favor, even indirectly, the development of comprehensive strategies or plans before funding. One of the deleted provisions had required local organizations to be "broadly representative" of communities; another had specified aid for a "limited period" to communities without plans, implying that comprehensive strategies might eventually be required everywhere. "It is not the intention of the committee," the majority report stated, "that the development of such a comprehensive community-wide plan be a prerequisite to the extension of financial assistance. . . ."

But Congress generally avoided these theoretical quagmires, preferring to concentrate on unambiguous matters of dollars and cents. Only once in the hearings did the committee look at the provisions dealing with participation of the poor, just long enough for Representative Frelinghuysen (R., N.J.) to say in frustration: "It can mean anything to everyone." The main addition which the House made to Title II—the $25 million adult education provision contained in Part B—was irrelevant to the main purposes of Community Action. The Democrats did not encourage sustained analysis of Community Action, since they were eager to pass the bill quickly and push the Republicans into a stance of opposition. Adam Clayton Powell, Jr. (D., N.Y.), chairman of the Education and Labor Committee, cut sessions short, despite complaints from Republicans that they had not questioned witnesses. "I am the chairman," he told them bluntly, "and I will run this committee as I desire." The Democrats caucused alone to "mark up" the bill, denying Republicans the traditional privilege of adding amendments during closed session. The Republicans would have to either swallow the administration's bill *in toto* or oppose it. And, as Powell observed with a wry smile, "It would be very embarrassing to be against poor people in an election year."

Cornered and resentful, the Republicans wanted to splinter the administration bill. But, as one reporter wrote, they were splintered among themselves over how to do it and not get hurt on election day. Frelinghuysen submitted an alternative Human Resources

Development Act which would have eliminated Community Action and assigned an extra $500 million to HEW. Albert Quie (R., Minn.) offered amendments which preserved Community Action but dropped programs for loans to poor farmers and small businesses. Goodell, as a last resort, attempted to break the Democrats' precarious compromises on parochial school aid and integration by throwing embarrassing questions at Carey and Landrum. Landrum, the bill's floor manager, accused him of "inflammatory speeches," though he later reckoned him, admiringly, "the best demolition expert I've ever seen."

The Democrats conceded a few small points unrelated to CAP to liberal Republicans just before the final vote. This was done to offset last-minute desertions by southern Democrats, who rushed to prove themselves true conservatives after the Republican party nominated Barry Goldwater as their presidential candidate. The concessions eventually appeared unnecessary; both Houses approved the act by large margins, the Senate in July, 62 to 33, and the House in August, 226 to 184. The vote produced familiar alignments, geographical and ideological. Southern Democrats joined most Republicans in voting against the bill. Moderate or liberal Republicans from east coast states like New York voted with the administration. The voting pattern appeared no different from those on other bills interpreted as "pro-Negro" or "progressive." CAP remained, according to one historian, "novel and poorly understood." "It was never my idea," says Congressman Landrum flatly, "that we would allow the program to be developed, operated, and run by those for whom it was created. If they were able to operate that kind of thing they wouldn't need the program."

Implementation by the Task Force

While Congress deliberated, the task force moved ahead to begin interpreting the bill's most important provisions in ways directly contradictory to the views of Landrum and other congressmen. The men assigned to implementing the program could not wait for final legislative approval to begin setting up the administrative machinery. As early as June, they undertook serious negotiations with cities across the country, and made plans to study thirty-odd candidates for good-sized grants. Even before then—in late March and April—they started determining the standards they would apply to those cities in funding local organizations and programs.

These activities brought the task force directly to the issue of the role of the poor. During the first meetings, the task force decided that people affected by Community Action must somehow be involved in running the program. In the ensuing months, they gradually made this notion of participation more central, so that by the fall of 1964, when guidelines were issued to the communities, the task force considered representation of the poor on Community Action policy boards a "vital feature."

In the final Community Action guide, the task force ruled that the "maximum feasible participation" clause required that policy boards include "at least one representative from each of the neighborhoods or areas in which the Community Action Program will be concentrated." The programs must provide the kinds of jobs that would "allow residents to influence the ways in which policy decisions are made and carried out." But residents would also be encouraged to form "grass-roots" involvement committees, organize block clubs, carry election petitions, and meet with political leaders.

This interpretation of the bill was, at the very least, a circumvention of congressional intent. Written during the summer as Congress debated and voted, it depended as much on the "broadly representative" clause as on the "maximum feasible participation" provision. Representative Green had purposely eliminated such references to "representation" on the grounds that they might give future implementers an excuse for requiring long periods of planning. The task force assented, but it preserved the phrase and used it for more revolutionary purposes. Instead of provoking institutional change from outside the communities by forcing agencies to prepare comprehensive strategies, the program would redistribute power by organizing the poor *within*.

The men who pushed the concept in this direction were the original guerrillas, many of whom had by now assumed official status as members of the task force. Boone, Hayes, and Kravitz were all full-time members; Ohlin was recruited for part-time service. They were led by Jack Conway, on temporary leave from the AFL-CIO, where he was director of the department of legislation. A labor organizer in Detroit during the early days of the auto workers' union, Conway thought of himself as an "action man" or "design merchant." He was responsible primarily for working with Congress and lining up personnel for the future Office of Economic Opportunity.

The movement to prohibit long-range planning, beginning with the president and culminating with Congress, had undercut at once the strategies of the CEA, the Budget Bureau, and the Hackett-Ylvisaker guerrillas. Planning had been the device supported by the CEA to ensure that the antipoverty program severed the poverty cycle simultaneously at as many important points as possible. The BOB had advocated planning as a means of forcing local agencies to coordinate their services in this attack more efficiently. Planning had been defended by the Hackett-Ylvisaker group as a lever for compelling fundamental changes in the attitudes and practices of local institutions. Now it could serve none of these objectives more than halfway. The promise of money and technical assistance might still be applied, but the preparation of comprehensive strategies could no longer be regarded as a major weapon in the arsenal. The lever would be very limited and the direction of change could no longer be controlled from outside the community.

The impetus for *fundamental* change, as the guerrillas on the task force quickly realized, now had to come from the poor themselves inside the community. Hence, among the guerrillas the consensus shifted in favor of the Boone and Cloward camps, both of which had aimed to compel the Establishment to accept the poor as co-decision makers. If the Establishment balked, they would rely on bureaucratic infiltration (Boone) or grass-roots revolt (Cloward) by the poor.

The program guide thus became a prospectus for revolution, or, as Sargent Shriver said, for "the business corporation of the new social revolution." As neatly and matter-of-factly as a corporate annual report, it suggested as one means to ensure involvement:

The provision of meaningful opportunities for residents either as individuals or in groups to protest or propose additions to or changes in the ways which a Community Action program is being planned or undertaken.

The guide was distributed in July, hot off the presses, to every community expressing interest in the new program. Congressmen might have read it, or at least might have talked to the men who were writing it. But they did not, and even if they had, they could easily have misjudged the consequences. For the men who were writing this prospectus, taken as a group, did not anticipate with any precision the effect of Community Action. Differing among themselves, they returned often to the rhetoric of "main fronts" and "wars" to describe the antipoverty strategy. Their battle plan was not the kind of well-mapped, precise campaign that could be unveiled on a pedestal at the flip of a curtain. They supplied a vision, not a catalogue of logistics, and they excluded from their following those who lacked enough poetic imagination to leap from free enterprise to revolution in one sentence. They made an effort to proselytize the congressmen, to make them see the vision, but the congressmen had their own idols.

Some Closing Interpretations

The formulation of the program guide during the summer of 1964 marked the end of a project which had started, a little over a year earlier, with the first suggestion of an antipoverty program. Following the passage of the act in August, and approval of appropriations, the task force applied these guidelines in funding the first Community Action projects. When the task force yielded authority to the newly established Office of Economic Opportunity, many of the guerrillas joined the federal antipoverty agency to administer the program. Fred Hayes, for example, became deputy director of OEO for CAP. It was they who had to resolve in a very short and chaotic period many crucial questions of policy left unsettled by the previous course of consideration within the executive and legislative branches.

The men involved in this process, the official participants and original proponents, had come to emphasize an element of policy which none of them really supported. In scrambling for their particular objectives and outlooks, they had somehow given the process a life of its own, a dynamic alchemy of personality and politics which finally ran its own course. An account of these events tells a great deal about these kinds of objectives and outlooks. It suggests first, the ways in which divisions of power within the government differentiate the goals of one segment of the federal apparatus from those of another. And it shows, second, how the objectives of this apparatus taken as a whole may be inherently different from the goals of men who propose new programs, particularly when such programs are designed to serve the poor.

Much of the federal Establishment misunderstood Community Action because the concept itself, being both complex and vague, could be tailored to many objectives. This Establishment had little in common with the guerrillas who developed the idea and proposed it to the Budget Bureau in the hope of shaking up the status quo and shifting power to the poor. Their misunderstandings were the result of fundamental distinctions in personality and position.

Moynihan traces the failure in communication between the two groups to the differences in outlook between what he characterizes as the "New York mind" and the "Washington mind." The latter is interested in cost-accounting efficiency, budgetary coordination, technical expertise—all the program indices which may be measured and tabulated for exhibit to voters and elected officials. This outlook values stability, well-established operational procedures, training, and professional standards. The New York mind, by contrast, thinks of social change, competing interest groups, class contention, and political influence. It cherishes innovation and upheaval. And it sees society as a steaming pot of soup, with ethnic and religious groups for vegetables, and the government as a lid. This outlook is concerned with keeping the mixture at a proper temperature; hot enough so that it is highly mobile, yet cooler than the boiling point. If we may apply labels for the sake of clarity, though at the expense of complete accuracy, the New York mind is much more theoretical, academic, sociological, and intellectual; the Washington mind is bureaucratic and pragmatic.

This dichotomy, however, does not capture fully the really essential difference in outlook between those who initially advocated Community Action and the federal Establishment that accepted it. The proponents were interested in eliminating an aspect of service programs which had always provided a vital objective for the Establishment. The great defect in past programs, they thought, was that the method of providing services and funds deprived the poor of self-confidence, self-respect, a sense of identity and personal worth. It did this, in a very superficial sense, by establishing rules which forced the poor to prove their failure in society: means tests to show substandard incomes and economic incapacity; "man in the house rules" to document failure in marriage (indirectly furnishing

an incentive for families to remain broken); administrative criteria
to distinguish the temporary from the chronic poor, and the like.

But these rules only reflected a more pernicious underlying deficiency. The government's programs were to call attention to the fact
that it was helping people—that it was extending assistance to men
and women in need. Despite references to self-help, the government
justified the program as a humanitarian gesture. Charity, in this
case, might take the form of services, instead of a direct money
grant. But the rationale of the government would be the same: this
was a worthy sacrifice which a wealthy country should be proud to
make for its less fortunate citizens, and one which those less fortunate men and women should regard as an act of beneficence. The
relationship of the government to the poor would still be that of
donor to donee.

The objective of those seeking the participation of the poor in the
program was to erase that relationship so as to give the poor the
sense of being masters of their own destiny, instead of being merely
inert statistics at the mercy of a strange and distant government.
The guerrillas did not want the poor to regard the program as a gift,
or to feel the obligation of expressing gratitude. Rather, this would
be a program they could claim as their own. They would join in
developing, implementing, and administering it at the local level;
and they would have no reason to feel beholden to anyone. Rather
than fearing that they were the special objects of government
charity, the poor could believe they had a right to such a program.

But the feeling of gratitude was precisely the political payoff the
federal Establishment craved. It was necessary, on one level, to gain
the votes and support of minority groups and other organizations
representing the disadvantaged. Much more important, it was vital
to justify the program to the main body of the electorate—mostly
middle class—that would demand some psychic reward for their
supposed material sacrifice. If the program could not gain the
gratitude of the leaders and membership of civil rights organizations
and labor unions, it probably would not earn their votes. And if it
could not be depicted to the nonpoor as an act of beneficence, it
probably could not play on the instincts of charity which ordinarily
motivate such humanitarian gestures. The members of the electorate, naturally, would want the program to affirm their own sense of
worth, to stand as a mark of their own success in the economic

system. By extending assistance to the poor, they wanted to define more sharply their own different identity. The rhetoric of a moral crusade justified the program as a dramatic effort to help the disadvantaged, but if the poor refused to be grateful, these words would prove as unsatisfying to the middle class as the promises of equal opportunity had been to Negroes.

It was almost inevitable, then, that the proponents and the federal Establishment should begin with different objectives and see Community Action from different perspectives. President Johnson would ultimately be held responsible for the program not only by minority groups, but by the electorate in general. If he did not appraise the program with public opinion polls spread before him, he nevertheless viewed the antipoverty program with the desires of his primary constituency in mind. In formulating the legislation, the agencies responsible to him were bound to demand some credit for their services, in addition to consciously taking account of the president's political needs. It was only natural that these official participants should be as concerned with the psychological "needs" of the nonpoor as with the material needs of the poor.

The proponents, by contrast, did not have to worry about winning elections, or justifying programs to the president. Their primary constituency was the poor—though the relationship probably was never understood by those they represented—and they wanted Community Action for a reason almost exactly opposite that of the official participants. Though the ultimate objective of the latter was, in some sense, to win gratitude, the proposers sought to abolish any feeling of dependency or obligation of the poor toward the ruling Establishment. In eradicating the relationship of giver and taker, they demanded a sacrifice from the Establishment that was not purely material—more money for services in education, employment, etc.—but psychic as well. They asked that economically successful citizens share their wealth with others and forego the rewards of self-satisfaction which normally accrue to generosity. They were unconcerned with who asked the middle class to make the sacrifice (or how), so long as it was made. The changes they demanded of institutions were thus bound to challenge the Establishment. For they aimed not only at particular agencies or elected officials but at the entire range of values and biases these institutions represented, precisely the values and biases which won elections and supported men in power.

The conflict in objectives between the guerrillas and the federal Establishment was summarized, in a way, by Sargent Shriver when he described Community Action as "the business corporation of the new social revolution." The interests of business corporations are not often compatible with those of social revolutionaries, and the values they represent usually are assumed to be contradictory. But the government managed to combine them in Community Action—never realizing the "boldness" of its invention—and left it to future antipoverty warriors to determine which characteristic of the program would prevail.

SOURCES

Almost all the information used in preparing this study comes from unpublished sources, principally interviews with the participants and use of their files. I am especially grateful to Daniel Patrick Moynihan, director of the Harvard-MIT Joint Center for Urban Studies, Adam Yarmolinsky, professor of law at the Harvard Law School, and Fred Hayes, director of New York City's Budget Bureau. In 1964, during the events described here, they were respectively: Assistant Secretary of Labor for Policy Planning and Research, Deputy Director of the Antipoverty Task Force, and Assistant Commissioner of Program Planning for Urban Renewal at the Housing and Home Finance Agency.

Further Reading

For those who are interested in the congressional phase of this story, I recommend the Congressional Hearings: U.S. Congress, Senate, Committee on Labor and Public Welfare, *Hearings on the Economic Opportunity Act of 1964*, 88th Cong., 2d session, 1964; and U.S. Congress, House, Committee on Education and Labor, *Hearings on the Economic Opportunity Act of 1964*, 88th Cong., 2d session, 1964.

Two of the most influential books at the time were:

Harrington, Michael. *The Other America* (New York: Macmillan, 1962).

Ohlin, Lloyd and Richard Cloward, *Delinquency and Opportunity* (New York: The Free Press, 1960).

STUDY

4

Political Parties:
House Republican Leadership

Robert L. Peabody

On election night, November, 1964, the Republican ticket, led by Senator Barry M. Goldwater of Arizona and Representative William E. Miller of New York, suffered its worst defeat since 1936.* President Lyndon B. Johnson and his running mate, Senator Hubert H. Humphrey of Minnesota, won by the largest share and margin of the popular vote in American history, namely 61 per cent and 15.9 million votes of more than 70 million cast. Goldwater and Miller carried only six states—Arizona and the deep South states of Alabama, Georgia, Louisiana, Mississippi, and South Carolina—with 52 electoral votes. A high rate of split-ticket voting enabled the Republicans to confine their net loss in the Senate to two seats, and in the House to 38. Still, in the 89th Congress, the Republicans held but 32 Senate and 140 House seats.

Their 1964 setback followed more than three decades of minority status for the Republicans. Since 1930, Republicans had controlled

*This study was made possible by grants from the Social Science Research Council and The Johns Hopkins University Committee on Public Affairs Research. I am particularly indebted to some seventy-five Republican Representatives and staff members who were willing to talk candidly about the strengths and weaknesses of their party.

Congress only twice, the 80th (1947–1948) and 83rd (1953–1954). They had elected but one president, Dwight D. Eisenhower, a war hero who lacked a strong party identification and whose tenure in office (1953–1960) did little to enlarge the number of voters who thought of themselves as attached to the Republican party. National surveys of the electorate had affirmed for years the 2–1 edge in party identification for the Democrats. Estimates published by the Survey Research Center of the University of Michigan following the 1964 presidential election pointed out that "in terms of underlying loyalties, the Democrats could expect to receive, all other things equal, something in the neighborhood of 54 per cent of the national popular vote; and if any change has been occurring in this figure in the past fifteen years, it [was] that this Democratic majority [had been] slowly increasing."

This study treats of the reactions of one important segment of the Republican party—its 140 members in the House of Representatives in the 89th Congress (1965–1966)—to the crisis in party leadership brought on by the 1964 election. It begins with the events leading to the overthrow of Charles A. Halleck of Indiana, House minority leader in the 86th, 87th, and 88th Congresses, by Gerald R. Ford, Jr., of Michigan at the beginning of the new Congress. It then focuses on Ford's efforts to consolidate his leadership position, and on developments within the House party organization and between the House party leadership and other centers of Republican power. Beginning with an election disaster, the case ends with a brief analysis of House Republican successes in the midterm elections of 1966. Throughout, the emphasis is on the difficulties facing the legislative leadership of a party controlling neither the Congress nor the White House, in contrast to the built-in advantages provided by the president's role as leader of the majority party.

Ford Defeats Halleck

On the morning of January 4, 1965, the Republican Conference met in the Ways and Means Committee Hearing Room of the Longworth House Office Building to select its candidate for Speaker of the House. From the Republican viewpoint, it was really a contest over their own leadership for the next two years, since the Democratic majority of the House could be expected to re-elect routinely John W. McCormack of Massachusetts to the

Speakership. Gerald Ford, a House member since 1948 and chairman of the Republican Conference since 1963, had been engaged since December 19, 1964, in an open attempt to take over the party leadership from Halleck, first elected to the House in 1935 and minority leader since 1959. Halleck had defeated his predecessor, Joseph Martin of Massachusetts, by a similar revolt in 1959. Over the Christmas holidays Halleck had countered the efforts of the Ford supporters with a lower-keyed campaign of his own. Both men sought to win and hold a majority of the 120 returning Republican congressmen and the 20 freshmen who had survived the November, 1964, election. Ford won by a secret ballot vote of 73 to 67. Halleck took his defeat hard, but with courage and good grace he moved to make Ford's election unanimous.

The 1965 minority leadership contest, at least on the surface, was not one of ideological contrasts. Both men represented districts from the midwest heartland of the Republican party. Both men had equally conservative voting records. These apparent similarities masked rather sharp differences in age, image, and beliefs about the strategy their minority party should adopt in the months ahead. Ford, at 51, six feet tall and sandy-haired with a football player's firm build, was the spokesman for a new generation of young, articulate, executive-type politicians. In launching his campaign he urged the promotion of a "fighting, forward-looking party seeking responsible and constructive solutions to national problems." Halleck, 64, short, red-faced, heavy jowled, an old pro of thirty years' service in the House, campaigned on a "record of solidarity in support of party principles," and for unified opposition to the "costly, unwise, and unnecessary proposals" put forward by Democratic administrations.

In contrast, the contest for Conference chairman, which took place immediately before the Ford-Halleck vote, involved both ideological and regional differences. Conservative Melvin R. Laird of Wisconsin had aroused the enmity of the eastern moderates and liberals by his firm and unbending management of the Republican party platform prior to Senator Goldwater's nomination in July, 1964. This animosity, together with the fact that Ford had been in the House four years longer than Laird, largely accounted for the preference for Ford over Laird among most of the young activists within the party. Ford and Laird agreed to keep their two cam-

Courtesy of Gib Crockett and *The Washington Evening Star*, November 10, 1966

"Down by the old mainstream . . . !"

paigns separate, although each was sympathetic to the other's aspirations. On the Sunday evening before the House Republican Conference, the Wednesday Group, composed of some twenty of the more moderate-to-liberal House Republicans, met and agreed to challenge Laird's nomination with the candidacy of Peter H. B. Frelinghuysen, Jr., of New Jersey. The next morning, however, Laird won rather easily by a vote of 77 to 62.

Ford sought to obtain firm commitments to his candidacy as early as possible following his December 19 declaration. Some thirty Republicans from all shades of the ideological spectrum pitched in behind Ford's principal campaign managers, Robert Griffin of Michigan and Charles Goodell of New York,* making phone calls and writing personal messages to wavering or uncommitted members. In so doing, they locked themselves in behind Ford.

Charles Halleck had flown back from Lake Wales, Florida, the day after Ford's announcement, upset and irritated by the challenge, but confident that he would win. After all, he had never lost an election in forty active years in politics. Elected sixteen times to the House since 1935, he rode the crest of the Republican surge in 1946 as the House Republican Campaign Committee chairman to become majority leader at the beginning of the 80th Congress (1947–1948). He was re-elected without opposition to that post for the 83rd Congress (1953–1954), and captured the top party leadership post from Joseph Martin in 1959. As minority leader from 1959 to 1964, Halleck expected to be able to capitalize on his record, his accumulation of credits for favors rendered, his prestige, and on the other obvious advantages of incumbency.

Reasons for Halleck's Loss

Why did Ford win and Halleck lose? Halleck's own cryptic explanation—"It's the only election I've ever lost, and it was because I got myself involved in a beauty contest"—conceals as much as it reveals. Much more was at stake than a choice between contestants based solely on age and physical appearance. In essence, the activists were able to convince a majority of their colleagues that Republican pursuit of majority status required a minority leader

---

*Both of these attractive young congressmen subsequently left the House to become Senators, Griffin in 1966 and Goodell in 1968. Laird was appointed Secretary of Defense by President Nixon in 1969.

who would project a more positive image to the nation and work toward more constructive alternative legislative programs within the House. By these standards, Ford clearly had an edge over Halleck.

The Republican election disaster of November, 1964, had created a climate for internal dissension and change. Some of the same pressures which eventually forced Dean Burch to tender his resignation as Republican national chairman in mid-January, 1965, were at work in the overthrow of Halleck. But Halleck, unlike party chairman Burch, was not primarily a scapegoat. Dissatisfactions with Halleck extended back to bitterness engendered by his defeat of former Speaker and minority leader Martin in 1959. This irritation and unrest were compounded by the continuing frustrations associated with the minority status of the Republican party. Agitation for change intensified throughout the long and trying sessions of the 88th Congress. A number of previously loyal conservative supporters broke with the minority leader when he joined Kennedy, Johnson, and Dirksen in pushing through the Civil Rights Act of 1964. Thus, it was a combination of those disgruntled with Halleck for a variety of reasons, plus those who genuinely favored change, which coalesced into the narrow majority which elected Ford.

Personal considerations inevitably are more influential in leadership contests than they are in major battles over legislation. Some members were so dominated by strong friendship, an old grudge, or intense personal ambition that they made up their minds early for one of the two candidates and never vacillated. The vast majority of the members approached the vote with ambivalence. As a key Ford lieutenant later observed:

Most members were trying to make an assessment on the merits of the two candidates and most were torn between. They were, themselves, in conflict. They were moving in different directions, struggling to decide which way to go. These were guys really trying to think about what was best for the party, not just what was best for themselves.

A Halleck supporter echoed these sentiments: "I doubt if any person who voted did not have mixed feelings at the time."

In the final analysis it was not so much the psychological climate or the personal factors, but the kinds of House Republicans who had been defeated in 1964, that made a change in leadership possible.

In the main, it was the more conservative and older House Republicans who were particularly hard hit by the election results. Of the 40 incumbents who ran for re-election and were defeated, more than two-thirds were among the most conservative in the party. Twenty defeated incumbents had been among the 62 House members who had endorsed Senator Goldwater's candidacy prior to the Republican party nominating convention in July, 1964. In contrast, only a scattering of liberal House Republicans, including but one Wednesday Group member, had gone down to defeat.

More significant in the Halleck-Ford contest, a substantial proportion of the 40 defeated Republicans were older and more senior members, and hence more likely to support the established leadership. Nineteen of the 40 had served ten years or more in Congress, including such senior members as Ben Jensen of Iowa and Walt Horan of Washington, the ranking minority members on the Appropriations Committee. As one of Halleck's chief supporters assessed the impact of the 1964 election:

There was a general feeling of dismay at the results. If the election had gone the other way, no doubt Charlie would have remained. . . . Many of the people defeated would have been Halleck supporters. In general, the more seasoned members of the House favored Halleck. It was the newer and less seasoned members who turned basically to Ford.

The bulk of Ford's support, and certainly the organizational nucleus of his campaign, came from members elected in 1956 and later. These five least-senior classes made up two-thirds of the total House Republican membership in 1965. Only 11 of the 140 Republicans were more senior than Ford. The continued frustrations of minority status and increasing dissatisfaction with Halleck's leadership probably made an eventual challenge inevitable, but without the heavy election losses among the more senior and conservative members it is extremely unlikely that Ford would have launched his challenge.

About an hour after Halleck's defeat, Republicans joined ranks to cast 139 votes in favor of Ford for Speaker of the House of Representatives. His Democratic opponent, John W. McCormack of Massachusetts, was, of course, overwhelmingly re-elected. During the opening days of the new Congress, the new minority leader was principally preoccupied with consolidating his own leadership.

Initial Tests of Ford's Leadership

All congressional leaders, majority or minority, are continually confronted with three broad areas of decision making: (1) questions about internal organization, including relationships with other leaders and the supervision of staff; (2) legislative strategy, both in formulating and implementing policy, and (3) external coordination, particularly relationships with the White House and the executive branch, the national party committee, other party leaders, interest groups, the mass media, and the American electorate. Decisions in these three broad areas are intertwined. A congressional leader may be more adept in one area than another, he may spend some days principally preoccupied by problems in one arena, but he cannot afford to ignore the other two very long without adverse consequences for his party and his own leadership.

Before Ford and his associates could begin to develop "an affirmative and specific Republican legislative program" or project the image of a "fighting, forward-looking party," they had to consolidate internal party organization. Two actions taken by the mid-December, 1964, Republican Conference shaped Ford's alternatives. The Conference had instructed its Committee on Minority Personnel to examine the whole problem of staffing, especially tendencies to treat minority personnel as purely patronage jobs despite the party's need for professional research support. The Conference also had created an eleven-member Committee on Organizational Structure, with five-term congressman Albert Quie of Minnesota as its chairman, and urged it to look into the organization and operation of such basic party organs as the House Republican Policy Committee and the Committee on Committees. The Republican Policy Committee, which had been reactivated under the chairmanship of John W. Byrnes of Wisconsin, following Halleck's defeat of Martin in 1959, was primarily responsible for establishing party positions prior to floor action on major legislation reported from the standing committees. The Republican Committee on Committees, composed of one representative from each state with Republican members in the House, made intraparty decisions as to committee assignments and transfers from one committee to another.

During his first two months in office Ford found his leadership

Figure 1

Organization of the Republican Minority Party,
United States House of Representatives,
89th Congress (1965–66)

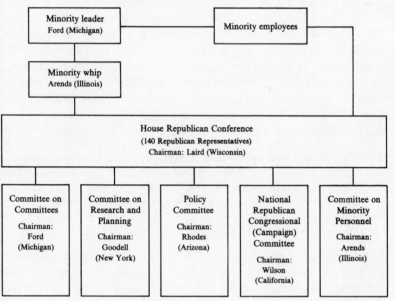

Source: Republican Conference, United States House of Representatives

challenged on five principal occasions: (1) on decisions affecting
minority employees; (2) on the choice of a minority whip; (3) on
committee assignments, particularly his endorsement of a New York
candidate for a seat on the Ways and Means Committee; (4) on the
choice of a Policy Committee chairman; and (5) on plans to
reorganize the Republican Conference and the Policy Committee.
Each challenge and its resolution contributed to the mixed record of
gains and rebuffs chalked up by Ford in his early attempts to
consolidate his leadership within the legislative party. At the beginning of his tenure of office, Ford had only a bare majority of
support, and members loyal to Halleck were by no means readily
inclined to accept the decisions of the new minority leader. The
resources at Ford's disposal—patronage, positions of influence, fa-

vored committee assignments, and so on—were both scarce and not solely his to dispense. He would have to negotiate and deal with other senior members who had their own bases of influence and power. In a minority party racked by election defeats and internecine warfare, effective power is even more widely dispersed than it is in an already highly decentralized Congress.

The Battle Over Minority Staffing. A number of House Republicans, most notably Thomas B. Curtis of Missouri, had long advocated more adequate minority staffing as a key aid in the development of a more rational and deliberative legislative process. As Curtis argued: "Without adequate minority staffing, we will be hard put developing the issues in hearings from the minority viewpoint. Also, we will be hard put to write intelligent minority views." Another Republican legislator put the case even more bluntly:

Too often in the past we've been out-propagandized, out-maneuvered, and out-researched by the Democrats. Of course, they have the personnel. They have the whole executive branch at their disposal. The staffs of the committees are largely made up of people sympathetic to the majority viewpoint and they have the staffs of the leadership. In the past, we've been content to sit back and get clobbered.

But before a strong case could be made for adequate minority staffing on committees, a deteriorating situation among the few patronage positions already allocated to their party had to be checked and reversed.

The minority party in the House maintains a skeleton staff which parallels such major offices as the clerk of the house, sergeant at arms, doorkeeper, postmaster, and pair clerk. If and when the Republicans became the majority their staff people would be waiting to assume positions now held by Democratic personnel. Regardless of party status, several positions are quite lucrative, paying better than $20,000 a year. Tradition allocated each position as a patronage appointment to a large-state delegation or to one of the principal party leaders. Most of the younger Republican activists were impatient with these traditions. They wanted professional services rendered for the high salaries paid, and furthermore, the requirement that the professional appointees should be responsible to the leadership and not to the delegation which had sponsored them. Argued one Ford supporter, "We've got to create a chain of command and provide for proper leadership supervision."

Despite the creation of a Personnel Committee in the 86th Congress to look into such complaints, little had been accomplished in the way of reform prior to the 89th Congress. Between the mid-December Republican Conference and the opening of the new Congress, both Halleck and Ford privately promised members of the Personnel Committee that they would enforce higher standards for minority employees, but agreed to delay action until a second Republican Conference of the new session.

Among the first decisions made by the new leadership was one to convert the position of minority sergeant at arms into a director of research for House Republicans. They sought to recruit Dr. William Prendergast, a former Republican National Committee research director, who had taken a research position with the National Association of Manufacturers. However, the Pennsylvania delegation, which had supported Ford almost to a man, balked at replacing their patronage appointee, William R. Bonsell, with Prendergast. Bonsell had come to work for House Republicans as majority sergeant at arms in the 83rd Congress, and had continued to serve as minority sergeant at arms from 1955 to 1964. On January 7, 1965, the new leadership was victorious against its first challenge. Prendergast defeated Bonsell by a secret-ballot tally of 84 to 40. Later that same day, Bonsell was elected minority doorkeeper in place of Tom J. Kennamer, a protege of former Missouri congressman Dewey Short. Kennamer subsequently became assistant doorkeeper.

Every attempt had been made to avoid the floor fight. As one participant later recalled,

We met with the Pennsylvania delegation several times but we couldn't satisfy them. They were jealous of their prerogatives. We said we would recommend Bonsell for another position. The Pennsylvania delegation—they've always been a maverick group anyway. We thought this was a pretty satisfactory compromise; they didn't.

The Pennsylvania delegation's discontent figured in Ford's next major controversy, an attempt to replace the incumbent minority whip.

Arends Survives a Contest. A member of the House since 1934 and party whip since 1943, Leslie Arends of Illinois had served as a loyal assistant to both Martin and Halleck. Recognizing the potential threat of Ford's challenge to his own leadership position, Arends had worked quietly behind the scenes for Halleck.

Now 69 years old, but still quite popular with many members, he quietly set about to assure his continuance in office even as Ford was meeting with his associates to decide who the new whip should be.

Arends had two grave disabilities from Ford's viewpoint. First, Ford needed someone who would work effectively in his interests and who would be wholeheartedly behind the new legislative strategy of constructive alternatives. Arends' general stance on legislation was regarded as too negative. Second, Ford felt that in order to unite the party, eastern liberals and moderates had to be given a larger share in the House leadership. If Arends continued as whip, midwesterners would occupy four of the five posts of party leadership. (Arends was from Illinois; Ford was from Michigan. Laird and Byrnes were both from Wisconsin, although the latter had already expressed his intentions to step down as Policy Committee chairman. The only non-midwesterner was the Campaign Committee chairman, Bob Wilson of California.)

Discussion of possible candidates to oppose Arends narrowed down to three easterners: Frelinghuysen of New Jersey; another member of the Wednesday Group, Robert Stafford of Vermont; and Goodell of New York. As we have seen, Frelinghuysen had made a surprisingly strong showing against Laird in the contest for Conference chairman. Compared to Frelinghuysen, first elected to the House in 1952, both Stafford and Goodell were low in seniority. While Goodell was the most acceptable of the three to conservatives, he was reluctant, having been one of Ford's two principal campaign managers, to become a candidate. One week after his own election, Ford finally decided to endorse Frelinghuysen as his candidate for whip.

Earlier that week, Ford had promised Arends that if a contest materialized, he would not follow the usual method of submitting his recommendation to the Committee on Committees but instead would take his choice directly to the Conference. A secret ballot vote was scheduled for Thursday, January 14, 1965. Ford, Frelinghuysen, Griffin, and Goodell threw themselves into an effort to align support, but three days proved to be far too short a time. Just ten days after his own election, Ford suffered his first major setback. Arends defeated Frelinghuysen by a vote of 70 to 59, and the Arends forces claimed the support of an additional nine of the eleven absentees.

In retrospect, Arends' victory was not difficult to explain. He began with most of the pro-Halleck support and the eleven-member Illinois delegation solidly behind him. Like Halleck, counting votes was Arends' stock in trade. But as whip he had not antagonized as many members as the former minority leader. His job was not so much to make party policy, but to implement it once established. He had rendered additional services to members as an influential member of the Committee on Committees. The kinds of issues which came before the Armed Services Committee, on which Arends had served as ranking minority member, were almost never as controversial as those which had continually preoccupied Frelinghuysen on his two committees, Foreign Affairs and Education and Labor. Finally, Arends, long popular with the Pennsylvania delegation, reaped the benefit of its disgruntlement over Ford's minority personnel decisions.

In contrast, Frelinghuysen's campaign got off to a late start and never really got rolling. There was almost no opportunity for cross-checking on votes, let alone to establish that Frelinghuysen had a chance to win. The support he drew in the contest for Conference chairman was misleading since it had included some anti-Laird votes. With his personal reserve and aristocratic Ivy League background, Frelinghuysen had never approached Arends' popularity among rank-and-file Republicans. Another major liability was his identification with the Wednesday Group. Two comments, the first from a conservative, the second from a Wednesday Group member, illustrate the problem:

When you come right down to it, whether we have 178 members or 140, the liberals don't have much to say about party policy. They have always been independent, gone their own way, and this has hurt their ability to influence anybody else.

We know we are not a popular group in the House. Popular isn't the word for it—we are a despised group. We're not team players and all that. Hell, we couldn't elect a guy dog catcher. With all the different shades of liberalism in our group, I doubt that we could get all 22 of us to vote for one of our own.

Finally, Frelinghuysen's internationalist voting record and his liberal stand on the nuclear policy plank at the San Francisco convention drove some of Laird's supporters, who might otherwise have gone along, into the Arends camp. Southern freshmen who had voted for Ford backed Arends almost to a man.

Subtract a half-dozen votes from southern conservatives, several votes in the California and Illinois delegations, and most of the Pennsylvania delegation and it is easy to see how Ford's 73 votes for minority leader declined to 59 votes for Frelinghuysen as whip. Another opportunity to recoup lay ahead. Ford could restore some of his prestige and reward his most loyal supporters through his influence on committee assignments.

Republican Committee Assignments: The Ways and Means Seat. By long tradition, the majority party takes 15 seats and the minority 10 seats on the powerful tax-writing and revenue-raising House Ways and Means Committee. Three of the ten Republican incumbents in the 88th Congress had been defeated in November, 1964. The extraordinary Democratic majority in the House led Speaker McCormack to alter the party ratio on the committee to provide for 17 Democrats and 8 Republicans. Thus, one minority seat was vacant at the beginning of the 89th Congress. Even as Ford's leadership was undergoing its second test in the contest for party whip, the ground was being prepared for another reversal—rejection of Ford's endorsement of Goodell's application to obtain this seat. Of the three states which had lost GOP members on Ways and Means—New York, Michigan, and Texas—the claim of the fourteen-member New York delegation seemed to outweigh the others, not just because of its size, but because the economic importance of northeastern financial interests being represented on the committee.

Five-term Howard Robison had replaced Mrs. St. George as the New York spokesman on the executive subcommittee of the Republican Committee on Committees. By tradition, this subcommittee is made up of a representative from all of those states with at least seven Republican members in their delegations, plus a small-state representative selected by the minority leader, and a member of each of the classes elected since 1960, the 87th, 88th, and 89th Clubs. Power is concentrated in the large states, since each member, save for the class representatives, has as many votes as there are members in his delegation. In the 89th Congress, it would take a majority of 39 votes to control the 77-vote executive subcommittee. For all practical purposes, a combination of any three of the five largest delegations—California (15), New York (14), Ohio (14), Pennsylvania (12), and Illinois (11)—could dominate the subcommittee, and hence the full Committee on Committees. Ford would have some influence as an ex-officio but non-voting chairman.

Goodell submitted his bid for the Ways and Means vacancy for consideration at the last possible moment and with considerable ambivalence. If he retained his present committee assignments, Education and Labor, and House Administration, he would be fourth-ranking on both. On the other hand, as eighth-ranking member on Ways and Means he would be offered a new challenge both in the substance of legislation and the opportunities to work with and learn from such respected senior Republican members as Byrnes and Curtis. His congressional predecessor, the late Daniel A. Reed, had served on Ways and Means with great distinction for many years, including a stint as chairman in the 83rd Congress. A recognition of the importance of this seat to New York, as much as any other factor, finally led Goodell to enter the contest.

The two most promising of the other ten applicants who applied for the single vacancy on Ways and Means were Robert Ellsworth of Kansas and James Battin of Montana. Each had been elected to Congress in 1960, and each had submitted bids for Ways and Means when vacancies occurred in 1962 on the retirement of Noah Mason of Illinois and again in 1964 on the death of Howard Baker of Tennessee. Illinois' large-state claim had prevailed in the first case, while the seniority claims of Joel Broyhill of Virginia were acknowledged in 1964. As soon as it became apparent that there might be a vacancy, both Ellsworth and Battin launched aggressive campaigns, following the usual practice of writing letters to party leaders, members of Ways and Means, and the holdover members of the Republican Committee on Committees, and striving to align interest group support.

Battin, however, had a number of uniquely favorable factors working for him. First, the young Montana conservative had served as a member of the executive subcommittee in both the 87th and 88th Congresses. As Battin later recalled: "I knew the members, I was familiar with the ball park, and I knew how the game was played." Second, Battin had the support of two of the most conservative large-state representatives, James Utt of California with 14 votes, and Leslie Arends of Illinois with 11 votes. Utt favored Battin because he felt the west was entitled to at least one more member on Ways and Means and because he had no doubts about Battin's conservative views. Arends had supported Battin's prior prestige appointments to Judiciary in 1961 and Foreign Affairs in 1963, and Battin in turn, had actively worked for Arends' re-election as party whip. Finally, in order to go on Ways and Means, Battin would have to give up his slot on the Foreign Affairs Committee, a position which a third member of the executive subcommittee, James Fulton of Pennsylvania, anxiously sought for himself. Fulton, a maverick liberal, had been forced off Foreign Affairs by Halleck in January, 1961, and thus it was with considerable relish that he voted for Ford as minority leader in 1965. Since Fulton could not return to Foreign Affairs until there was a vacancy—which could only come about if Battin or another member left Foreign Affairs—his otherwise improbable alignment with conservatives Utt and Arends was undertaken.

Thus, even as Goodell submitted his bid, the contest was all but over. On January 15, on the first ballot, Battin won the coveted seat with 39 votes, comprised of Utt (15 votes), Arends (11), Fulton (12), and the single vote of a close friend, Laurence J. Burton of Utah, the representative from the 88th Club. Later that afternoon, the same combination of large-delegation votes put Fulton back on the Foreign Affairs Committee. Both Battin's and Fulton's assignments were routinely endorsed by the full committee, the Republican Conference, and subsequently by the House itself.

Although these appointments were interpreted in the press as a further setback for Ford, there was little he could have done to prevent Battin's appointment, once the alliance of Utt, Arends, and Fulton was put together. Ford's supporters fared better on other committee assignments. At least three of the five appointees to Appropriations were members who had been active in support of his candidacy. His influence was also felt on assignments to less prestigious committees.

The risks may be great, but there are important benefits to those who back a winning candidate. Of the six congressmen who served as Ford's inner circle of campaign workers—Griffin, Quie, Conte, Goodell, Ellsworth, and Rumsfeld—not one of them had served on the Republican Policy Committee in the 88th Congress. Only Quie represented his state on the Republican Committee on Committees. Conte was the only one of the six serving on the Republican Congressional Campaign Committee. Their positions in the party hierarchy following Ford's victory at the opening of the 89th Congress were considerably improved. Four of the six became members of the Republican Policy Committee. Three of the six were selected by their state delegations to represent them on the Republican Congressional Campaign Committee. Griffin was one of three Republicans chosen for the Joint Committee on the Organization of Congress. In the 88th Congress Ellsworth was the only member of the House to serve on three standing committees, all relatively minor: Merchant Marine and Fisheries, Post Office and Civil Service, and Veterans Affairs. He gave up the first to accept appointment to the prestigious Joint Economic Committee. Conte was selected as the one House Republican on the Migratory Bird Conservation Commission, a position he had actively campaigned for in the 88th Congress, only to be rebuffed by Halleck. He also became a member of the Select Committee on Small Business and the Joint Commission on the Coinage.

Perhaps the most important appointment was Ford's choice of Goodell as the sole minority representative on the House Office Building Commission. This obscure but powerful commission, by its control of space and its supervision of service personnel other than capitol police, gives its members multiple opportunities to do favors for other congressmen. Its importance is indicated by its majority members: the Speaker of the House, John McCormack, and the dean of House Democrats and chairman of the Judiciary Committee, Emanuel Celler of New York. Goodell was also appointed chairman of a new Republican Conference Committee on Research and Planning, which was to figure in a further trial for Ford in February.

Choosing a Policy Committee Chairman and Creating a Committee on Research and Planning. In mid-January, John Byrnes of Wisconsin announced his resignation as Policy Committee chairman in order to devote full time to his responsibilities as ranking minority member of the Ways and Means Committee. On January 22, the day after the House of Representatives ratified Republican committee assignments, the *Washington Evening Star* carried a story declaring that John Rhodes, six-term member from Arizona, hoped to succeed Byrnes as Policy Committee chairman. Once again Ford was faced with a dilemma. Rhodes was not his first choice for that post, but he could not afford to run the risk of another contest. If he lost, it would all but destroy his effectiveness as a leader. Even if he won, it might well remove his remaining hopes for uniting the party.

Ford's first choice to head the Republican Policy Committee was Charles Goodell, a 38-year-old conservative from a rural district in the southwestern corner of New York state. First elected in 1959, Goodell had quickly earned a reputation as a promising young legislator and potential leader. He and Griffin had organized Ford's race for Conference Chairman in 1963 and had helped engineer Ford's defeat of Halleck in 1965. Goodell's intelligence, organizational talents, and political sagacity were well recognized, but so were his liabilities. At the time a contest seemed possible, a midwest conservative friendly to Goodell commented on them:

Just between you and me, I think Charlie [Goodell] would do a hell of a good job as Policy Committee Chairman. His biggest liability, of course, is his juniority . . . Goodell has also encouraged some resentment from some of the other members. He has been tabbed as a hatchet man. The fact of the matter is you need such people. They are an integral part of a campaign. . . . But you can't expect to do one and then come along and reap the rewards of the other. You can't expect to be a jockey and a horse at the same time.

From Ford's point of view, John Rhodes' two principal limitations were that he had been one of Goldwater's strongest supporters in 1964 and that he had remained loyal to Halleck in 1965. These were not seen as liabilities, of course, by many other Republican legislators. On the other hand, the 49-year-old Rhodes had several major advantages compared with Goodell. He had twelve years of service to Goodell's seven years. Since 1961, Rhodes had served as chairman of a Policy Committee subcommittee on special projects, which made him the most likely heir to John Byrnes.

Ford and his associates considered several alternative ways to maintain their influence while avoiding another contest. Although he hinted to reporters that Goodell might be a good man for the Policy Committee post, Ford made no formal recommendation. A number of Republicans, chief among them Laird, had been urging Ford to bring the Policy Committee more closely under the Republican Conference. A division of the two functions performed by the Policy Committee—(1) the development of long-range policy papers through task forces and (2) the adoption of specific policy stands on legislation—had been contemplated as early as December. At a joint press conference on February 3, Ford, Laird, and Arends announced the creation of a new committee of the House Republican Conference, to be called the Research and Planning Committee, and to be chaired by Goodell. In addition to supervising Republican task forces, this new committee was assigned the job of coordinating the research team being developed under the direction of Dr. Prendergast.

Three weeks later at another Republican Conference on February 23, Goodell's appointment as chairman was routinely confirmed along with seven additional members of the Research and Planning Committee. That same afternoon, John Rhodes was unanimously elected chairman of a restructured Policy Committee. In a press conference which followed, Ford and Laird went out of their way to stress that the new positions were coequal in the party hierarchy. But the difference in the methods by which Goodell and Rhodes were selected was not lost on most Republican members. Rhodes had been elected by the Conference; Goodell's appointment merely confirmed. Nonetheless, by these arrangements a major confrontation had been avoided, and able members from the east and west were now part of what had been a predominantly midwestern leadership. Unfortunately, these accommodations were marred by one final setback for Ford.

The Quie Committee Recommendations. Meanwhile, the ad hoc Quie Committee on Organizational Structure was bringing off a quiet revolution in Republican party organization. Its eleven members represented all shades of ideology, geography, and age-grouping. Once recommendations had been thrashed out in committee, their adoption in the Republican Conference was greatly facilitated by the diverse composition. At the January 14 Conference before the whip vote, its first recommendations were routinely approved. The five principal party leaders—floor leader, whip, and the chairmen of the Republican Conference, Policy Committee, and Congressional Campaign Committee—were prohibited from serving as ranking minority members or chairman of standing committees. A floor amendment offered by John Rhodes provided that deposed leaders would have the right to go back on their former committees with full seniority. The positions of vice chairman and secretary of the Conference, held respectively by William Cramer of Florida and Richard Poff of Virginia, were given added status by being made part of the top leadership. These changes, together with the creation of the Research and Planning Committee and the building up of a research staff under Prendergast, substantially consolidated the powers of the Republican Conference.

The Quie Committee fared less well with its recommendations made to the Committee on Committees. Its first recommendation, that a member should not serve as chairman or ranking minority member on more than one standing or select committee, was adopted by the executive subcommittee with but two exceptions for veteran Ohio members, Clarence J. Brown and William M. McCulloch. Several ranking minority members did step down a rank on their less important committees, among them, Corbett of Pennsylvania (House Administration), Springer of Illinois (District of Columbia), and Ayres of Ohio (Veterans Affairs). Other recommendations, such as the proposal that ranking minority members of major committees be prohibited from serving on other committees, came too close to the power base of too many important senior members, and were quietly dropped.

Perhaps the major reform instituted by the Quie Committee was reorganization of the Policy Committee, whose principal task is to hammer out a party consensus on legislation prior to floor debate. It was during the adoption of these changes at the February 23 Conference that Ford once again ran into difficulty.

The major changes in the Policy Committee went through quite smoothly. The resolution, as originally introduced, called for a Policy Committee of 25 members: eight regional representatives, eight leaders, seven members-at-large, and two class representatives. The most important change gave the floor leader the power to select the seven members-at-large in order "to give balance and provide membership from each major committee." Three amendments were introduced from the floor, only one of which was accepted. Arends proposed that the Policy Committee be enlarged by adding former minority leaders, namely Martin and Halleck. Adopted in a spirit of reconciliation, the presence of Halleck on the Policy Committee later gave the Ford supporters some cause for regret when the former party leader aggressively criticized some of the bills developed by the Ford wing as constructive alternatives to Johnson's proposals.

A proposal to add one more class representative from the 87th Club was rejected. The final amendment proposed by Howard Robison of New York provided for the inclusion of the chairman of the newly created Research and Planning Committee as a member of the Policy Committee along with the incumbents of seven other leadership positions: the floor leader; whip; chairman, vice-chairman, and secretary of the Conference; chairman of the Policy Committee; and chairman of the Campaign Committee. Had the language been written into the resolution prior to its introduction, it probably would have slipped through without objection. Although sympathetic to the proposal, Quie was reluctant to reconstitute his committee in order to add the provision after Goodell's position had been created in late February. Coming as a floor amendment, it gave the Halleck-Arends camp one last opportunity for revenge. With Ford off the floor on the telephone discussing Vietnam policy with Richard Nixon, and with Laird unable to comment because he was presiding officer, the Arends-led opposition defeated Goodell's bid to obtain equal status, 38 to 30. Later that week, Ford announced that among his seven appointees to the Policy Committee, his first two choices would be Byrnes and Goodell.

Ford, Laird, and Quie had in many respects accomplished a major coup at the February 23 Conference. First, they had had Goodell's nomination confirmed and the Committee on Research and Planning approved by a unanimous vote. Second, the task forces had been transferred from the Policy Committee to the Research and Planning Committee. This group had been given the right to create new task forces without coming back to the Conference. Third, major reforms had been brought about in the Policy Committee and accepted by the Republican Conference. Perhaps the most important change was the right of the minority leader to appoint seven members, thus substantially strengthening his control. Fourth, Ford had avoided a direct confrontation by accepting Rhodes as chairman of the Policy Committee, a contest which he almost certainly would have lost. Unfortunately, some of the gain that these leaders had engineered was lost sight of when an AP wire story featured a further setback to Ford because Goodell had not automatically been accorded leadership status. As usual, it was conflict rather than accomplishments that made news.

Out-Party Legislative Strategies

Even before the 89th Congress convened and in the very act of selecting their leaders, House Republicans were faced with the problem of overall legislative strategy. Three basic alternatives are available to a party which does not control the White House: (1) cooperation with the presidential majority, (2) partisan opposition, or (3) promotion of constructive alternatives to administration proposals. No party ever practices one alternative exclusively, but different House and Senate leaders may come to be identified with one or another policy stance. On any piece of legislation, adherence to one of these alternatives derives as much from day-to-day decisions on legislative tactics as from ideological commitments and overall strategy. Minority party legislators can never escape the pressures of deciding when to suggest perfecting amendments or agree on compromise language, when to oppose a provision or section of a bill outright, or when to develop their own substitute for a bill offered by the administration. Often by the time the minority party's leadership gets involved, many of their options have already been foreclosed by the pace of events or the actions of the majority party. Among recent Republican congressional leaders, Senator Everett Dirksen and Representative Joseph Martin have most closely approximated the policy of cooperation with the majority; Senator William F. Knowland and Halleck, the policy of partisan opposition; and Senator Robert A. Taft, Senator Thomas Kuchel, and Ford have come closest to a policy emphasizing constructive legislative alternatives to Democratic programs.

The Democratic congressional leadership had confronted similar alternatives during the Eisenhower administration (1953–1960). However, unlike Dirksen, Halleck, and Ford, Democrats Lyndon Johnson and Sam Rayburn had majority control over their respective houses for the last six of the eight years, which heightened their flexibility and their capacity to push successfully for Democratic-sponsored legislation. The two Texas congressional leaders at first adopted a policy of cooperating with the popular Republican president, but later shifted to preparing Democratic alternatives and working toward modification or defeat of Eisenhower proposals. As they approached the presidential elections of 1956 and especially 1960, they were frequently as interested in manufacturing issues by forcing Eisenhower to use his veto powers as they were in passing legislation. Pro-Stevenson forces on the Democratic Advisory Council, and, later, pro-Kennedy liberals both inside and outside Congress, often felt that neither Johnson nor Rayburn went far enough in their criticism of Eisenhower or in developing significant Democratic alternatives. Both sets of experiences—attempts by Democratic congressional majorities from 1955 to 1960 and the frustrations encountered by Republican minority leaders from 1961 to the present—illustrate the difficulties that any out-party must face in trying to combat and surmount the inherent advantages of presidential leadership and executive branch support in the initiating and implementing of legislative programs.

Cooperation With the Presidential Majority. Cooperation with the majority assures the minority party of maximum involvement in the governing process since the majority party often must make substantial concessions to secure cooperation from the minority. But the costs to the out-party can be high since it gives it less flexibility as the legislative process proceeds and its ability to criticize after the fact is virtually eliminated.

Perhaps the classic example of such a policy stance was the emphasis of Republican Senator Arthur Vandenberg of Michigan on a bipartisan foreign policy—"a politics which stopped at the water's edge"—during the Truman administration. Senator Dirksen's support of the nuclear test ban treaty in 1963 provides a more recent example of cooperation. On critical decisions of foreign policy, the veteran Republican floor leader frequently backed not only his own President, Eisenhower, but also Democratic Presidents Kennedy and Johnson.

The crisis brought about by racial violence also led to a bipartisan approach on civil rights legislation. The threat of a Senate filibuster by southern Democrats makes Republican cooperation essential to the passage of such laws. Thus, Dirksen played a crucial role in the passage of the Civil Rights Acts of 1957, 1960, and 1964. The cooperation of former minority leader Halleck and the ranking minority member of the House Judiciary Committee, William McCulloch of Ohio, was essential to the passage of the Civil Rights

Act of 1964 in the House. The Voting Rights Act of 1965 found Dirksen continuing to cooperate with the majority, while Republican House leaders led by Ford and McCulloch took a different tack and presented a constructive alternative, a bill hammered out in cooperation with senior southern Republicans on the Judiciary Committee. Overwhelming Democratic majorities in the House carried the day for the administration version.

Republicans practiced a modification of a cooperative strategy on the Vietnam war issue in 1966 and 1967. They amended a policy of general support for the president by attacking Democratic critics of Johnson's Vietnam policies, thus keeping themselves in an enviably flexible position as the 1966 and 1968 elections approached.

A policy of cooperation with the majority is especially appropriate on less controversial legislation such as the Water Quality Act or the International Education Act. On bills of such import neither side expects to get much political mileage. The majority accedes to minority amendments as a price of obtaining consensus and ease of passage. Yet some conservative Republicans would reject even this kind of cooperation. Their attitude is, "Hell, don't improve legislation, you won't get credit for it anyway." Most minority members, however, take a more conciliatory attitude. As one House Republican commented:

This is a dilemma we continually face, whether to go for issues or to try to improve the bill. It comes down to what is the best way of accomplishing our responsibility as a minority party. Should we improve the bill in committee at the risk of losing credit, or should we oppose it and seek issues for the campaign?

And, of course, when Republicans can make improvements in a bill, but still develop an issue, that is the best of all possible worlds.

Partisan Opposition. Republican House and Senate minority leaders over the past several decades have most frequently adopted the stance of partisan opposition. The principal objective is to defeat Democratic measures. Its great advantage as a strategy is that it is much easier to unite the party in opposition than it is to obtain agreement of alternative solutions. Senate minority leaders Wherry of Nebraska, Bridges of New Hampshire, and Knowland of California were practitioners of this approach. As Robert Taft of Ohio, chairman of the Senate Republican Policy Committee from 1947 to 1953 and majority leader under Eisenhower in 1953, summed up this philosophy: "The business of the opposition is to oppose. Minority leaders . . . have no responsibility for presenting a program. Their role is one of opposition and criticism." (Like all great legislative leaders Taft would not let himself be bound by such rhetoric. During his long and distinguished legislative career he sponsored a number of major bills, most notably his housing bills and the Taft-Hartley Labor Relations Act of 1947.)

Halleck, majority leader in the 80th and 83rd Congresses and Republican minority leader in Eisenhower's last two years, was adept at unifying Republicans behind their own legislative programs. But he was especially skilled at defeating Kennedy and Johnson administration bills, often in alliance with conservative southern Democrats. Halleck's December, 1964 defense of his record as minority leader acknowledged the need to cooperate with the majority when Eisenhower was president. He also stated that "most of the constructive legislation" passed during the Kennedy-Johnson Administration bore "a very definite Republican imprint." Still, the main thrust of Halleck's December statement emphasized a policy of partisan opposition:

Many costly, unwise, and unnecessary proposals were either defeated or abandoned by virtue of almost solid Republican opposition. . . .

On vote after vote, Republicans from north, south, east and west—from urban and rural areas—have stood shoulder to shoulder on issues of vital importance to America. On six major issues over the past two years, our roll calls votes averaged 162 to 3, an amazing example of teamwork. A study of Republican votes in the House from January, 1961, to mid-1964 shows that where we had a policy position, the Republicans averaged 150 to 14 on fifty-one House roll calls.

Two factors were to inhibit Republican opportunities to inflict defeats on administration programs in the 89th Congress. The first was the size of the minority. With but 140 members, a score of whom came from urban and suburban districts whose interests made them sympathetic to liberal Democratic domestic programs, Republicans could not realistically expect to win many legislative victories. Even the support of the 60 to 70 conservative Democrats, most of them southerners, would seldom provide enough votes to overturn the overwhelming majorities enjoyed by the Democratic House leadership. In many previous Congresses, and again in the 90th Congress (1967–1968), a combination of Republicans and conservative southern Democrats had the votes to thwart liberal Democratic programs. Since that condition was absent for the 89th Congress, the need for a different strategy was apparent. As a southern Republican observed:

Jerry [Ford], I think, will be more likely to have unofficial and more limited relations with southern Democrats, whereas Charlie [Halleck] would have more formalized relations—the Indiana horse-trader—you do this for me and I'll do that for you. . . . Now, we only have 140 votes. Surely, negotiation with the southern Democrats, the so-called coalition, is less viable.

And a midwestern moderate voiced similar views:

In the past when we had larger numbers it was possible to have a different kind of leadership, to get everyone together, a shoulder-to-shoulder type of leadership. Particularly, when we were trying to combine with enough southern Democrats, sometimes to block legislation, and also, to change the legislation—Halleck was very effective at this.

Now we are at a period where that type of leadership is no longer what we need. To think that the coalition could continue to work effectively is not realistic and that is the only kind of leadership Halleck is capable of. Therefore, I felt that the best hope is not unity, but diversity. We need new ideas. We need to stimulate sharp-shooting from a variety of approaches. We need to consider ideas from a fresh view and to look for new solutions. We have to work toward appealing to the American people with alternative policies that make sense.

These attitudes lead us to expect the so-called conservative coalition (a majority of Republicans and a majority of southern Democrats voting together) to be far less effective in the first session of the 89th Congress. In 1965, this combination was able to win only one-fourth of the 24 per cent of the roll calls on which it appeared. Its record in 1966 was only slightly improved. In contrast, on 28 per cent of the roll call votes in 1961, the conservative coalition won almost three-fourths of the time. (In 1967, the conservative coalition was again operating at full strength. It appeared on one-fifth of the votes and again won almost three-fourths of the time it appeared.)

The second factor inhibiting Republican adherence to a policy of partisan opposition in the 89th Congress was partially attributed to the costs of the minority leadership contest. Locked in an intraparty struggle, Republicans were ill-prepared to contest proposed Democratic rule changes enhancing majority rule. Pre-planning and strategy were largely left up to Clarence Brown of Ohio, the old-guard ranking Republican on the Committee on Rules. Over the final weekend and during the morning Republican Conference before the new Congress convened there was almost no time to develop or promulgate the Republican alternatives. Other than floor debate, attempts to rally the party in opposition to the Democratic proposals were practically nonexistent. On the opening day, the vote on the motion to cut off debate and prevent amendments to the proposals of the Democratic leadership carried by 224 to 201. Seldom again during the session would as many southern Democrats oppose the Democratic leadership. Seventy-four of them plus four conservative northern Democrats joined Rules Committee chairman Howard Smith of Virginia and the bulk of Republicans in opposing the changes. But sixteen Republicans, all but three of them from east coast states, voted with the Democratic majority to provide the winning margin. Two of the three rules changes took further powers away from the House Committee on the Rules and made it easier to schedule legislation, control the time of debate, pass conference reports, and, in general, eased the tasks of the Democratic leadership. As Democratic majority leader Carl Albert summed up the consequences of the rules changes: "It was the greatest victory ever won on behalf of the president's Great Society program, because on this day the Great Society was saved."

Perhaps the greatest shortcoming of partisan opposition is that it does not seem to be a very successful policy for election success. The American public is seldom satisfied with mere criticism. The days of "caretaker" government have long since passed. If the Republican party was to become a majority party, critics of this approach argued, it had to convince many more voters that it could meet the needs of the country with positive programs, and meet them more efficiently and with less danger of conflicts of interest than the Democrats. After the election disaster brought on by Goldwater's candidacy, Ford's call for new and innovative legislative plans fell on receptive ears within his own party.

Constructive Republican Alternatives. Ford's election as minority leader promised a party shift from partisan opposition to the promotion of fresh, constructive Republican alternatives. In a

January, 1965 *Fortune* article, Ford outlined the projected new directions:

We must come forward on a planned and thoughtful basis with attractive, workable alternatives to administration proposals. Our aim should be an affirmative and specific Republican legislative program for the Eighty-ninth Congress, produced as early as possible in the session. We must stake out our positions independently of any preplanning with the southern Democratic leadership so as to correct the frequently distorted image of a Republican—southern Democratic coalition.

Republican governors comprised another office-holding group promoting constructive alternatives after the 1964 election. Generally more liberal than Republican national legislators, the governors were anxious to assert themselves as authoritative spokesmen for the out-party. Meeting in Denver, in early December, the Republican Governors' Association called for a new approach based on the formulation of "positive policies."

We need to appeal to all Americans. We need to become inclusive rather than exclusive. We need to win elections and serve America as a great broad-based political party, far greater and far more effective than any narrow, exclusive political clique can ever hope to become.

But after voicing the need for unity the governors tended to go their separate ways.

It was not until the end of January, 1965, that Ford could take time out from his organizational trials to solicit his colleagues for concrete legislative suggestions. Only in the loosest sense did Republicans ever unite on a planned program. In most instances, the leadership relied on its ranking minority members to set policies for them. During the first session of the 89th Congress, Republicans offered substitutes for six of the major bills proposed by the administration: (1) the Appalachia Regional Development Act, (2) the Social Security Amendments Act, including Medicare, (3) an act creating a Department of Housing and Urban Development, (4) the Voting Rights Act, (5) the Elementary and Secondary Education Act, and (6) the public housing bill, including rent supplements. Republicans had a direct opportunity to vote on the first four of the six Republican substitutes. (During debate on the remaining two, the Republican leadership seized upon different targets of opportunity for their motions to recommit the bills to committee.)

As Table I suggests, the Republican leadership was reasonably successful in rallying support for three out of four of their constructive Republican alternatives. Their average support of 85 per cent on these four measures is only slightly lower than an overall support of 86.8 per cent on twenty-six votes on which the Republican Policy Committee took a position in the first session.

However, formulation of constructive alternatives generated a series of further problems for Ford and his associates. Some conservative colleagues resented what they interpreted as "me-tooism," efforts "to outbid and outpromise" the Democrats. Yet when Republican leaders attempted to modify legislation to accord with the views of all elements within the party, as they did on the voting rights substitute of 1965, the results were likely to be criticized because they did not go far enough. Thus, some newspapermen and numerous Democrats accused "the party of Abraham Lincoln" of selling out its principles in order to accommodate the views of its more conservative southern members.

TABLE I

Votes on Four Recommittal Motions to Substitute Constructive Republican Alternatives for Administration Proposals, 89th Congress, 1st Session (1965)

	Republicans Yea Nay % for	Democrats Yea Nay % for	Total vote
Appalachia (Cramer motion), March 3, 1965	92 44 67.6	8 279 97.5	100–323
Medicare (Byrnes motion), April 8, 1965	128 10 92.8	63 226 78.0	191–236
Department of HUD (Dwyer motion), June 16, 1965	122 5 96.1	19 254 94.5	141–259
Voting Rights (Collier motion), July 9, 1965	115 21 84.6	56 227 80.0	171–248

Source: *Congressional Quarterly Weekly Reports*, Vol. XXIII (March 5, 1965), pp. 368–369; (April 9, 1965), pp. 662–663; (June 18, 1965), pp. 1204–1205; (July 16, 1965), pp. 1402–1403.

The vote on the Appalachia substitute offered by Cramer of Florida illustrates another problem associated with such a strategy.

The identification of legislative proposals as matters of Republican party policy sometimes promotes a counter-unifying force on the Democratic side. Not only did Republicans lose a third of their own membership, many of these from the eleven-state Appalachian region; they drove all but eight Democrats into opposing the Republican recommittal motion (see Table I). As one Republican leader later recalled: "That was an unfortunate first choice for a constructive alternative. We ended up falling flat on our face."

The Byrnes substitute on Medicare illustrates several further complications. When Republicans offered innovations, they ran the risk of having their ideas incorporated into the administration bill with little hope of their sharing in the credit. Democrat Wilbur Mills, chairman of the Ways and Means Committee, recognizing that some form of Medicare would pass in the 89th Congress, was quick to seize upon the Byrnes proposals calling for voluntary, comprehensive coverage of doctor bills and other medical expenses to be paid through general revenue and contributions from participants. This, together with other Republican contributions, substantially improved the administration's bill. But in the end it was not Mills or Byrnes, but President Johnson who reaped most of the credit for passing Medicare.

Republicans were able to unite behind the Byrnes substitute on the recommittal motion, 128 to 10. They split almost in half on final passage, however, 65 voting for, and 73 against. (As Table I indicates, the recommittal motion was rejected 191–236. On final passage Medicare won overwhelmingly, 313–115.) Ford joined Byrnes in voting "nay" with a slight majority of his colleagues, but he was the only Michigan Republican to do so. Byrnes had reluctantly gone along with the GOP Policy Committee stance. A moderate Republican, who voted against final passage, explained the dilemma confronting Republicans on these votes:

There were two schools of thought—many wanted to promote the contributions made by John Byrnes and vote for final passage; others sided with Campaign Committee Chairman Bob Wilson. His relationships with the AMA, Omaha Mutual, and others who contribute to Republican campaign coffers [they felt] made it necessary to vote against the bill. . . .

The feeling was we would stand together on the recommittal motion and then, on final passage, we would let guys do what they have to do to save their own skins.

Thus, a slight majority of House Republicans voted against the program and in accord with views held by some of their strongest sources of campaign support. A strong minority favored Medicare, particularly representatives from large urban states who, in essence, were voting district sentiments. For example, all fourteen Republicans in New York state voted for Medicare on final passage.

Other factors besides the personality and political ideology of a leader affect the propensity to adopt one policy alternative rather than another. As we have suggested, when the Republican minority shrinks so that its members, together with the conservative southern Democrats, no longer make up a majority, then partisan opposition will become less appropriate. Permanent minority status leads to what reporter David Broder has called "influence politics," payoffs to special interests and more subtle forms of compromising with the majority. As one House Republican put it: "Members get used to side deals; they become content to take crumbs from the Democratic table."

Differences between the first and second session, between the demands on a congressman's time in the first year as compared with an election year, also affect legislative strategy. The development of constructive alternatives requires "deep and powerful thinking, a lot of time and effort on the part of a member, and good staff support. In an election year, all these things are harder to come by."

House Republican legislative policy in the second session of the 89th Congress reflected these and other pressures. As the party approached the midterm elections of 1966, the hazards of searching for constructive alternatives became more acute. Moreover, it was far easier to rally party members against the administration and its policies. As one representative summed it up: "When the party gets the scent of blood, it wants to deal a death blow. It wants to knock out what the other side is proposing, completely." Finally, the outcomes of primary election contests in 1966, in many cases favoring the conservative candidate, increased pressures to return to a policy of partisan opposition.

Reviewing the years 1965–1966, the lesson seems clear that the optimum strategy for the minority legislative party is not one, but a blend of all three policy stances. The key questions are those of issue selection and timing. At the opening of the 89th Congress, a stress on new and innovative programs made sense to counter Goldwater's image as a negative candidate. As the midterm election of 1966 approached, opposition for its own sake became more important as Republicans deliberately sought to put the majority party on the defensive.

The House Minority Leader's External Relations

Who speaks for the out-party, the party not in control of the White House? In most instances, leadership devolves upon its congressional leaders, its national party chairman, governors, past or prospective presidential candidates, and other party notables. Congressional leaders of the out-party must allocate far more of their time to external relations than their counterparts who enjoy control of the White House. Chief among Ford's external preoccupations throughout 1965 and 1966 were coordinating policy making with the Senate minority leadership and the Republican National Committee, cultivating press and television contacts in order to gain maximum exposure for the Republican viewpoint, and fund raising and campaigning for his party's congressional candidates. These activities would have their ultimate payoff in developing campaign issues, promoting a successful comeback in the midterm election of 1966, and improving Republican prospects for the presidential election of 1968.

Relations with Senate Republicans. A traditional problem for the out-party, as V. O. Key has written, is that it "lacks the machinery to produce a decision on party policy that will be accepted as binding by all the important segments of the party."* One party organ, the Joint Senate-House Republican Leadership, had been partially performing this function since 1961. More active in the 89th Congress than before, this group also became the core of a much larger policy-making body, the Republican Coordinating Committee, which came into being in January, 1965. The institutional jealousies which frequently characterize House-Senate relationships, the mutual distrust between congressional leaders and the National Committee, the deep ideological cleavage which divided the party following Goldwater's unsuccessful campaign, and the ever-present potential for personal conflict and rivalries be-

---

*V. O. Key, Jr., *Politics, Parties, & Pressure Groups*, 5th ed. (New York: Thomas Y. Crowell, 1964), p. 564.

tween ambitious politicians made it a wonder that Republicans were able to organize at all, let alone succeed as well as they have.

On the eve of his departure from office, President Eisenhower had suggested that House and Senate Republican leaders continue to meet as a collective group on Capitol Hill. The Joint Senate-House Republican Leadership had never been very successful as a policy-coordinating body, but it has provided a convenient public forum. Typically meeting two or three times a month, usually on a Wednesday afternoon, it concentrates on reworking the press conference statements which will be delivered by the Senate and House minority leaders the following morning at 11:00 a.m.

During most of the 89th Congress its membership was composed as follows:

The Joint Senate-House Republican Leadership

Senate	House of Representatives
Everett M. Dirksen, Minority Leader	Gerald R. Ford, Minority Leader
Thomas H. Kuchel, Minority Whip	Leslie C. Arends, Minority Whip
Bourke B. Hickenlooper, Chairman, Policy Committee	Melvin R. Laird, Chairman, Republican Conference
Leverett Saltonstall, Chairman, Republican Conference	John J. Rhodes, Chairman, Policy Committee
Thruston B. Morton, Chairman, Republican Senatorial Committee	H. Allen Smith,[a] Ranking Member, Committee on Rules
	Bob Wilson, Chairman, Republican Congressional Committee
	Charles E. Goodell,[a] Chairman, Committee on Research and Planning

[a]Goodell and Smith were added to the Joint Leadership at Ford's request following the death of Clarence Brown of Ohio, Smith's predecessor as ranking minority member on the House Committee on Rules.

Ray Bliss, the chairman of the Republican National Committee, presides over the meetings. His full-time efforts, organizational talents, and preference for avoiding stands on issues have facilitated the greatly improved relationships between congressional leaders and the National Republican Committee.

These meetings also provide a mechanism for healing potentially damaging rifts between House and Senate leaders. On Tuesday, April 19, 1966, at one of his ad hoc press chats in the Senate press gallery, Senator Dirksen took issue with Ford's April 14 charge that the Johnson administration was guilty of "shocking mismanagement" of the Vietnam war. As the *Washington Post* reported the conflict: "In what respect is it shocking?" Dirksen wondered. "Who are the shockers?" Dirksen said that Ford "went pretty far" with his charges. When pressed to elaborate upon his criticism of Ford, Dirksen replied: "I can do the watusi and the frug, but I don't squirm." Ford was irritated and dismayed, but he withheld comment until he could confront Dirksen personally. When the Joint Leadership met the next day, other House Republicans were more hostile. According to one observer, "Dirksen listened to their criticisms, heard them all out and then completely disarmed them with his conciliatory attitude." He returned to the Senate gallery that same afternoon, maintained that he had been misunderstood, and denied that there was any split between Ford and himself. Most of the Joint Leadership press conference on Thursday, April 21, 1966, was spent on further reinterpretation of previous statements and denying the existence of any leadership conflict. It was critical not that Ford and Dirksen held differing views of appropriate Republican strategy on the Vietnam war, but that Republicans seem to have developed a vehicle for reconciliating conflict when it occurs. As the two men developed confidence in each other's judgments, the likelihood of such flare-ups was substantially reduced.

The Republican Coordinating Committee. Republicans appear to have brought off an even more critical innovation in out-party organization by creating the Republican Coordinating Committee. Unlike the short-lived Democratic Advisory Council, which operated under national chairman Paul Butler during the latter part of the Eisenhower Administration, this committee was organized around its congressional leaders and functioned with their complete cooperation. In addition to the Joint Senate-House Republican Leadership, its members during the 89th Congress included former President Eisenhower and four previous presidential candidates, Barry Goldwater, Richard Nixon, Thomas Dewey, and Alfred Landon; five representatives from the Republican Governors' Association, George W. Romney of Michigan, William W. Scranton of Pennsylvania, Nelson A. Rockefeller of New York, John

A. Love of Colorado, and Robert E. Smylie of Idaho; the chairman of the Republican National Committee, Ray Bliss; the assistant chairman, Mrs. Mary Brooks; and four vice chairmen, Mrs. Collis P. Moore of Oregon, Donald R. Ross of Nebraska, Mrs. J. Willard Marriott of the District of Columbia, and J. Drake Edens of South Carolina. Meeting about four times a year, the Republican Coordinating Committee promoted a series of task forces on such subjects as human rights and responsibilities, the conduct of foreign relations, intergovernmental relationships, job opportunities, and federal fiscal and monetary policies. These position papers, as well as reports emanating from congressional groups such as the House Committee on Research and Planning, aided Republican candidates in the 1966 elections and provided guidelines for the Republican party platform in 1968.

The Republican Coordinating Committee, like the Joint Senate-House Leadership, cannot be evaluated solely on its ability to coordinate policy and serve as an effective forum for the promotion of campaign issues. Perhaps its major benefit is that it provides periodic meetings at which the diverse party elements can interact to develop stronger personal and party ties. By hammering out differences in closed sessions, Republicans, for the most part, avoided the wrangling which has characterized their party in the past. Through the Republican Coordinating Committee they were able to present a more solid front to the electorate as they worked toward victory in the midterm elections of 1966.

Television and Press Coverage. Not the least of the reasons for which Ford was elected minority leader in 1965 was to counteract unfavorable images created by the "Ev and Charlie Show," the Joint Leadership press conference which had featured Senate minority leader Dirksen and Ford's predecessor, Halleck. As one observer commented, "This twosome had become as celebrated among Washington reporters as Gallagher and Sheean used to be to theatergoers." Although Ford found it difficult to match the fine sense of timing and phrase-making of the mellifluous Senator Dirksen, from the beginning he presented a more handsome personal impression than his predecessor. As he gained more experience and confidence, Ford demonstrated a hard-hitting style of criticism, which made the evening news programs with more and more frequency. In the spring of 1966, Dirksen and Ford embellished their television appearances by working with a large backdrop with block letters suggesting such questions of the week as: "Mr. President, what are YOU doing about the rising cost of living?" and "Mr. President, what CAN we believe?" These Joint Leadership press conferences offered the minority its best available alternative in an uphill effort to compete with the world's greatest forum—the White House.

In most instances the Republican leadership could not hope to compete successfully with President Johnson and the extensive natural press exposure that the incumbent of the White House automatically enjoys. A typical presidential press conference receives wide television coverage, front-page newspaper attention, several stories commenting on newsworthy aspects of the conference, and a reprinting of the complete proceedings in the papers like *The New York Times* and *Washington Post*. In contrast, Ford and Dirksen were fortunate when a picture made the front page and they found one or more of their press releases covered in stories usually relegated to the middle sections of the paper. More than two hundred representatives of the mass media will attend a typical full-dress White House press conference; the Joint Senate-House Republican Leadership conference seldom attracts more than fifty to sixty.

The minority party introduced another innovation in 1966 by countering the president's State of the Union Message with its own Republican appraisal one week later. On Monday evening, January 17, 1966, Republican senators and representatives assembled with their wives in the historic old Supreme Court Chamber in the Capitol to hear Dirksen and Ford. Again, the minority party was at a disadvantage. The best that they were able to obtain was thirty minutes of late-evening viewing in a futile effort to match the president's fifty-two minutes of prime television time.

Fund Raising and Support of Congressional Candidates. Another principal activity of the congressional leaders is campaign fund raising and the support of their party's candidates for Congress. In 1965, Ford participated in more than forty fund-raising ventures and found time to speak in the home districts of almost thirty incumbents. His pace in 1966 was even more intensive. By August, he had made more than 110 speeches, appeared in 27 states, and addressed more than 70,000 people. As the fall elections approached, an even greater amount of his time and effort was concentrated in the 48 districts, previously held by Republicans, which elected freshman Democrats in 1964. House Republicans focused on other districts also, in line with criteria explained by Congressional Campaign Committee chairman Bob Wilson:

To begin with, there are 63 target districts where Republicans lost by 5 per cent or less of the vote. We add to that about 10 districts where incumbent Democrats are retiring and we go after those. And then, finally, there are a number of districts with vulnerable Democratic incumbents either because they have been complacent, or they have had a poor show of attendance on the floor, or for other reasons which make them less secure. By early summer about 80 of these 100 districts are set. We keep about 20 others in limbo. We don't want to throw money away unless we have a good chance of winning. And of course, we have to do a good job of hanging on to the 140 Republican districts which we now control.

One problem the Republicans did not encounter was a lack of campaign funds. In 1964, Wilson organized a Republican Congressional Boosters Club. A series of campaign dinners held in forty major cities throughout the country raised more than $1 million. Members of the Boosters Club were asked to contribute $1,000 in 1965 and a similar amount in 1966, with the funds pledged to assist the campaigns of non-incumbents only. Richard Nixon served as honorary chairman and the principal speechmaker. (Later, in 1967 and 1968, Nixon would begin to cash in on the long hours and extensive travel he had devoted to the Republican cause.) Other Republican leaders, including Arends, Laird, Rhodes, Wilson, and Goodell also gave extensively of their time. Another successful fund-raising device was the Republican Congressional Committee *Newsletter*, which brought in over a million dollars in subscriptions in 1965–1966.

The Development of Campaign Issues. The search for campaign issues was a common thread running through all of Ford's activities. Since the Democrats had better than a two-to-one majority in the House, they had little need to work closely with Republicans. By 1966, Republicans frequently were attaching greater weight to the development of campaign issues than to cooperative efforts to improve legislation. They stressed, as primary issues of the 1966 midterm elections, the rising cost of living and the war in

Vietnam. Republicans exploited the inflation issue in various ways: attempts to impose 5 per cent cuts in the administration's appropriation bills, numerous speeches on the floor of the House and Senate, Joint Leadership press conferences, and publishing such reports as the Republican Coordinating Committee's "The Rising Costs of Living."

The escalation of the war in Vietnam posed more tricky problems. Initially, most Republicans had backed the president's policies, either from conviction, a belief in bipartisan foreign policy, or a reluctance to appear to be "playing politics" with the war. But at the same time Republicans missed no opportunity to exploit deep Democratic divisions. Above all, the GOP leadership tried to preserve enough flexibility to be able to shift their policies should the situation change drastically before November, 1966. Republicans, looking toward 1968, could not ignore the fact that General Eisenhower was in essence a "peace candidate" in 1952 during the Korean War. Throughout 1966 the stance of individual Republican party leaders varied—in general, Dirksen and Arends were more supportive of President Johnson's policies than Ford or Laird.

By June, 1966, the American public's evaluation of the president's conduct of office was at its lowest standing in thirty months. According to the Gallup poll, 46 per cent said they approved Johnson's performance in office, 34 per cent disapproved and 20 per cent did not express an opinion. One month later, the bombings of petroleum facilities near Hanoi and Haiphong seemed to temporarily restore confidence in the president's handling of his job. But as the elections approached, opinion ratings on the president's performance dropped still further.

In addition to inflation, the war in Vietnam, and declining confidence in the president, Republicans sought to exploit other issues, such as farm-belt dissatisfaction with Secretary of Agriculture Freeman's policies, mismanagement of the war on poverty, and uneasiness about corruption in government, intensified by the Bobby Baker case and the Senate investigation of Democratic Senator Thomas Dodd's conduct. Republicans also stressed the need for a strong two-party system and a Congress which would stand up to the president.

Republicans were badly divided as to how to approach the most potentially explosive issue of the 1966 campaign, the possibility of a white backlash caused by Negro rioting in northern cities and the proposed open-housing title of the civil rights bill which preoccupied Congress through most of the summer and fall of 1966. On a key roll call vote on an amendment offered by moderate Republican Charles Mathias of Maryland which would have excluded single-family dwellings from coverage, House Republicans split 69 to 69. Although a compromise version passed the House, only 12 of 33 Senate Republicans voted to invoke cloture. The northern and southern wings of the Democratic party took their customary stances and the motion fell ten votes short of receiving the necessary two-thirds majority to limit debate. What would have been the Civil Rights Act of 1966 was dead for the 89th Congress.

By early fall, House Republican leaders were cautiously optimistic about their chances to pick up seats in the 90th Congress. The figure most often mentioned was a minimum net gain of 30 seats.

The Effects of Leadership Change

Ford, Laird, and their associates launched their campaign for control of the House Republican party with three major objectives in mind. First, they wanted to develop a more positive legislative strategy. Second, they hoped to improve party organizational machinery. Third, they felt they had to make substantial election gains in 1966 if their party was to move toward majority status. The results of a partial shift from partisan opposition to promoting constructive alternatives have already been examined. Before turning to an analysis of the 1966 election results, a brief evaluation of the organization developments introduced in 1965 and a tentative assessment of Ford as a minority leader will be undertaken.

The new minority leadership was able to bring off at least five major modifications of party institutions and methods of operation in the 89th Congress.

First, more so than under either Halleck or Martin, leadership decisions became shared decisions. Basic policy was largely determined by an inner circle composed of five formal leaders: minority leader Ford, Conference chairman Laird, Research and Planning Committee chairman Goodell, minority whip Arends, and Policy Committee chairman Rhodes. Laird and Goodell were closer, personally, to Ford, and hence, appeared to have more influence with the minority leader than either Arends or Rhodes did. But the cooperation of the latter two conservatives, representing the wing of the party once led by Halleck, was crucial to party reunification. These five leaders frequently were joined by some or all of a somewhat broader group of formal leaders, personal friends, and influential committee members. On day-to-day questions involving legislation, particularly decisions on motions to recommit or to modify Democratic bills, the top leadership worked closely with the ranking minority members of the committees involved. Actual leadership in the 89th Congress corresponded closely to formal leadership in the House minority party.

Second, the Republican Conference, composed of all House Republicans, operated more effectively than in previous Congresses as the official coordinating body. It did not meet as frequently as Laird first anticipated, nor was it used to any great extent to ratify decisions made by the Policy Committee. It did, however, serve its primary purpose as an organizing mechanism at the beginning of the Congress and as a forum for party reform.

Third, under the House Republican Conference, the minority leadership developed a professional research staff composed of director of research Prendergast (the minority sergeant at arms), three research assistants, and two secretaries. In addition to their own public relations assistants, Ford, Laird, and other leaders could call on the services of Robert Hartmann, former chief of the Washington Bureau of the *Los Angeles Times*. Here again, expectations were not fully realized. Prendergast and Hartmann were sometimes torn between service to two or more masters. Long-range research frequently gave way to the immediate demands of issue development and public relations.

Fourth, by the end of the first session of the 89th Congress, thirteen task forces were operating under the Research and Planning Committee. Their subject matter give some indication of the kinds of issues which Republicans attempted to exploit: agriculture, congressional reform and minority staffing, economic opportunity, education, federal civil service, Latin America, NATO and Atlantic community, nuclear affairs, platform implementation, unemployment compensation system, United Nations, urban and suburban affairs, and voting rights.

Fifth, the Republican Policy Committee did an effective job of coordinating day-to-day policy making. Thirty-one policy positions were taken in the first session. On twenty-six floor votes on these bills, Republican support ranged from a low of 64 per cent on the Republican motion to recommit the Arts and Humanities Act of 1965 to a high of 100 per cent on four non-controversial bills such as the Water Quality Act and the Uniformed Services Pay Act. Overall Republican support averaged 86.8 per cent, or an average loss on these policy position roll call votes of about seventeen members. During the second session (1966), Republican support of Policy Committee positions increased to 94.4 per cent on twenty roll call votes. These results closely approximate the Policy Committee acceptance scores of 90.5 and 93.7 per cent achieved in 1961 and 1962 under Halleck's leadership.

As a result of Ford's seven appointments, the Policy Committee was somewhat more responsive to the leadership than it was in previous Congresses. Moderates had a larger voice on the committee than before. Liberals fared less well, especially after John Lindsay, who represented New York and the New England states on the Policy Committee, left Congress to campaign successfully for the position of mayor of New York City.

Ford is the man who should reap most credit for the organizational changes and movement toward unity, but who must take most of the blame for an absence of significant legislative victories in the 89th Congress. It soon became clear that parliamentary maneuvering and floor in-fighting were not Ford's strong points.

A few Republicans thought that Ford made a good overall impression on the floor, despite his lack of debating skill and parliamentary adeptness. As one midwestern moderate put it:

Ford is the kind of guy you can stand up with, be proud of. With Charlie Halleck we used to cheer when he gave the other side hell. He had this ability to go to the heart of the matter, but he sometimes said some pretty mean things.

Others thought that Halleck, unlike Ford, drove some of his colleagues too hard. If anything, Ford appeared to err in the opposite direction. As another party leader commented:

The worst I've ever seen Ford do is get mad at one or two members and shake his finger at them. And then, it's because they said they were going to vote with us and they turned around and didn't.

Certainly, his openness and sense of fairness were sources of strength. Members admired and appreciated these qualities. But other members deplored what they conceived to be a basic lack of political instinct and a hesitancy on Ford's part to utilize the full powers of his office. A comment from another party leader sums up the situation:

Ford is very open minded. Most of his problems come from the fact that he is too damn fair. . . . You can't help but like and admire him. But when it comes to implementing a plan which requires a delicate sense of timing, a concern for the intricacies of details, an interweaving of the component parts, Ford is at a loss.

The different leadership styles of Halleck and Ford did seem to have some impact on party regularity in voting. According to *Congressional Quarterly* calculations, House Republicans supported their party 72 per cent of the time under Halleck in the 88th Congress, whereas under Ford in the 89th Congress party unity dropped to 65 per cent. But these percentage differences must be interpreted with caution. There were fewer chances when united Republican efforts would have reversed roll call outcomes and more Republican absenteeism—both factors which tend to lower party unity scores.

When asked early in 1965 how he would summarize Ford's strengths, a southern conservative replied:

One, he's easy to talk to. Two, he's easy to get to—he's a person who will take you into his confidence. Three, he has been able to keep track of what is going on before things happen—the voting rights bill would be a good example of that. Four, his Press Club statement the other day was very effective. For someone new he's doing a helluva job. He's bound to take some lumps. If you don't do anything, you'll never be criticized. If you do something you are going to be hurt—it's as simple as that.

In capsule form, this comment summarizes the main preoccupations of a minority floor leader. In contemplating organizational improvements and his day-to-day dealing with his colleagues, he must win their confidence by being accessible and willing to make decisions. As a legislative strategist, he must sense his opportunities well in advance and convert his limited chances into positive outcomes. He must be capable of withstanding criticism, both for his actions and his inactions. He must be able to convey a positive image of his party before the mass media and the electorate. On balance, Ford seems to have met most of these criteria sufficiently well to be judged a success in his initial term as House minority leader.

The Congressional Election, 1966

A minority legislative party has to have a minimum base of strength—incumbents in office, staff support, campaign funds, and other resources—if it is to operate effectively. In the 435-member House of Representatives, 140 Republicans clearly were not enough. However, by virtue of new leadership, better organization and staffing, and substantial campaign contributions, the House GOP in 1966 was in better shape to contest a midterm election than at any time since 1946.

A number of factors were riding on the outcome of these races, not the least of which was Ford's continuing tenure as minority leader. Ford readily acknowledged the high stakes and the importance of making a substantial comeback in the number of House seats won: "If we can pick up 30 or more seats, we're all right. If we make less than 30, my future is in jeopardy."

On November 8, 1966, Republicans made substantial gains all across the nation. In a major shift of party control, GOP candidates won ten governorships away from Democrats, losing only two, Kansas and Maine. Three new Republican seats were added in the Senate for a post-election balance of 36 Republicans to 64 Democrats. In the House, the GOP won 52 seats from Democrats, losing only five, for a net gain of 47 seats. Overall, Republican nominees received 48.7 per cent of the vote cast for House candidates, their party's best performance since 1956.

Republicans made their most striking gains in the midwest, picking up five seats each in Michigan and Ohio, two in Wisconsin, and one in Illinois and Indiana. Elsewhere across the nation the net gains were most substantial in the plains states and the South with seven additional seats each, followed by five-seat additions in the Rocky Mountain and mid-Atlantic states, four new seats each in the border and Pacific coast states, and a one-seat gain in New England. The Democrats regained four of their five seats from Republicans in the South—two in Alabama, one each in Georgia and Mississippi—plus one in Maine.

The net increase of 47 seats from 1964 to 1966 more than ensured Ford's re-election as minority leader. Without a major comeback in

1966, his party would have little hope of waging a successful presidential campaign in 1968, let alone a chance to become the majority party in the House. Yet the 1966 election should also be viewed as a restoring election, which put House Republicans in only a moderately better position than their position following the 1962 elections. In fact, outside the South and border states, Republicans in the 90th Congress actually held four seats fewer than they did in the 88th Congress.

What factors brought about the Republican comeback? In many House races local personalities and local issues all but decided the outcomes months in advance. Perhaps in only 80 to 100 districts did the non-incumbent have a real opportunity to defeat the incumbent. When incumbent House members decide to seek re-election—year after year, in Democratic and in Republican tides—better than seven out of eight are winners. Incumbents, after all, have numerous advantages—at least two years to become well known, the congressional mailing privileges, a full-time staff of eight to ten persons, and ready opportunities to tap campaign funds which are much more difficult to come by for non-incumbents.

The 1966 election was one in which most of the factors promoted Republican victories within the closely contested races. As we have seen, President Johnson's popularity with the American electorate was decreasing and issues were converging in such a way as to further the probability that more than a 30 to 35 seat net recovery would be achieved. In addition to Johnson's credibility problem, dissent over the conduct of the war in Vietnam, and inflation, Republicans stood to benefit from a traditional pattern which has seen the out-party gain a net average of 37 seats in the sixteen midterm elections held from 1902 to 1962. Of the 48 Democratic freshmen who rode the Johnson tide to victory in 1964, 20 were defeated in 1966. The seats of four Democratic freshmen who did not seek re-election also went back into the Republican column.

Just how much Ford, Wilson, and other House Republican leaders contributed to the overall victory is difficult to assess. By election time, Ford had traveled more than 138,000 miles and made more than 180 speeches in behalf of candidates or in fund-raising efforts. Wilson's attempts to recruit especially attractive Republican candidates such as Donald Riegle of Michigan and Robert Mathias of California were made easier by a promise of $5,000 to $15,000 in campaign assistance once the candidate had won the Republican primary nomination. Just as Halleck was forced to share the blame for the 1964 disaster, Ford was entitled to reap some credit for the 1966 success.

Effect on the 90th Congress. It was clear long before the new 90th Congress convened on January 10, 1967, that its productivity would be far different from that of the record-breaking 89th Congress. The 187 House Republicans were in a much stronger position to contest the programs of the Democratic majority at every stage of the legislative process, in committee, on the floor, and in conference. From the beginning, Republicans were more united, and Ford operated with more positive style and greater confidence. By the end of the first session (1967), in 24 matters on which the Republican Policy Committee took a position, they were on the winning side in 18. The conservative coalition—the voting alliance of Republicans and southern Democrats against northern Democrats—won more victories (37 out of 51 roll calls on which such voting patterns appeared) than at any time since the *Congressional Quarterly* began to measure its performance (1957).

Yet the first session of the 90th Congress could not be construed as a total defeat for Johnson and the House and Senate Democratic leadership. The Senate remained much more liberal than the House on almost all issues save civil rights, and the resulting compromises between House and Senate versions of legislation were, more often than not, Democratic administration victories. Appropriations were often the opposite—fiscal conservatives frequently had a field day, in rhetoric if not always in results. Johnson failed to get a tax surcharge increase until 1968, and this at the price of a promise to cut $6 billion in federal expenditures. He could, however, be somewhat comforted by the passage of major social security amendments, revision of several education acts, and a host of lesser administration measures. Just how constructive the 90th Congress had been, and who was responsible for its successes and failures, became one of the issues in the election of 1968.

Some Major Themes Reconsidered

What can be learned from this study of House Republicans in the mid-1960's about American political parties and congressional behavior in general? One of the first things is the relationship between election results and congressional activity. Collective decisions made by the electorates of 435 House districts every two years are important for our two-party political system. It is not just that the aggregate results determine which congressional party shall be the majority and which the minority, with the resulting right to organize the House, select the Speaker, and name the committee chairmen. As the defeat of Halleck by Ford after the 1964 election and the re-election of Ford as minority leader after the 1966 election illustrate, the magnitude of the net gain or loss sets the climate for continuity or change in party leadership.

Furthermore, the size of the majority largely sets the limits for success or failure of the president's legislative program. Since 1930, the Democratic party has been the majority party in the United States. Until Nixon's victory in 1968, Republicans elected only one president—Eisenhower—and controlled Congress but twice—the 80th (1947–1948) and 83rd (1953–1954). Thus, only during the first two years of his first term did Eisenhower have an opportunity to work with Republican legislative majorities. Even then his majorities were so narrow—221 to 214 in the House and a one-vote majority in the Senate—that the loss of but a few dissident members was usually enough to thwart his legislative objectives. And, in general, most congressional Republicans, especially House members, are more conservative than other state and national party leaders.

Democratic presidents have also required far more than a bare majority in the House and Senate to secure passage of their legislative programs. Though the ratio of northern moderates and liberals to southern conservatives varies from one Congress to the next, it is seldom enough to effectively offset a combination of southern conservatives and Republicans voting together to create the so-called "conservative coalition." The 89th Congress, with 295 Democrats and 140 Republicans in the House, gave President Johnson the largest working majority that any Democratic president has enjoyed since Roosevelt and the 75th Congress (1937–1938). The result was an unusually successful legislative record, which included the passage of Medicare, an elementary and secondary education act, voting rights legislation, and a host of other administration bills.

Still another theme appears in our study: the plight of the out-party compared to the advantages enjoyed by a majority party in command of the presidency and both Houses of Congress. The president is the pre-eminent party leader even in ordinary times. In Johnson, Republicans confronted an especially skilled partisan, who was intimate with the workings of Congress and prepared to utilize all the resources at his command to implement his Great Society programs. The attempts of Ford, Laird, Goodell, and others to develop constructive alternatives, to promote a more positive party image, and to rally their supporters around their programs were inhibited by the personal conflict, factionalism, and decentralization characteristic of both major parties, but especially pronounced within the out-party. Possessing only limited sanctions over other congressmen primarily responsible to diverse constituencies, the House Republican leaders' ability to achieve even the moderate successes in reunification and improvement in party organization was a source for wonder.

Brief mention should also be made of what Frank Sorauf has called "the chief unsolved organizational quandaries of the parties"— the role and relationship of congressional party figures to other party office holders at the precinct, ward, county, state, and national levels. Traditionally, the problem has been one of the legislative groups remaining somewhat aloof from the other party organs, their members primarily interested in their own re-election and barely tolerating other party activities such as defining and articulating national party platforms and policies. By making their Joint Senate-House Republican Leadership the core of a broader Republican Coordinating Committee, the GOP has moved a long step toward ameliorating the problem. It remained to be seen how effective this coordinating body would be in a presidential election, as contrasted with a midterm election, in which most factors favored a Republican comeback.

Relationships between House Republicans and other national party leaders received further tests as their party strove to nominate a presidential winner in 1968. With all House seats up for re-election in 1968, Republican representatives who elected to run had a major stake in selecting their presidential candidate, Richard M. Nixon. Above all, they wanted a winner, someone who could help them gain control of the House. To secure a majority, Ford and his associates had to hold all of their present seats and pick up at least 31 more; since they were bound to lose a few marginal seats, they had to win 40 to 50 seats to achieve a majority in the House. In

1968, election results across the land were mainly favorable for Republicans. The net gain of four seats in the House of Representatives fell far short of expectations, however.

Still, through their continuing efforts in the 90th Congress, Republican representatives strongly influenced the shaping of issues and the writing of the 1968 Republican platform. Chief among the preoccupations of each was the complex and recurring task of balancing the representation of local, state, and national interests with his conception of the "public good," both in the short and long run. Seldom are these factors divorced from political realities, the incumbent's assessment of what is in his party's interest, and the effect on his own political career and chances for re-election. Nor should questions of what is in the public interest be separated from individual and collective decisions based largely on self-interest. For that is what politics is all about.

Sources

The major source materials for this study were informal and semi-structured interviews with more than 75 Republican Representatives and congressional staff members from December, 1964, through January, 1967. Many of its themes were initially developed in "House Republican Leadership: Change and Consolidation in a Minority Party," a paper delivered at the 1966 annual meeting of the American Political Science Association, New York City, September 9, 1966. Events which preoccupied House Republicans just before and during the opening days of the 89th Congress are given more elaborate treatment in my Eagleton Institute Case Study, "The Ford-Halleck Minority Leadership Contest, 1965" (New York: McGraw-Hill, 1966). Other useful sources were *Congressional Quarterly Weekly Reports*, especially Special Reports on the Elections of 1964 and 1966; various documents issued by House Republican Party Committees and the Republican National Committee; and newspaper accounts of party and congressional activities from 1964 until 1968, especially those in *The New York Times, Wall Street Journal, Washington Evening Star*, and *Washington Post*.

Further Reading

Converse, Philip E., Aage R. Clausen, and Warren E. Miller. "Electoral Myth and Reality: The 1964 Election," *American Political Science Review*, Vol. 59 (June, 1965), 321–336.

Cosman, Bernard, and Robert J. Huckshorn. *Republican Politics: The*

1964 Campaign and Its Aftermath for the Party. New York: Frederick A. Praeger, 1968.

Cummings, Milton C., Jr. *Congressmen and the Electorate: Elections for the U.S. House and the President, 1920–1964.* New York: The Free Press, 1966.

Froman, Lewis A., Jr. *The Congressional Process: Strategies, Rules, and Procedures.* Boston: Little, Brown, 1967.

Hess, Stephen, and David S. Broder. *The Republican Establishment: The Present and Future of the G.O.P.* New York: Harper & Row, 1967.

Huitt, Ralph K. "Democratic Party Leadership in the Senate," *American Political Science Review,* Vol. 55 (June, 1961), 333–344.

—— and Robert L. Peabody. *Congress: Two Decades of Analysis.* New York: Harper and Row, 1969.

Jones, Charles O. *Party and Policy-making: The House Republican Policy Committee.* New Brunswick, N.J.: Rutgers University Press, 1964.

——. "The Minority Party and Policy-Making in the House of Representatives," *American Political Science Review,* Vol. 62 (June, 1968), 481–493.

Key, V. O., Jr. *Politics, Parties, and Pressure Groups,* 5th ed. New York: Thomas Y. Crowell, 1964.

Peabody, Robert L. "Party Leadership Change in the United States House of Representatives," *American Political Science Review,* Vol. 61 (September, 1967), 675–693.

—— and Nelson W. Polsby (eds.). *New Perspectives on the House of Representatives.* Chicago: Rand McNally, 1963; 2nd ed., 1969.

Polsby, Nelson W., and Aaron B. Wildavsky. *Presidential Elections: Strategies of American Electoral Politics,* 2nd ed. New York: Charles Scribner's Sons, 1968.

Ripley, Randall B. *Party Leaders in the House of Representatives.* Washington, D.C.: The Brookings Institution, 1967.

——. *Majority Party Leadership in Congress.* Boston: Little, Brown, 1969.

Sindler, Allan P. *Political Parties in the United States.* New York: St. Martin's Press, 1966.

Sorauf, Frank J. *Political Parties in the American System.* Boston: Little, Brown, 1964.

Truman, David B. *The Congressional Party: A Case Study.* New York: John Wiley & Sons, 1959.

STUDY

5

The Supreme Court:
Entering the "Political Thicket" of Reapportionment

Andrew Hacker

The Supreme Court of the United States consists of nine men, each of whom is appointed to serve in effect for as long as he chooses. Though these Justices are "above" politics in that they are neither elected by nor accountable to the voting public, their duties often force them into making decisions that affect the political arena. Such decisions trace their origins to the willingness of a single citizen to file a suit at one of the thousands of courthouses throughout the United States. If he presses his case through appeals, and if higher-court judges are willing to give him further hearings, his grievance may ultimately come before the highest tribunal of our Republic.

The ruling rendered by that bench will apply not only to the individual who initiated the suit, but also to many other citizens in similar situations across the country. And some of these decisions will compel a deep-seated change in the nation's legal and political arrangements. On these occasions there can be critical repercussions at many levels of government, some of which challenge the power and authority of the Supreme Court itself.

In this study we look into one of those occasions: wherein a suit filed by a Tennessee citizen named Charles Baker became the

231

opening salvo in a political and constitutional struggle which has yet
to reach its final resolution.

Eleven Angry Men

Charles W. Baker had a grievance. Though he had
never encountered any obstacles to casting his ballot, he felt that he
was not receiving the political representation to which he was
rightfully entitled. Charles Baker's problem stemmed from the very
simple fact that he happened to make his home in Memphis,
Tennessee. (For the record, Baker was not an ordinary citizen. He
had long been active in local politics and had ascended to the
chairmanship of the governing board of Shelby County, the most
populous county in the state.)

In 1959, Shelby County—where the city of Memphis is situated—
sent seven representatives to the lower house of the Tennessee
legislature. Inasmuch as the voting population of that county numbered 312,345, Baker could be said to have had approximately
1/45,000th share of a representative to voice his opinions and
interests at the state capitol. But Baker's perturbation grew out of
the fact that his representational fraction was appreciably smaller
than that of many other voters in Tennessee. Since the 2,340 votes
of rural Moore County, about 300 miles east of Memphis, were able
to elect a single representative, each Moore County voter had 19
times as much representation in the Tennessee legislative process as
Baker had. In addition to Moore County there were 22 other rural
counties, each with less than 7,000 voters, which sent one representative each to the state's 99-seat lower chamber—even though their
total voting population, as Baker computed it, should have entitled
the whole group to only two legislators.* The same kind of anti-
urban discrimination applied to the apportionment of the state's
upper chamber, and the under-representation suffered by Memphis
had also been imposed on at least four other large cities in the state.

Baker decided to take his problem to the federal courts. His mode
of attack was to sue the Tennessee Secretary of State, Joe C. Carr,
and five other state officials who administered the prevailing voting

*Baker used the number of *voters* in each county as the basis for his calculations. An alternative method is to base such computations on the *total* population of an area, for the proportion of people who actually vote varies among
districts.

laws, asking the court to compel those officeholders to give him a ballot equal in worth and weight to that of any other voter in the state. To strengthen his case, Baker enlisted as co-plaintiffs ten friends who lived in Nashville, Knoxville, Chattanooga, and Clarksville, other under-represented cities. On July 31, 1959, they presented their case before Judge John D. Martin of the Nashville Division of the United States District Court of Tennessee.

Recourse to the Courts

Why did Baker and his friends take their case to the courts—and to the federal courts at that?* The answer to the first half of this question, one destined to become an object of judicial controversy, was that they felt the Tennessee legislature would never voluntarily reapportion its districts so as to give city dwellers more equitable representation. During the previous half-century every bill proposing redistricting had failed of passage. This was hardly surprising, because the majority of the legislators, having come from over-represented areas like Moore County, had no inclination to vote away their political power. Thus Baker asserted that the deck was so stacked that *even if* he got a majority of Tennesseans to support his position, legislative redress would still not be forthcoming. For as matters stood in 1959, fewer than 30 per cent of the voters—those located in rural counties—elected legislative majorities in both of the state's chambers. Moreover, the Tennessee constitution did not provide for either the initiative or the

*The United States has fifty-one separate judicial systems: one in each of the states and one at the national level. Cases involving state or local laws must first be brought before state or local courts for their initial hearing; and a case may only be submitted to a federal court if, in the language of the Constitution, it arises "under this constitution, the laws of the United States and treaties made . . . under their authority." Thus the federal courts will only give a first hearing to cases relating to laws that have been passed by the United States Congress. In such instances a suit is tried first in one of the 86 United States District Courts; from there it can be appealed to one of the 11 United States Courts of Appeals; and after that the United States Supreme Court may be petitioned to make a final adjudication. If a state or local law has been appealed all the way through to the top court of a state's judicial system, it can still be submitted directly to the United States Supreme Court on the ground that the state or local statute violates some section of the United States Constitution. Hence federal courts are entitled to refuse to accept a case dealing with a state law until it has been shown that all available avenues in that state's court system have been tried.

referendum, thus precluding any attempt to forge a statewide popular majority to coerce the legislature to act on reapportionment. These reasons, Baker claimed, compelled him to bypass the customary political processes and to ask the judicial branch for aid.

Baker took his suit directly before a federal judge for two major reasons. First, the state courts had already been approached on this issue, but to no avail. Back in 1956 a Nashville resident named Gates Kidd had asked the Supreme Court of Tennessee to give him proper representation in the state legislature. He was turned down by that five-man tribunal on the grounds that, under the separation of powers, the "courts have no power to compel the legislative department" in the reapportionment area. The Tennessee high court also took the rather curious position that if they invalidated the then prevailing districting arrangements in the state, the judges would be forced to abolish the legislature and the result would be "the destruction of the state government." Baker reasonably inferred from the response to Kidd's suit that he too would be rebuffed by the state judiciary.

The more important reason for Baker's filing suit in federal court was his contention that his under-represented condition was really a "Federal question," rather than simply a state or local matter. For the Fourteenth Amendment of the Constitution of the United States commands that "No state shall . . . deny to any person within its jurisdiction the equal protection of the laws." Baker urged that his deprival of an equal ballot effectively stripped him of equal protection under Tennessee's laws. He and his fellow city dwellers, permanently lacking the political power merited by their numbers, were continually subjected to discrimination at the hands of their legislature. Rural areas, acting through their enduring (and "artificial") legislative majority, overtaxed the cities and suburbs and bestowed disproportionately generous sums on themselves for school aid and road construction. Baker's compelling argument was that he and thousands of his fellow citizens suffered such injustices merely because of where they happened to live.

Judge John Martin of the United States District Court for Western Tennessee agreed that Baker's case against Carr did indeed involve a federal question. He went on to say that it was an important national issue and that its resolution would have significant constitutional implications. Consequently, he ruled that the case was too critical to be decided by himself alone and recommended that a special panel of judges be set up which in effect would combine the District Court and the Circuit Court of Appeals levels at one trial. Thus a few months later a three-man panel consisting of one circuit judge and two district judges—one of the latter being Martin himself—convened to hear argument in *Baker v. Carr*. And because this tribunal embodied the two lower levels of the federal judicial system, whichever party lost the case could—and most surely would—appeal directly to the Supreme Court.

The State of the States

The special procedure invoked for Baker's case reflected the fact that Tennessee's inequitable representation was the characteristic condition of city and suburban voters across the nation.* The postwar years had witnessed accelerated changes in the physical distribution of the American people. Within even one ten-year period—the decade separating the censuses of 1950 and 1960—the movements of population were sufficient to change the complexion of the Republic. Thus between 1950 and 1960 more than half of the country's 3,000-odd counties, most of them rural, actually lost population even though the nation as a whole was growing by almost 20 per cent. Yet while rural America was losing its residents and many people were migrating from farms to the cities, the largest urban centers were actually growing smaller *despite* the influx of these new arrivals. In 1960 Cleveland had 4 per cent fewer people than in 1950, San Francisco almost 5 per cent,

---

Apportionment is the act whereby each of the seats of a legislature is assigned to a particular piece of territory. Thus in 1962 the state of California was "apportioned" 38 of the 435 seats in the United States House of Representatives. *Reapportionment* occurs when the number of seats in a legislature is increased, decreased, or—more usually—when seats are taken from one area and given to another. Thus the United States House of Representatives was "reapportioned" in 1962, at which time New York's delegation was reduced from 43 to 41 members while Florida's was raised from 8 to 12. *Malapportionment* generally describes the condition which prevails when pieces of territory have representation differing from what they would have were all members of the legislature to be elected from areas containing relatively equal populations. Thus if a county in a state has a population four times as large as another, but both have the same number of representatives, "malapportionment" exists. *Districting* is the drawing of a map outlining the actual geographic boundaries of each seat of a legislature. Inequitable "districts" occur when some have appreciably more residents than others.

Detroit 10 per cent, and Boston over 13 per cent. (Medium-sized cities grew slightly over the decade, but just about enough to keep their relative place.) The big gainers were the suburbs, which in fact recruited more city dwellers than the cities could replace by attracting migration from rural areas. Suburban Americans numbered 21 million in 1950 and 38 million by 1960, a rise of more than 80 per cent. Indeed, suburbia accounted for almost two-thirds of the nation's 28 million population rise between 1950 and 1960. Thus the cities tended to be the most constant factor in this period while rural and suburban America were the variables. (To be sure, the *composition* of the cities was not "constant"; those leaving for the suburbs tended to be middle-class, and the people taking their place were poorer Americans from rural areas.)

State legislatures were unresponsive to the new distributions of population. Rural and small-town lawmakers continued to comprise majorities in the legislatures, and they displayed a marked indifference to the needs of both cities and suburbs. Urban and suburban citizens were cheerfully taxed, but their demands for legislation and appropriations were virtually ignored. A typical complaint was voiced by a labor union spokesman before a congressional subcommittee studying apportionment in the late 1950's:

Urban and suburban under-representation is one of the most notorious and shameful facts in American political life today. . . . Because of urban representation—because a city vote is worth only a fraction of what a country vote is worth—the severe, pressing problems of urban and suburban America are being neglected. . . . America is, today, an urban nation. A majority of the people of the nation live in urban centers and their immediate environs. . . .

There were other effects as well. The unwillingness of rural-oriented legislatures to face up to urban problems provoked the cities to by-pass their state capitols and go to Washington with direct requests for federal aid and comfort. In large measure the growth of federal activities in the urban area is a result of legislative lassitude in the states. Rural over-representation also had the consequence of hobbling the two-party system in many states. For example, the party which could muster a statewide popular majority to win the governorship was often unable to capture a majority of seats in the legislature. In such circumstances, each party tended to concentrate its efforts, interests, and leadership in a different section of the state, with the result that neither party had an incentive to take a truly statewide view.

At the same time it would be wrong to hold malapportionment primarily responsible for all the vicissitudes of state government and politics. Research into the ways in which legislators actually voted revealed that many urban representatives often sided with their rural colleagues in denying appropriations and amenities to the cities. And further investigations have shown that the relationship between the degree of a state's malapportionment and its expenditures on programs which cities favor was not as strong or as consistent as might have been expected. One explanation for these findings is that few city voters keep a watchful eye on the activities of their legislators, thus permitting or leading them to be more susceptible to the blandishments of conservative interest groups.

For a variety of reasons, state legislatures neglected to adjust their apportionment to the population redistributions within their borders. A National Municipal League report showed that 14 states had let at least a decade elapse without having redistricted their lower chambers. Nebraska, Wyoming, and Rhode Island made their most recent revisions in the 1930's, and Indiana's was in 1921. Mississippi redrew her map in 1914, and Alabama, Connecticut, and Tennessee's latest efforts were in the first decade of the century. Delaware, Maryland, Vermont, and New Hampshire all had lower houses based on districts created *prior* to 1900.

Most commonly, a state's constitution provided that every county had to have at least one representative in one or both houses. While populous counties were usually accorded several seats, they could be outvoted by the numerous smaller counties. Each of Iowa's 99 counties had a representative in the lower house, whereas each of the nine largest counties was given a second seat. Fifty-eight of the counties in Iowa had populations of less than 20,000. Yet their 58 members, representing a total of only 834,750 Iowans, carried over three times as much weight as the 18 members from the nine largest counties, even though the latter represented 1,024,485 people.

The Tennessee situation, where a Moore County voter had a ballot worth almost 20 times one cast in Memphis, was by no means the most egregious. In Georgia the most-favored voter's ballot was worth 98 times that of the state's least-favored citizen. There were people in Florida with votes weighted 108 times over those of others, and in Connecticut the most-favored least-favored ratio rose to 424:1. In Vermont and New Hampshire, whose districting maps were rooted in colonial times, a rural voter had 1,000 times as much electoral power as did those who chose to make their homes in the cities. In fact, even the most arithmetically equitable state in the country still had one chamber which gave the voters of one district twice as much per capita representation as those of another. In no state were all citizens, wherever resident, close to being electorally equal.*

Thus if the Tennessee apportionment were declared unconstitu-

*Two methods are generally used to measure the degree of malapportionment prevailing in a legislature. The first involves calculating what proportion of a state's population could elect a majority of the members of a legislative chamber. Thus in 1962 Idaho's upper house had 44 members, one from each of the state's counties regardless of the number of inhabitants. While Idaho's total population was 667,191, the 23 smallest counties taken together contained only 110,898 people. That 17 per cent of the state's population could therefore elect the 23 members necessary to comprise a legislative majority. A *second* method is to discover the equitable (or "ideal") population that each district should have, and then ascertain how far each of the existing districts deviates from that norm. Thus in 1962 the "ideal" Idaho district would have had 15,163 people in it (667,191 divided by 44 seats). This meant that an Idaho district with a population of 8,679 was 43 percentage points below the norm (and was hence over-represented) while one with a population of 21,170 was 15 points above that norm (and hence under-represented). It is then possible to compute the average of all the districts' deviations to obtain some idea of how that state compares with others.

Malapportionment is frequently used as a gerrymandering device whereby one party uses the votes cast for its candidates to gain as many legislative seats as it possibly can. In such an effort two strategies are used. The first is to maximize the number of "excess" votes cast for the other party's candidates; this is achieved by drawing up districts which concentrate the other party's supporters so that their candidates win with majorities of 75 per cent or even more. Such "excess" majorities are not only far larger than what is needed to win, but this device also prevents those "excess" votes from helping the other party's candidates in more closely fought contests elsewhere in the state. The second strategy is to maximize the other party's "wasted" votes as well, and this is accomplished by making sure that as many as possible of its ballots (apart from its "excess" votes) are cast for candidates who eventually lose. Thus one of the goals pursued by the party which controls the drawing of the electoral map is to make as many of its own votes effective by rendering the other party's votes either "excess" or "wasted." Thus in the 1966 California elections, Democrats won 53 per cent of the seats in the State Assembly (42 out of 80) even though only 46 per cent of the statewide legislative vote was cast for Democratic candidates (2,835,173 out of 6,129,383). This 7 per cent "bonus" in seats for the Democrats stemmed from the fact that disproportionately more Republican votes throughout the state were in the "excess" or "wasted" categories.

tional, that ruling would probably affect most—if not all—of the other states as well. Baker's was a "federal case" not only because it invoked a clause of the federal constitution but because it alleged a wrong characteristic of state legislatures generally across the nation.

Baker Rebuffed

The initial judicial treatment of the Tennessee case was a triumph for the confirmation of precedent, not the assertion of innovative law. On December 21, 1959, the three-judge panel unanimously ruled in favor of Joe Carr and the other Tennessee officials who presided over the preservation of the status quo. Heavily stressing past decisions, they held that "the federal courts, whether from lack of jurisdiction or from the inappropriateness of the subject matter for judicial consideration, will not intervene in cases of this type to compel legislative reapportionment."

The judges did, however, express sympathy with Baker's plight, remarking that Tennessee's constitution required reapportionment to take place every ten years following the census, and yet the legislature had not redrawn district boundaries since 1901. Even so, the judicial arm could offer no tangible assistance to Baker and his fellow litigants.

With the plaintiffs' argument that the legislature of Tennessee is guilty of a clear violation of the state constitution and of the rights of the plaintiffs, the Court entirely agrees. It also agrees that the evil is a serious one which should be corrected without further delay. But even so, the remedy in this situation clearly does not lie with the courts. It has long been recognized and is accepted doctrine that there are indeed some rights guaranteed by the Constitution for the violation of which the courts cannot give redress.

The overriding reason for this apparently callous ruling—saying in effect, "you are right, but there is nothing at all we can do"—was that all precedents were against Baker. Lower courts are expected to follow the law of the land as determined by the Supreme Court in previous cases. District and Circuit Courts do not normally regard it as their prerogative to overrule earlier decisions of the nine-man tribunal in Washington, no matter how outdated, inappropriate, or unjust those precedents may seem. And the Supreme Court's opinion on malapportionment matters had been expressed, thirteen years earlier, in the case of *Colegrove v. Green*. That decision continued to be binding on lower courts—until such time as the Supreme Court changed its mind.

The Professor's Precedent

To those familiar with the path of the law, Charles Baker's suit was neither new nor surprising. The arguments he marshaled had a familiar ring, for a similar case had been before the courts a scant 13 years earlier. There was, in fact, only one noteworthy difference: the previous case had dealt with a citizen's under-representation in the national House of Representatives, rather than in the state legislature.

Professor Kenneth Colegrove, a member of the department of political science at Northwestern University, sued Governor Dwight Green of Illinois. Colegrove complained of being unfairly represented in the United States Congress and alleged that the cause was simply that he happened to live in the Seventh Congressional District of Illinois, a constituency with a population of 914,053. By contrast, Illinois' Fifth Congressional District contained only 112,116 people, each of whose votes were worth eight times as much as Colegrove's.

The Supreme Court of the United States handed down its decision in *Colegrove v. Green* on June 10, 1946. With only seven Justices taking part in the decision, the Court decided against Colegrove by a vote of 4 to 3. Speaking for the four-man majority, Mr. Justice Frankfurter stated that it was not for the judicial branch to decide a question so clearly "political" in character. In his famous "political thicket" passage, he wrote:

To sustain this action would cut very deep into the very being of Congress. Courts ought not to enter this political thicket. The remedy for unfairness in districting is to secure State legislatures that will apportion properly, or to invoke the ample powers of Congress.

The boundary between "legal" and "political" questions is certainly not clearly defined. Indeed some commentators would say that such a line does not exist at all, and the history of the Court has shown that the justices have often disagreed over whether a particular issue is so "political" as to fall outside the realm of "justiciability"—that is, to be beyond the jurisdiction of the judicial branch. But instances can be cited of "non-justiciable" questions. Courts have been reluctant to interfere with the activities of legislative investigating committees except on the most narrow and technical grounds, nor have courts thus far decided that foreign military operations mounted by the Executive branch are illegal or unconstitutional. Nevertheless, it is clear that in recent years courts have been willing to pass judgments in areas which many observers define as "political." The issue of apportionment presented just such a challenge.

Frankfurter's view was that if inequities in representation in fact exist, two types of remedy are available. On the one hand the Congress itself has the power to regulate by law the "manner" in which its own members will be elected. Thus it could require that all representatives come from districts of equal, or roughly equal, population. On the other hand the state legislatures, which draw up congressional districts, can be pressured or persuaded to create constituencies relatively equal in size. But in either event, this responsibility was construed as being part of the legislative rather than the judicial process. Colegrove and others who felt underrepresented would have to work for the election of congressmen and state legislators sympathetic to the equalitarian principle. They must convince voters and legislators, not judges or courts, of the rightness of their cause. Frankfurter concluded: "The Constitution has left the performance of many duties in our governmental scheme to depend . . . on the vigilance of the people in exercising their political rights."

How helpful was this advice? For 57 years, from 1872 to 1929, Congress's apportionment acts had required that House districts contain "as nearly as practicable an equal number of inhabitants." But this provision was not included in the 1929 act, nor in subsequent acts, and Congress had shown little inclination to revive it. Moreover, even when the requirement of equal-sized districts was on the books it was never enforced. In that 57-year period not a single Representative was denied his seat because he had been elected by an undersized district, although there was no shortage of challengeable candidates. The chances of congressional action as a remedy, therefore, were slender.

Frankfurter's alternative advice was to elect state legislators willing to draw up congressional districts in an equitable manner, but here Colegrove came upon another roadblock. The districts for the Illinois legislature were also malapportioned, with a similar over-representation of rural voters. One state senate district was sixteen times as large as another; moreover, Cook County, with 51 per cent of the state's population, elected only 19 of the 51 state senators. In consequence a minority of the people of Illinois could fill 63 per cent of the seats of the upper chamber. Thus there would be little chance of electing a state legislature willing to create equal-sized congressional districts even if Colegrove managed to persuade a majority of Illinois' voters to do so. There were, then, built-in obstacles insurmountable by even the most vigorous exercise of democratic procedures.

Therefore Colegrove felt justified in launching a second suit, this time against Edward J. Barrett, the Secretary of State of Illinois. Here he asked the federal courts to order the Illinois legislature to redistrict itself along more equitable lines. It was obvious that the legislature would not do this unless it was compelled to, and a judicial directive seemed to be the only recourse. A three-judge panel of the Northern District of Illinois assumed jurisdiction in the case in December, 1946, and the following February it handed down an adverse judgment. The case was appealed directly to the Supreme Court of the United States. On March 10, 1947, that tribunal issued a brief statement refusing to grant certiorari in *Colegrove v. Barrett*, explaining that the districting of state legislatures was outside its jurisdiction.

Felix Frankfurter was one of the six-judge majority voting to deny Colegrove a hearing on his second case. Yet it was Frankfurter who, in *Colegrove v. Green*, had advised him to take this grievance directly to the people of his state. "The remedy for unfairness in districting," Frankfurter had said, "is to secure state legislatures that will apportion properly...." However, when, in *Colegrove v. Barrett*, the plaintiff asked for judicial intervention to enable the citizens of Illinois to have a true voice in electing the body that draws up the state's congressional districts, Frankfurter and a majority of his colleagues nevertheless refused to act. The suspicion might reasonably arise that the 1946 Court may have been less than charitable in suggesting a program of action in one breath, and then, in the next, refusing to provide the assistance needed to implement that suggestion.

1946 vs. 1959

Since Baker's case against Tennessee officialdom was the mirror image of Colegrove's suit against Illinois, why did he file suit? Baker suspected that with the replacement during the intervening thirteen years of some of the Justices who had served in 1946, he would face a tribunal that might reverse the Colegrove rulings. Certainly the gamble seemed worth it. Of the eight men who had formed the Court on June 10, 1946, only three remained on the bench in 1959.* One of these was Justice Frankfurter and the other two were Hugo Black and William O. Douglas, both of whom had voted for Colegrove in his Green case and supported giving him a hearing in his Barrett suit. However, the six new Justices were a mixed—and an unpredictable—group. Among them only two could probably be counted on to take Baker's side: Chief Justice Earl Warren and Associate Justice William Brennan, both of whom had already shown a sympathy for liberal causes and an affinity for judicial activism. But Black, Douglas, Warren, and Brennan only added up to four votes, one short of the necessary majority.

Facing them would be Frankfurter, and probably Justice John Marshall Harlan, who was generally conservative in temper and disinclined to Court intervention in "political" matters. This lineup left three "swing" men—Justices Tom Clark, Potter Stewart, and Charles Whittaker—all of whom had often shown conservative tendencies in their opinions. Even though Baker needed the agreement of but one of them, it was entirely possible that the three would decide to support Frankfurter's Colegrove position.

Baker at the Bar

It took exactly sixteen months for Baker's appeal to journey from the federal courthouse in Tennessee to the Supreme Court building in Washington. Not only are the courts' dockets crowded, which means that cases must wait patiently in line, but it takes time to prepare briefs and pleadings suitable to withstand close scrutiny and severe questioning.

*Chief Justice Harlan Fiske Stone died in April of 1946 and a successor had not yet been named at the time of the *Colegrove v. Green* decision. Thus the Court consisted of only eight Justices until the end of the 1945–1946 term, when Fred C. Vinson was named Chief Justice.

On the 19th and 20th of April in 1961, counsel for both Charles Baker and Joe Carr appeared to present oral arguments before the Supreme Court. The lawyers for both sides are each given a full hour to elaborate their side of the case. However, the Justices are at liberty to ask questions during that time, and those interruptions count as part of the allotted sixty minutes. Representing Baker was Charles S. Rhyne, a distinguished Washington, D.C., attorney and a former president of the American Bar Association, who frequently appeared before the Supreme Court. Counsel for Carr were James Glasgow and Jack Wilson, assistant attorneys general of Tennessee. Also present and scheduled to speak was Archibald Cox, the Solicitor General of the United States. For the Department of Justice had filed an *amicus curiae* ("friend of the court") brief in support of Baker, attesting that President John F. Kennedy's administration was officially on record favoring equitable state legislative apportionment.

Counsel Rhyne opened by stating that the Tennessee legislature had "affirmatively, purposefully, and systematically nullified the voting right" of Baker and his ten co-appellants; and he went on to point out that they had no recourse save to enter the courts. Since Tennessee did not permit popular referendums, amending the state constitution rested with the already malapportioned legislature and that body had shown no inclination to alter the inequities of the status quo. At this point in Rhyne's argument, Justice Whittaker interrupted to ask what would happen if the legislature itself amended the state's constitution: "Even if it did pass an amendment, wouldn't you have just what you have now?" Baker's attorney was happy to accept that hypothesis, adding, "I mentioned it to show that we have no other remedy." (Clearly this was a sympathetic, indeed a helpful, question; and it seemed to suggest that Whittaker was pro-Baker.)

Solicitor General Cox chose to stress that the Tennessee system violated the "equal protection" provision of the Fourteenth Amendment which, he argued, forbids not only racial discrimination but any unreasonable distinctions on the part of a state. "If this is so with regard to legislation affecting economic or social interests," Cox proceeded, "it is particularly so as to the right to vote, which is at the heart of democratic political processes." The Solicitor General was referring to the view that a state may not limit or curtail the freedoms of certain categories of citizens—unless it can give good reasons related to a legitimate legislative purpose why the people in those categories ought to be treated differently. People who are bald cannot be arbitrarily barred by law from restaurants or occupations that are open to their more hirsute fellow-citizens, but heavy trucks may be appropriately prohibited from using certain kinds of roads. By the same token, Cox suggested, a person cannot be assigned an underweighted vote just because of where he happens to make his home—or, indeed, for any other reason.

Once again Justice Whittaker put a leading question. "If there is a clear constitutional right being violated," he asked, "is there not both power and a duty in the courts to enforce the constitutional right?" Cox replied that of course the judiciary had the authority and the obligation to intervene. At that point, Justice Stewart inquired about the hands-off ruling of *Colegrove v. Green.* To this the Solicitor General answered, perhaps somewhat cryptically, that in the earlier Court's handling of that case "the cure might have been worse than the disease."

Assistant Attorney General Glasgow of Tennessee rose to speak for Joe Carr. "The obvious purpose of this suit," he insisted, "is to control the exercise of state legislative power," and to transform "the federal judiciary into a supervening federal authority to control the political activities of a sovereign state." Glasgow relied heavily on the Colegrove precedents, emphasizing not only states' rights but the principle of non-intervention in presumably "political" matters. Justice Whittaker, however, had other matters to explore, such as the requirement of the Tennessee constitution that called for periodic reapportionment. "As long as it is there, is it to be ignored?" he asked. "Are you complying with it?" he pressed. To these queries Glasgow could only respond: "No, Sir, it has not been complied with since 1901."

Glasgow's colleague, Jack Wilson, then took over to point out that if the Supreme Court chose to use its power on Baker's behalf, that "action would put the state in a sort of receivership." For judicial intervention in this area would amount to saying that "the people of Tennessee are incapable of self-government and never will be able to solve this problem."

Given a few minutes for rebuttal, Baker's attorney emphasized that his client was only concerned with the overall constitutionality of the existing apportionment arrangement. He was not asking the courts to draw up a districting plan or to impose any particular scheme on the Tennessee legislature. "Suppose Tennessee started in anew on all this," Justice Harlan hypothesized, "do you recognize a right in the state to make a classification between rural and city voters?" "We would recognize any reasonable classification," was the answer. Harlan probed further: "You do not insist on absolute mathematical equality?" And here counsel's reply, perhaps surprising because of all that had gone before, was a simple "No."

With this termination of oral argument, it emerged that *Baker v. Carr* was being fought on the level of high principle. The eleven Tennessee citizens were asking for a broad determination on constitutional grounds. They wanted a decision that would reverse the Colegrove precedents, so that in the future courts could be petitioned to correct specific apportionment inequities. They wanted the Court to agree to the adoption of a new principle of jurisdiction and a broad standard of equitable representation. How to put that standard into practical operation was a matter that could be decided later on.

Lobbying and Litigation

Both custom and common sense decree the inappropriateness of applying pressure to courts and judges. While legislative assemblies and administrative agencies are regarded as fair targets for lobbies and interest groups, the judicial branch is supposed to be both immune to and insulated from such tactics. Certainly it is unthinkable for an interested party to call on a Supreme Court Justice in an effort to influence his impending decision.

Nevertheless, there is a legal and respectable way by which concerned parties may make their feelings known to those charged with adjudicating cases. Individuals or groups are permitted to submit *amicus curiae* briefs which give support to one of the litigants. In theory, these briefs are supposed to provide strictly legal arguments that have not been covered by the attorneys for the plaintiff or defendant. In fact, however, *amicus* briefs often go beyond presenting precedents and argumentation to supply economic and sociological information believed worthy of judicial attention. (This was the case with the famous "Brandeis briefs" at the turn of the century, which argued in favor of upholding early workmen's compensation laws by amassing an array of official statistics on industrial accidents. Sociological and psychological research findings were incorporated in NAACP briefs in the school desegregation cases of the 1950's.) On other occasions *amicus* briefs alert a court that the question before them is not simply a quarrel between two unique litigants, but greatly concerns other individuals and groups.

It so happens that in the Tennessee apportionment case all the *amicus* briefs supported Baker's position. The most impressive came from the National Institute of Municipal Law Officers, and it was signed by the city attorneys of such cities as Los Angeles, New York, Dallas, Detroit, Richmond, and Minneapolis. Here, certainly, was testimony that large urban centers wished to redress the under-representation they suffered under antiquated districting systems. But there was also a brief on behalf of 50 residents of New York's suburban Nassau County, for the suburbs typically were also deprived of an equitable voice in the legislature. Another was submitted by the city of St. Matthews, Kentucky, a small town of 11,000 people, that nevertheless felt aggrieved because its citizens' votes were undervalued. A fourth brief came from J. Howard Edmondson, the governor of Oklahoma. Though he was himself elected by a popular majority, he had to share power with a legislature in which—as in Tennessee—lawmakers elected by less than 30 per cent of the population could legislate in the state's name. Yet another brief was filed by the head of the AFL-CIO in the state of Michigan, voicing his union's concern over the diluted ballots of their predominantly urban members. And finally, as we have indicated, the Kennedy administration put its prestige behind Baker's appeal.

How much these expressions of outside opinion influenced the Justices is impossible to gauge. Officials of other malapportioned states did not, at this time, offer *amicus curiae* support to Joe Carr of Tennessee. Perhaps they were unaware of the potential significance of the case for their states or perhaps they were complacent that the Colegrove finding would be renewed. But at all events they did not elect to engage in the legal lobbying that was their right.

The Decision

On March 26, 1962—almost 1,000 days after Baker first initiated his suit—the Supreme Court handed down its decision in his case. By a vote of 6 to 2, the Justices ruled that the grievance of the eleven Tennessee voters was a legitimate judicial question and that legislative apportionment was an issue that the courts could properly review.* Two of the "swing" Justices, by joining their four activist colleagues, had brought about a reversal of the Colegrove precedent. Six Justices submitted written opinions in this landmark case. Justice William Brennan expressed the broad view of the six-judge majority; and in this he spoke for himself and two of his colleagues, Chief Justice Earl Warren and Justice Hugo Black. However, three other Justices—William O. Douglas, Tom Clark, and Potter Stewart—felt compelled to write "concurring" opinions. That is, though they agreed with the majority's decision, each had a different set of reasons for supporting that position. Justice Felix Frankfurter wrote the main minority opinion, and Justice John Marshall Harlan appended some additional remarks which Frankfurter endorsed.

As a result of this unusual surge of literary activity, the opinions in *Baker v. Carr* cover 86 double-columned pages in the Supreme Court Reports. Although we can examine only selected issues, we must emphasize that a wide array of problems were involved in the case. There was the question of whether Charles Baker had "standing." That is, could a citizen—or even a dozen citizens—demand the wholesale restructuring of the apparatus of a state's government? By the doctrine of "standing," they had to show that their grievances were not peculiar to themselves and that their suit was sufficiently serious to warrant a judicial response. In other words, courts will not accept as a case to be heard every suit that a citizen cares to bring against a government policy or procedure. And that is one basic reason why taxpayers have had so little success in attacking government appropriations by court actions. One aggrieved taxpayer may not try to stop the expenditure of public money on rockets to the moon by attempting to exaggerate the direct harmfulness of the

---

*The ninth Justice, Charles Whittaker, did not participate in the deliberations or the voting due to illness. Indeed, he retired from the Court shortly thereafter.

space program to him and others who he claims feel the same way. Yet there are occasions when the Courts are willing to accept an individual's claim that the injury he is suffering is both direct and is being experienced by a whole class of citizens in situations similar to his own. The Baker case was such an instance.

Justice Brennan, speaking for the majority, pointed out that citizens who are politically under-represented do indeed have a "personal stake" and thus are entitled to bring suit for relief. If an individual city dweller can show that he is so disadvantaged by prevailing arrangements, he has the right to ask for general reform of legislative districting. But the Tennessee appellants had a more specific complaint. The state's constitution and the implementing 1901 act required a reapportionment every ten years, yet demands had been ignored for six decades. Justice Brennan wrote:

These appellants seek relief in order to protect or vindicate an interest of their own, and of those similarly situated. Their constitutional claim is, in substance, that the 1901 statute constitutes arbitrary and capricious state action, offensive to the Fourteenth Amendment in its irrational disregard of the standard of apportionment prescribed by the State's Constitution or of any standard, effecting a gross disproportion of representation to voting population. The injury which appellants assert is that this classification disfavors the voters in the counties in which they reside, placing them in a position of constitutionally unjustifiable inequality vis-à-vis voters in irrationally favored counties.

Back in 1946 the Court had ruled that Professor Colegrove's apportionment suit was a "political" question and hence not "justiciable." The issue was whether, under the doctrine of the separation of powers, a question should properly be decided by the legislative or the judicial branch. As we have indicated, the lower court had ruled that Baker's case was like Colegrove's in that it involved a "political" question and hence was not a legitimate question for the courts. But this lower-court reliance on the Colegrove precedent, Justice Brennan now ruled, was a "misinterpretation" of the holding in the earlier suit. For Colegrove's case dealt with the apportionment of seats for the United States House of Representatives, whereas Baker's referred to the apportionment of his state's legislature. The United States Supreme Court cannot invade the rightful preserve of Congress, Brennan implied, for that would be "political." However, it can supervene the activities of state legislatures: that is not "political." Thus he wrote:

In . . . "political question" cases, it is the relationship between the judiciary and the coordinate branches of the federal government, and not the federal judiciary's relationship to the states, which gives rise to the "political" question.

With these words the Colegrove holding was deemed to be a precedent not relevant to Baker's suit, thereby permitting the Court to make a decision on the merits of the case.*

The Supreme Court majority based its substantive decision primarily on the "equal protection of the laws" clause of the Fourteenth Amendment. Unequal citizen participation in the selection of lawmakers, leading directly to legislative under-representation for some citizens and over-representation for others, was held to be a denial of equal protection of the laws. The Court, however, did not go so far as to fix the precise meaning of "equal participation," or to insist that all districts for *both* legislative chambers had to be based on constituencies of equal or nearly equal population. The Justices were content, at this stage, to adumbrate the general principle without setting up specific guidelines on how far the districts of Tennessee's legislature might deviate from an "ideal" population figure or from each other. This was rather like the earlier school-desegregation cases, where the Supreme Court turned back to the lower courts the task of determining acceptable degrees of desegregation consistent with the broad principle of the unconstitutionality of state-enforced segregation.

Baker's case thus would have to be argued all over again back in Nashville, and a judge at the District Court level would decide whether the existing system or a proposed alternative system was equitable under the general strictures of the Fourteenth Amendment. "We have no cause at this stage to doubt the District Court will be able to fashion relief," Justice Brennan said. He left unsaid what would occur if judges around the country began to use widely disparate criteria in ruling on the equitability of apportionment

---

*Would this preclude the Court from passing judgment on the districting arrangements of the House of Representatives of the United States? This was hardly an academic problem, for at that very moment a case was before a Federal District Court in Atlanta challenging the gross disparities in Georgia's congressional districts.

systems. It could be presumed that the Court would not make its decision on how to cross that bridge until compelled by necessity.

In a concurring opinion Justice Douglas summarized the key point at issue as he saw it: "The question is the extent to which a State may weight one person's vote more heavily than it does another's." In another concurrence Justice Clark answered that question by showing the disparate weightings assigned to votes cast in each of the state's counties. "The apportionment picture in Tennessee is a topsy-turvical of gigantic proportions," he wrote. "Tennessee's apportionment is a crazy quilt without rational basis." Clark went on to point out that Tennessee could not even claim that it was adhering to the principle of favoring rural residents according to some consistent calculation:

Since discrimination is present among counties of like population, the plan is neither consistent nor rational. It discriminates horizontally by creating gross disparities between rural areas themselves as well as between urban areas themselves, still maintaining the wide vertical disparity already pointed out between rural and urban.

Clark's concurring opinion differed from the others in that he was willing to consider the actual mathematical merits (and demerits) of the Tennessee apportionment. Thus he appended a series of statistical tables to his comments, going so far as to devise an arithmetic formula by which to test the incidence of representational inequity throughout the state. This exercise presaged the sort of expertise that judges would have to muster once the principles of *Baker v. Carr* came to be applied in a practical way. In his exposition Clark did not assert that precise numerical equality was necessary, but that in the case before him the inequalities were more than reason could allow.

In addition, Clark underlined the propriety of judicial intervention in this area. Though the Colegrove decision of 1946 had said that citizens had the "practical" option of voting in legislators mandated to redress the apportionment balance, this rule failed to recognize that in many states the majority, try as it might, was unable to rule. Clark said:

The majority of the people of Tennessee have no "practical opportunities for exerting their political weight at the polls" to correct the existing "invidious discrimination." Tennessee has no initiative and referendum.

I have searched diligently for other "practical opportunities" present under the law. I find none other than through the federal courts.

This statement seems to imply that had the state's constitution permitted an initiative or referendum Clark might not have supported judicial intervention, because Tennesseans would then have had a political avenue for redress. (But suppose that a state does allow referendums and the majority nevertheless votes for maintaining a malapportioned legislature? The Court, as we shall see, soon had to face up to that eventuality.)

Quite obviously the Justices were not unaware of the momentous potentialities of their decision. They had signaled the end of rural domination of legislative politics, and the consequent increase of urban and especially suburban power in the state capitols. Nevertheless, none of the majority members based their opinions on conjecturing about what policy outcomes might follow reapportionment. They did not suggest that city schools should or would receive more state aid or that such considerations were relevant to their judgment. The Court's concern was that Tennessee's citizens have votes of roughly equal weight, not the use voters chose to make of their equalized ballots.

Thus the judiciary entered the "political thicket" against which Justice Frankfurter had warned in *Colegrove v. Green*. Yet Frankfurter himself continued to adhere to his earlier view, although now, in 1962, he wrote as a dissenter rather than as spokesman for the Court's majority.

Frankfurter's Dissent

The majority in *Baker v. Carr* had indicated that equal votes for all citizens was a legitimate goal that might properly be pursued in the courts. Justice Frankfurter, joined by Justice Harlan, vigorously disagreed on both counts. They raised this fundamental question: whether equal representation in the lawmaking process was in fact a valid principle. Brennan, Douglas, and Clark, in lieu of developing historical or philosophical underpinning for their decisions, had merely assumed that equally weighted votes and majority rule were incontrovertible facts of democratic political life. To the two dissenters, however, majority rule was still an open issue: minorities might, in some circumstances, be entitled to disproportionate representation. Frankfurter said:

One cannot speak of "debasement" or "dilution" of the value of a vote until there is first defined a standard of reference as to what a vote should be worth. What is actually asked of the Court in this case is to choose among competing bases of representation—ultimately, really, among competing theories of political philosophy.

Frankfurter, quite candidly, preferred one philosophy over another. He regarded the equalitarian theory as based more on emotion than on reason or practicality, and by his reading of the historical record, numerical equality had no claim to be treated as an unquestioned tenet of American government.

Those pressing for pure majority rule, he went on, were apparently unaware that minority rights have played a vital role in American institutions. Relatively few states apportioned both their houses by the population criterion—did this not demonstrate that the standard of equal numbers lacked universal support? Frankfurter sharply put forth an affirmative answer to that question:

The notion that representation proportioned to the geographic spread of population is so universally accepted as a necessary element of equality between men that it must be taken to be the standard of a political equality preserved by the Fourteenth Amendment—that it is, in appellants' words "The basic principle of representative government"—is, to put it bluntly, not true. However desirable and however desired by some among the great political thinkers and framers of our government, it has never been generally practiced, today or in the past.

Frankfurter's statement implied that the prevailing arrangements, being the embodiment of the historical and philosophical components, of the American tradition, should be permitted to continue. On the other hand, if this history and philosophy were to be abrogated, then the equalitarian claim should be viewed as a novel proposal for reform, rather than disguised as a distillation of American tradition and practice.

Frankfurter's opinion made as compelling a case for malapportionment as seems possible. Not only did he adhere to his well-known practice of engaging in historical and philosophical interpretation, but his long dissent was replete with evidence of impressive scholarship. Frankfurter's citations ranged from Dorr's Rebellion in Rhode Island and the English Reform Act of 1832 to Jefferson's *Notes on Virginia* and Madison's writings in *The Federalist*. There is a discussion of the ratification of the Fourteenth Amendment, an analysis of apportionment in the American colonies prior to the Declaration of Independence, and a description of the workings of the British Boundary Commission which draws up constituencies for the House of Commons. Yet if all this research was to no avail in convincing six of his fellow Justices, his views reflected and articulated sentiments held outside the marble halls of the Supreme Court Building. Time would show that his position was not as beleaguered as the 6–2 vote in *Baker v. Carr* might have suggested.

Finally, Frankfurter felt that the Court had no business in intervening in this area. He found it curious that the proponents of wider democracy were asking the judiciary, an undemocratic institution, to make the decision rather than leave it to the public at large:

In this situation, as in others of like nature, appeal for relief does not belong here. Appeal must be to an informed, civically militant electorate. In a democratic society like ours, relief must come through an aroused popular conscience that sears the conscience of the people's representatives.

Frankfurter presumably knew that less than 30 per cent of the Tennessee electorate could select the representatives who would constitute a majority of the legislature. The opposition of those rural lawmakers to equitable apportionment required a "militant electorate" to recruit as many as 70 per cent of the voters to produce a legislature sympathetic to equal representation. Perhaps Frankfurter felt that such an extraordinary majority was necessary to upset tradition and alter the existing pattern of representation. At all events he would have allowed the status quo to persist until the "popular conscience" had become close to unanimous in favoring change.

Unfortunately for Frankfurter's view, simple majority rule was operative in the Supreme Court itself, and Baker's case against Carr became the law of the land. Frankfurter's last words, however, were not without an ominous overtone. He wondered if his colleagues were not indulging in "merely empty rhetoric, sounding a word of promise to the ear, sure to be disappointing to the hope." The implication, to which only the future would supply the answers, was that the interests benefiting from the status quo would somehow negate or circumvent the changes called for by the Baker decision.

The 6–2 lineup in *Baker v. Carr* did not contain surprises so much as it settled speculations. The four "liberal" Justices—Warren, Black, Douglas, and Brennan—backed Baker's position, which was consistent with their customary support of civil rights. The two more "conservative" members of the Court, Frankfurter and Harlan, adhered to the theory they had often expressed: that it is for the states and their citizens to solve their own political problems by political methods of their own devising. Clark and Stewart, the two "swing" Justices, had frequently tended to the conservative side in the past; especially in civil liberties cases in which the issues were freedom of speech and association. However, the plaintiffs in the current case, far from being dangerous or unorthodox dissenters, were upstanding citizens and leaders who were simply petitioning for equality of representation in the governmental system. Hence Clark and Stewart encountered no initial inconsistency in siding with their more liberal colleagues on March 26, 1962. Whether they would remain part of that group if the apportionment issue appeared to take a more radical turn at some future time was problematic.

Applying the Principles

It is rather sad that Justice Frankfurter's last major opinion prior to his retirement should have been so pessimistic in tone and so wrong in prediction. The courts moved into the apportionment area with alacrity, and within twenty months of the original decision they were hearing suits brought by citizens in 39 of the 50 states. Moreover, in this same period no less than 20 states actually changed their apportionment schemes, more often than not because of an impending judicial order or the threat of one. The willingness of judges, on both federal and state levels, to implement *Baker v. Carr* was in itself noteworthy. "Lower courts did not wait for guidance from above," Anthony Lewis wrote. "They moved ahead in the expansion of a new constitutional doctrine with a speed for which legal observers can find no recent parallel."*

This surge of judicial activity, however, was not matched by any great spirit of self-reform on the part of the legislatures. Many assemblies made only marginal changes or corrected only the most egregious of their imbalances. Thus in state after state, the courts examined the newly submitted districting patterns and—in most

*The New York Times, November 10, 1963.

cases—found them sorely inadequate. In Tennessee, the birthplace of *Baker v. Carr,* plans were sent back and forth from capitol to courthouse three or more times. "The rural bloc has demonstrated that it will seek every means of avoiding compliance—even cheating by a few seats—in an effort to preserve as much of its authority as possible," a correspondent in Nashville reported. As a final resort Tennessee issued a call for a constitutional convention to draw up an apportionment scheme. But even here the question would arise as to the manner in which the delegates to such a convention were chosen; clearly one ground for challenging an apportionment plan would be to say that legislative districts created by an unrepresentative convention were themselves invalid. All in all, the states that redistricted during 1963 and 1964 only went through the motion of reform, and litigation against these new plans began to follow *Baker v. Carr* up the well-trod road to the United States Supreme Court.

There was, moreover, considerable confusion at the judicial level due to the failure of the Supreme Court to specify precise standards of equality. Thus a three-judge Federal District Court in Atlanta decided the validity of Georgia's then prevailing "county-unit" system (where each county, in the elections for governor and other statewide officers, was accorded at least one "unit" vote regardless of its population) by devising a formula whereby the disparity of representation among Georgia's counties could not be "in excess of the disparity that exists as against any state in the most recent Electoral College allocation." Just how or why the national Electoral College became their touchstone for solving Georgia's problem is not clear. But such an exercise did support the contention that concrete guidelines would soon be needed if the Baker decision was to have rational and consistent application.

Unfinished Business: Standards Are Specified

The Supreme Court turned from general principles to specific cases when, on June 15, 1964, it handed down judgments relating to six states: Alabama, New York, Colorado, Maryland, Virginia, and Delaware. Interestingly, four of these six dealt with apportionment plans that had been drawn up after March, 1962, and hence purported to meet the standards implicit in *Baker v. Carr.* In *Reynolds v. Sims* and five companion cases the Justices sought to resolve questions that had been left outstanding. The Court ruled, most significantly, that "the seats in both houses of a bicameral legislature must be apportioned on a population basis." Chief Justice Warren, speaking for majorities that ranged from 8–1 to 6–3 depending on the case, rejected the theory that each state was a miniature "federal" system and could thus base one of its legislative chambers on local governmental units—such as counties or townships—rather than population. And in the Colorado case the Court ruled that even if a majority of a state's voters approved an apportionment plan in an initiative or a referendum, such a scheme would be held invalid if it failed to base districts on population.

Chief Justice Warren reiterated most of the arguments that Justice Brennan had made for the Court in *Baker v. Carr* two years earlier. "Legislators represent people, not trees or acres," he said. "Legislators are elected by voters, not farms or cities or economic interests." When one district has ten times the population of another and both are assigned but a single representative, it is as if both districts were equal in population but the voters in one were handed a sheaf of ten ballots to cast. "It would appear extraordinary," Warren remarked, "to suggest that a state could be constitutionally permitted to enact a law providing that certain of the state's voters could vote two, five, or ten times for their legislative representatives, while voters living elsewhere could vote only once." The constitutional ground remained as before: equal protection under the Fourteenth Amendment. But that guarantee was now extended to a citizen's voting rights for both chambers of his state's legislature.

The effect of the *Reynolds v. Sims* group of decisions was to call for a re-examination of state bicameralism. A justification frequently heard was that just as the United States Senate represented the states in the Congress, so one state might give representation to counties or townships or some other governmental units regardless of what their populations might be. Many of the states provided that each of their counties must have a minimum of one seat in one of the chambers no matter how few people might reside within its borders. The Supreme Court rejected that justification:

Political subdivisions of states—counties, cities, or whatever—never were and never have been considered as sovereign entities. Rather, they have been traditionally regarded as subordinate governmental instrumentalities created by the states to assist in the carrying out of state governmental functions.

Denial of the theory of "miniature federalism" did not, in the Court's view, render bicameralism purposeless. Those states wishing to retain duplicate debates, hearings, and roll calls as part of their legislative processes might continue with such an arrangement. Even with equal populations for districts, Chief Justice Warren wrote, "different constituencies can be represented in two houses":

One body could be composed of a single-member district while the other could have at least some multi-member districts. The length of terms of the legislators in the separate bodies could differ. The numerical size of the two bodies could be made to differ, even significantly, and the geographical size of districts from which legislators are elected could also be made to differ. And apportionment in one house could be arranged so as to balance off minor inequities in the representation of certain areas in the other house. In summary, these and other factors could be, and are presently in many states, utilized to engender differing complexions and collective attitudes in the two bodies of a state legislature, although both are apportioned substantially on a population basis.

Once again Justice Harlan dissented. Reiterating most of Frankfurter's arguments in the Baker case, he now denied that the Fourteenth Amendment required that both houses of state legislatures be based on equally populated districts. "I think it is demonstrable," he wrote, "that the Fourteenth Amendment does not impose this political tenet on the states or authorize this Court to do so." And, again following Frankfurter's earlier lead, Harlan pondered that the new series of apportionment decisions would bring about "a radical alteration in the relationship between the states and the federal government, more particularly the federal judiciary."

What About Voluntary Under-representation?

Finally, an intriguing question was raised in the Colorado case. In the 1962 general election the voters of that state, by a margin of 305,700 to 172,725, amended their constitution to provide at least one seat in the upper house to certain districts despite their meager populations. Since the amendment was endorsed by a popular majority in every county, it could only be concluded that voters from populous counties were willing to dilute their own legislative strength and give disproportionate power to rural minorities elsewhere in their state. Here was the very opposite of a "majority tyranny" at the polls.

The Court, however, was not concerned with the rights of the minority—or at least those of rural minorities—but rather with the rights of individuals. It declined to acknowledge that there existed any constitutional justification for arrangements wherein the political power of some citizens might be greater than that of others:

An individual's constitutionally protected right to cast an equally weighted ballot cannot be denied even by a vote of a majority of a state's electorate. . . . We hold that the fact that a challenged legislative apportionment was approved by the electorate is without federal significance, if the scheme adopted failed to satisfy the basic requirements of the Equal Protection clause.

It is a precept of American constitutional law that a citizen cannot trade, barter, or even give away certain rights. These rights, the end-products of a historical evolution that is often but dimly understood by those who possess them, express the freedoms upon which the individual's pursuit of the good life depends. It is not inconceivable that some Americans, under some circumstances, might be induced to trade away their right to worship, to express their political views, or to maintain domestic privacy. By avoiding the results of the Colorado referendum, the Court reaffirmed its classic role as defender of individual rights, even when, as in this case, many urban voters consented to dilute their own rights.

At the time of the original Baker decision there had been a great deal of speculation whether the two middle-of-the-road Justices, Tom Clark and Potter Stewart, would support subsequent reapportionment reform. The Colorado case answered this question; here both Clark and Stewart broke away from the majority and joined Harlan in his dissent. Clark noted that Colorado, unlike Tennessee, permitted the initiative and referendum and that the electorate had supported the lopsided apportionment plan. "This indicates the complete awareness of the people of Colorado to apportionment problems and their continuing efforts to solve them," he noted. "This court should not interfere in such a situation." Justice Stewart was troubled that a uniform standard of equitable districting would impose hardships on states with peculiar geographic contours. Citing Colorado, he showed in some detail how the very existence of the Rocky Mountains cut that state into natural regions which could form the reasonable boundaries for legislative seats even if they were not of equal populations. Colorado's voters knew what they were doing, he suggested, for "it was not irrational to conclude that effective representation of the interests of the residents of each of these regions was unlikely to be achieved if the rule of equal population were mechanically imposed." The Colorado case, then, was the point at which the "swing" Justices indicated that while they approved of reapportionment in some situations, they were unwilling to do so in all situations.

The Court Becomes Controversial

During the 1961–1964 terms in which it handed down *Baker v. Carr* and *Reynolds v. Sims* the Court had, of course, been making many other decisions, some of which proved to be highly controversial. It was not only that a majority of the Justices were now of liberal persuasion, but that they displayed a compassion for the plight of citizens whose deviant or unorthodox behavior disturbed the sensibilities of many in society.

Thus in the 1961–1962 term the Justices vindicated Negro sit-in demonstrators who had been arrested by Baton Rouge, Louisiana, authorities for disturbing the peace. Those who sit in at lunch counters may be nuisances to the proprietors, the Court said, but a constitutional system must tolerate nonviolent trouble-makers as well as less demonstrative citizens. A unanimous bench also struck down a Florida law which required all state employees to take a loyalty oath; and, with only one Justice dissenting, it voided a Post Office ruling that certain magazines featuring photographs of nude males were obscene. Perhaps most sensitive of all was the Court's declaration that prayers in public classrooms were unconstitutional, even if they were denominationally neutral and pupils who objected to reciting them were allowed to remain silent or leave the room.

In 1962–1963 the Court hammered home some of the rulings it had inaugurated a year earlier. A group of South Carolina Negroes had their arrests voided on the ground that their right to freedom of speech and petition permitted them to march through the downtown streets of Columbia en route to a picketing demonstration outside the state capitol. The procedures of Rhode Island's Commission to Encourage Morality in Youth were deemed to be unconstitutional exercises of censorship; and the city of Baltimore was told that it could no longer have the Lord's Prayer recited in its schools. And in a Florida case a unanimous Court freed a man who had been convicted of breaking into a poolroom, declaring that even defendants charged with such crimes as burglary must be provided with counsel—and at public expense if necessary.

The following term witnessed not only the landmark *Reynolds v. Sims* group of cases but also a 6–3 decision requiring districts of the United States House of Representatives to be of equal populations as well. The Justices went on to strike down another loyalty oath, this one required of teachers and other public employees in the state of Washington. And by a 6–3 vote they released from prison an Illinois man who had been accused of fatally shooting his brother-in-law, because he had not been permitted to have a lawyer present with him during his interrogation at the police station house.

To many commentators it looked as if the majority on the Warren Court was bending the Constitution to protect some of the more unruly and unsavory elements in American society. President Kennedy's appointments of Byron White and Arthur Goldberg to fill the seats of Whittaker and Frankfurter had strengthened the "liberal" bloc and it appeared that the "conservatives" would never again be able to muster a majority. To conservative critics of the Court, the rulings were perceived as encouraging demonstrators to make even greater nuisances of themselves, exempting public employees of dubious patriotism from swearing loyalty or allegiance to their state and nation, banishing God from public classrooms, flooding the mails and drugstores with obscene books and magazines, and coddling criminals from virtually the moment of arrest so that even reasonable police efforts to secure confessions would be thwarted by smart lawyers.

Here, in three years' time, appeared to be more than enough ammunition for those growing restive over the pace of judicial activism. Hardly a state did not have at least one of its laws or procedures overturned or undercut by a Court majority that seemed bent on allying its authority with individuals and causes easily seen as inimical to patriotism, morality, and order. The reapportionment decisions were, to these critics, only the last straws in an already unbearable bundle. At the same time it must be realized that although the issue of equality of representation may not have carried as emotional an appeal as some of the other unpopular decisions, it nevertheless became the chief battleground on which the Court's antagonists decided to mount their attack.

Congress vs. the Court

The *Reynolds v. Sims* group of cases were handed down in mid-June of 1964, and the summer and early fall of that year witnessed a vigorous and often vitriolic debate over the reapportionment decisions. The chief forum for these discussions and diatribes was the Congress. First to act was the House of Representatives. Congressman William Tuck, a Virginia Democrat, introduced a bill that would take from the Supreme Court its jurisdiction over apportionment cases. Its operative provisions read: "The Supreme Court shall not have the right to review the action of any court concerning any action to apportion or reapportion any legislature of any state."

The limiting of judicial jurisdiction is one of the most potent of Congress's powers against the courts. Article III of the Constitution states that "the Supreme Court shall have appellate jurisdiction, with such exceptions and under such regulations as the Congress shall make." This means that the Congress is entitled to rule that, for some types of cases, the final word may rest within the states' judiciaries. In this event the consequence would be that parties who were dissatisfied with a decision handed down by one of those tribunals would be precluded from appealing their case to the Supreme Court of the United States. A decade earlier, the Congress had come within one vote of stripping the Court of its power to pass on state laws concerning internal subversion. The Tuck bill was an attempt to use this technique to prevent any more decisions of the *Baker* and *Reynolds* type.

Tuck outlined his view in these words:

I favor apportionment of legislative bodies and . . . reapportionment of the same whenever it becomes necessary or desirable on the part of the citizens of any state. But I am opposed to our states and people being subjected to the utterances and arbitrary commands of the Supreme Court of the United States. Congress has the power to lay the hand of restraint upon the Federal judiciary and stop these judicial indiscretions and abuses. I hope and believe it has the will.

His position was supported from the Republican side by Representative Leslie Arends of Illinois:

The Supreme Court decision last June unfortunately has created a chaotic situation throughout the nation. The question involved here is whether the people of the respective states shall themselves determine how they will be represented in their own state legislatures. The Court's decision is tantamount to an abandonment of the principle of a republic of federated states.

On August 19, 1964, the House passed the Tuck bill by a 218–175 roll call. Its passage was due largely to the votes supplied by a coalition of Republicans and southern Democrats: 80 per cent of the Congressmen in those two groups voted for the Tuck bill; the opposition was composed primarily of northern Democrats. Since the House is generally considered to be closest to popular sentiment of the moment, the vote may well have reflected the opinion of a substantial portion of the American people.

The Senate, however, is a more deliberative and a less democratic body. Not a few Senators were frankly concerned over the severity of the retribution that the House was willing to visit on the Justices. It is one thing to say that you do not approve of some of the Supreme Court's decisions; it is quite another to amputate its authority with a blunt instrument. At all events, the Senate was unwilling to go along with the House bill (in one test only 21 votes could be recruited for it), but there was sentiment for at least a symbolic acknowledgment of the issue. After a debate of filibuster proportions, a "sense of Congress" resolution was passed by a 44–38 vote asking District Court judges then considering apportionment cases to allow the 1964 elections for state legislature to be held with the existing malapportioned districts. The resolution was a victory for liberal Democrats, who did not want the Senate to take any action critical of the Supreme Court. This very mild resolution was proposed by them as a means of heading off severer measures from other quarters. Thus most Republicans and virtually all of the South's Senators made up the 38 negative votes. Because the Senate resolution had so little in common with the House bill, a brief meeting of a conference committee concluded that compromise action was impossible and the whole issue was therefore shelved.

That the House's reaction was the more vehement may well have stemmed from the Supreme Court's *Wesberry v. Sanders* decision in February of 1964, which ordered that chamber to equalize its own districts. (Though the disparities in populations among House seats were by no means as glaring as those in state legislatures, its districts did range in size from 177,431 to 951,527.) Although this decision would not directly affect all congressmen, a goodly number were clearly disturbed over this judicial intervention in their own housekeeping.*

Changing the Constitution

During the Senate debate, Republican leader Everett McKinley Dirksen expressed concern that the Court's decision would enable Chicago to control both houses of the Illinois legislature. "I think we will have to look and see if this is a proper field for a constitutional amendment," he pondered aloud.

By the opening of the 89th Congress, in January of 1965, Dirksen had concluded that an amendment was indeed necessary. He doubtless felt that although the Supreme Court was entitled to interpret the Constitution, its members also were bound to adhere to the wording of that document. Where the phrasing is vague or ambiguous (such as "equal protection of the laws") the Justices might read their own prejudices or predilections into the clauses they were purporting to apply and interpret. However, if the Constitution were amended so as to read in a very specific manner (as "the manufacture, sale, or transportation of intoxicating liquors . . . is hereby prohibited"), then the Court would be obliged to adhere to those specifications.

Thus in the spring of 1965, Senator Dirksen introduced a Senate Joint Resolution—which soon came to be called the "Dirksen Amendment"—designed to overturn not only the Baker and Reynolds decisions, but also the Lukas case, which had dealt with the Colorado referendum. For this reason there were two key clauses to the amendment:

The members of one house shall be apportioned among the people on the basis of their numbers and the members of the other house may be

---

*The Court's action here dealt directly with one part of a coequal branch of the federal government. Thus the Justices might appear to have intruded into the very area they had defined as "political"—and which, in *Baker v. Carr*, they said they could not enter. The Court based its decision on an interpretation of Section 2 of Article I of the Constitution ("The House of Representatives shall be composed of members chosen . . . by the people of all the several states") and refrained from mentioning the "political" issue at all. Rather their argument was that the Framers had intended all citizens to have equal representation in the House of Representatives and that the prevailing disparities in districts violated that intention.

apportioned among the people on the basis of population, geography, and political subdivisions in order to insure effective representation in the state's legislature of the various groups and interests making up the electorate.

A plan of apportionment shall become effective only after it has been submitted to a vote of the people of the state and approved by a majority of those voting on that issue at a statewide election. In addition to any other plans of apportionment which may be submitted at such election, there shall be submitted to a vote of the people an alternative plan of apportionment based solely on substantial equality of population.

The intent of Dirksen's amendment was clear, and to many it seemed a reasonable proposal. On the one hand it would reverse the Reynolds decision by permitting one of the chambers of a state legislature to be apportioned on the basis of "groups and interests," rather than simply a counting of heads. On the other hand, however, such a nonarithmetic apportionment would have to gain the approval of a statewide majority—as it had in the Colorado referendum—where the voters are given a chance to choose between two different districting plans. Thirty colleagues co-sponsored Dirksen's resolution, and not all of them were Senators from rural states. Among his supporters were Democrats and Republicans from Ohio, California, Massachusetts, and Pennsylvania.

Dirksen initially used a curious but permissible tactic to bring his amendment to a speedy vote. After introducing a minor bill authorizing a "National American Legion Baseball Week," he replaced it on the agenda with the apportionment amendment. The roll call on his proposal proved to be both a victory and a defeat. It "won" by a vote of 57–39, but a two-thirds majority of the Senators is needed for proposing a Constitutional amendment, so in fact the measure was defeated. In the spring of 1966, the alignments and outcome were virtually the same, this time by 55–38. Though the core of support for Dirksen's resolution came from Republicans and southern Democrats, in both years ten to a dozen northern Democrats from smaller, less urban states also voted for the amendment. It became apparent by 1967, however, that the Illinois senator could not muster the votes needed for a two-thirds majority, which is another way of saying that an obdurate minority had successfully prevented the amendment from being sent to the states for ratification.

Although the debate in Congress centered on the apportionment issue itself, reactions to the recent behavior of the Supreme Court were also evident. Thus Senator Birch Bayh of Indiana warned his colleagues against using their deliberations as a "springboard for vilification of the Supreme Court of the United States," asserting that there was "little to be gained by getting Congress fighting the Supreme Court." Others, however, would not be put off by these admonitions. Senator James Pearson of Kansas saw the controversy as a counterpart of the "great struggle over the future of the Supreme Court in 1937," and Senator Peter Dominick of Colorado regarded the Court's recent exercises of power as a "sobering example of what can, and in fact did, happen when our federal judiciary steps into the state political arena." Arizona's Senator Paul Fannin supported Dirksen's proposal by exclaiming that "all this amendment does is restore to the people a right which the Supreme Court has wrongfully taken away from them."

If these Senators meant that the issue was between the rulings of an appointed Court and the will of a democratic people, then it was to be expected that representatives of public groups would begin to speak of "judicial legislation" by a handful of Justices. Just because the Dirksen amendment could not win its way out of the Senate did not mean that no other ways of attaining the same end existed.

Pressure for Passage

Dirksen's amendment was never voted on by the House because of the efforts of Emanuel Celler, the chairman of that chamber's Judiciary Committee, who kept it from reaching the floor. Despite its failure in Congress, there was strong support for his resolution elsewhere in the country. Rallying behind the attempt to reverse the Court were a phalanx of well-organized and well-financed groups. Among these, needless to say, were associations with a strong rural base: the American Farm Bureau Federation, the American National Cattlemen's Association, the Dairymen's League Cooperative Association, the National Cotton Council, the National Grange, and the National Livestock Feeders Association. Even the normally liberal National Farmer's Union voted 112,540 to 89,447 to support the anti-reapportionment movement. Joining forces with rural Americans were not a few organizations both urban-based and usually urban-oriented. Thus the House of Delegates of the American Bar Association, meeting in New Orleans, voted 115–94 to overrule the Reynolds decision. William R. Brown, speaking for the Chamber of Commerce of the United States, stated publicly that "the recent apportionment decisions of the United States Supreme Court have tended to hack up the whole man while attempting to cure one sick member of the body." He was joined by John A. Clem, representing the National Association of Real Estate Boards, who warned that "electing both houses of a state legislature by population is to abandon state affairs to the class and interest which happens to be in the majority." Similar sentiments were voiced by spokesmen for city-situated groups like the National Association of Manufacturers and the American Retail Federation.

Support of the Dirksen amendment by these urban-based interests was grounded on a hard-nosed sense of self-interest. An observer of California politics once pointed out that "privately owned utilities, banks, insurance companies, and other concerns with crucial legislative programs have discovered some 'cow county' legislators more responsive to their demands and less committed to contrary points of view on key social and economic questions than are urban representatives."* Not only are rural lawmakers more conservative by temperament, but many of them have been willing to set up informal alliances with urban businessmen, realtors, and lawyers in an effort to slow down social and economic reforms proposed by metropolitan legislators. Some city residents have found their own interests better served by rural representatives than by the men for whom they vote at their own polls.

The most significant strategy, though, was being worked out by groups which were frankly political. The General Assembly of the States, an organization comprised chiefly of state legislators from around the country, had met as early as 1962 to express its displeasure over the Supreme Court's original *Baker v. Carr* decision. Among the more vehement expressions was that of a midwest lawmaker who was angered over the continual overruling of state statutes by the federal judiciary. The Tenth Amendment to the Constitution, said Warren Wood of Illinois, had been "raped twice a day for ten years." By a 26–10 vote, the Assembly proposed an amendment of its own that would prohibit the Supreme Court from

*Dean McHenry, "Urban vs. Rural in California," *National Municipal Review*, Vol. 35 (1946), pp. 353–354.

adjudicating any case "relating to apportionment of representation in a state legislature."

By 1965 this campaign had been taken over by the like-minded National Commission on Constitutional Government, whose officers included state legislators from Nebraska, Florida, Texas, and Missouri. Eschewing publicity, commission members traveled up and down the country, stopping at state capitols and attempting to persuade legislatures to pass resolutions calling for a reversal of the reapportionment decisions. Their initial purpose was to use these state resolutions to put pressure on Congress to pass the Dirksen amendment. However, though 23 state legislatures had enacted suitable resolutions, petitions, or memorials by the summer of 1965, the anti-reapportionment amendment, as we saw earlier, failed to pass. Still, almost half of the state legislatures had been enlisted in the crusade to override the Supreme Court, and the movement's arsenal was not yet depleted.

Call for a Convention

Those opposed to reapportionment may have been doing their work quietly, but they were surprisingly effective. It came as a shock to many observers when, by the spring of 1967, the legislatures of no less than 32 states had issued a call for a new Constitutional Convention—the first to be proposed since the original assemblage of 1787. Article V of the Constitution does indeed provide for this avenue of action: "On the application of the legislatures of two-thirds of the several states," it reads, the Congress must "call a convention for proposing amendments." This meant 34 of the 50 states, only two more than the 32 which had already acted.*

To be sure, students of constitutional law were not agreed on what constituted a valid call for a convention. The resolutions submitted by the 32 states were not uniform in wording: some simply embodied the Dirksen amendment, while others rephrased

*All the southern states were represented in the 32, and the remainder were mostly smaller states in the midwest and plains regions. Notable by their absence were larger states having substantial urban and suburban populations: New York, Pennsylvania, Ohio, California, Massachusetts, and New Jersey. Indeed, Illinois was the only large state to call for a convention, an action taken by a coalition of rural and suburban legislators large enough to outvote Chicago's representatives.

the Tuck bill that would have stripped the Supreme Court of its jurisdiction over apportionment questions. There was also the issue, raised by Senator William Proxmire of Wisconsin, that 26 of the 32 legislatures were malapportioned at the time they passed their anti-reapportionment petitions. Nor did anyone really know how Congress goes about calling a convention, who its members would be, or how that body of delegates should itself be apportioned. Finally there was the puzzle over whether such an assembly would limit itself to the topic of apportionment or if it could propose amendments on other subjects. Not a few people were worried lest a "runaway convention" invalidate not only the Supreme Court's decisions on apportionment but on loyalty oaths, school prayers, obscenity, and fair criminal procedure as well.

By the beginning of 1968, however, no additional states had acted. But with victory apparently so near at hand, it was clear that the campaign for a convention would continue with the quiet vigor that had already brought it within close reach of at least symbolic success.

An Ivory Tower Tribunal?

Was the Supreme Court frightened, intimidated, or in any way forestalled by the activities of its antagonists in Congress and the state capitols? The House majority for the Tuck bill, the Senate majority behind Dirksen's amendment, and the majority of state legislatures favoring a reversal of their decisions, might have persuaded the Justices to reconsider their controversial rulings. After all, as Mr. Dooley had pointed out in an earlier day, "No matter whether th' constitution follows th' flag or not, th' Supreme Coort follows th' iliction returns." And though there had been no popular poll on the apportionment issue, certainly enough elected representatives of the people had made clear their opposition to the Court's decisions.

But the Warren Court was not one to backtrack on major matters. Indeed, the Justices acted as if they were either ignorant of or oblivious to the stirrings their rulings provoked. By the middle of 1966, all but 4 of the nation's 50 state legislatures had been compelled to reapportion both their chambers to make their districts encompass approximately equal populations. The Supreme Court, assisted by lower federal and state courts operating under its guidelines, refused to settle for anything less than substantial numerical equality of representation. Thus the *Congressional Quarterly* could report:

In virtually every one of the states where reapportionment action occurred, there was a continuing but losing struggle by rural elements to retain a controlling voice in the legislatures. Prodded by the courts, however, most states have moved gradually . . . to change representation to reflect the new urban-suburban majorities. Moreover, where the legislatures were hesitant or refused to act, the courts directly intervened to speed legislative action and even to hand down reapportionment plans of their own.*

The judicial guideline that first appeared permitted no more than a 15 per cent tolerance. That is, if a state had a population of 10 million and a legislative chamber of 100 members, each district should ideally contain 100,000 residents. In practice, courts were permitting deviations of up to 15 per cent either way: in this example, districts had to fall within a population range of 85,000 to 115,000. As time went on the standard became far more rigorous. Michigan showed how far equalitarianism could be carried by creating 38 districts for its upper chamber, each with population totals which deviated by less than 1 per cent from the 205,874 norm. Spurred on by examples such as this, a Federal District Court in St. Louis rejected as inequitable a Missouri apportionment even though its greatest deviation was only 3.1 per cent.†

In six years, from the *Baker v. Carr* decision in 1962 until mid-1968, the legislative map of the United States underwent a revolutionary transformation. Almost all the country's 100 major representative assemblies—99 in the states and one in the nation's capital—had been compelled to abolish or at least coalesce several thousand rural districts and to create hundreds of new seats for urban and suburban areas. The question that only the future can answer is whether this presumed revolution has been anything more than a triumph of equalitarian mathematics. It is too early to know whether the sorts of laws and policies emanating from the reconsti-

*"State Legislative Apportionment," *Congressional Quarterly*, June 17, 1966, p. 1285.

†On April 1, 1968, the Supreme Court in a 5–3 decision on a Texas case applied its "one-man-one-vote" ruling to lawmaking bodies at the local level; thus bringing the Baker principle to almost 40,000 cities, counties, and townships throughout the nation.

tuted legislatures will substantially differ from those enacted by their malapportioned forebears. And even if legislative policy does appear to take a new turn in many states, it will require serious study to determine whether to assign the cause to reapportionment or to other political factors. The fears spurring opposition to the Court's reapportionment decisions may prove to have, in fact, been exaggerated. Yet if people believe they are being threatened, then their beliefs are in themselves an important political fact.

But by all outward signs the Supreme Court seemed unaffected by the currents of controversy it had created. If the Justices had been made uneasy by the Tuck bill, the Dirksen amendment, or even the eventuality of a Constitutional Convention, they showed no inclination to trim their sails to the political winds. To some observers, the Court was adhering to its constitutional principles despite the onslaughts of opponents who showed little appreciation of the meaning of equal justice under law or regard for the essential role of the Court in the American scheme. To others, the Justices were a band of headstrong and interfering men who sought to impose their personal opinions on the American people and their elected representatives. But to the student of politics, the accumulating consequences of Charles Baker's case combine to illustrate what can, in fact, happen when the Supreme Court of the United States makes so bold as to enter a "political thicket."

Some Concluding Observations

What Role for the Courts?—"The only check upon our exercise of power," the late Chief Justice Harlan Fiske Stone once remarked, "is our own sense of self-restraint." The power of the judicial branch in the American political system has been a perennial subject of controversy. It is easy enough to say that it is the job of the Justices to interpret the Constitution. And in analyzing the aims and the administration of particular statutes, the Supreme Court does indeed have the opportunity to declare laws unconstitutional. The issue, of course, is whether the Justices should display a sense of forbearance in these instances, or whether they should be encouraged to nullify legislation they see as running counter to the Constitution.

In the area we have examined in this study, Frankfurter and Harlan made the case for judicial self-restraint. Except on rare and widely separated occasions, they said, an appointed tribunal should not override the will of elected legislatures. "The Court's authority," Frankfurter wrote in the Baker case, "must be nourished by its complete detachment, in fact and in appearance, from political entanglements and by abstention from injecting itself into the clash of political forces in political settlements." Warren, Black, and Douglas, in contrast, were proponents of judicial activism and took the view that all too many laws abridged or invaded the constitutional rights of individuals. The passive view of Frankfurter and Harlan is customarily supported by those whose business it is to make the laws, and many congressmen and state legislators are disturbed over the recurrent application of the activist philosophy by the Court majority in recent years.

Judicial Legislation? The apportionment experience also indicates that the Justices legislate as well as adjudicate. For in striking down inequitable districting arrangements, the Supreme Court created a vacuum which had to be filled according to its guidelines. There were, indeed, cases in which new districting plans were deemed unsatisfactory by judges, who imposed plans of their own. Judges, however, are involved in the politics of legislation no matter what they decide to do. Had the Supreme Court refused to hear Charles Baker's suit against Joe Carr, the decision of the lower tribunal would have stood as the final word on apportionment. The Justices thereby would have been granting their tacit approval to the continuation of Tennessee's 1901 statute which bestowed on some voters ballots worth 20 times the value as those of other citizens. Thus the Court cannot escape the practical effect of making a decision even when it declines to pass judgment on a case.

Interpretation or Manipulation? "No state shall . . . deny to any person within its jurisdiction the equal protection of the laws." These are plain words of part of the Fourteenth Amendment of the United States Constitution. Yet just what do they mean? How does one know when some citizens of a state are being made to suffer unconstitutional instances of discrimination? The Justices have to know, or at least they are compelled to make a decision in each case coming before them. They will often disagree: where one judge will see the denial of equal protection, another will say that the plaintiff has in fact been receiving equitable treatment. "The fact that an individual lives here or there," Chief Justice Warren asserted in *Reynolds v. Sims*, "is not a legitimate reason for overweighting or diluting the efficacy of his vote." How did Warren and those Justices who concurred with him reach this conclusion? Clearly the transition from "equal protection of the laws" to "districts of equal population" is as much a human judgment as it is a progression in pure logic. And critics have accused members of the Warren Court of manipulating the words and phrases in the Constitution to accord with their personal preferences. Thus, it is suggested, the prevailing liberal majority on the bench is initially predisposed to invalidate conservative laws, and the lengthy reasons given in their opinions are simply after-the-fact justifications for the impulsive indulgence of ideology. This is a difficult charge to answer, for everyone is to some degree the captive of his political emotions and even judicial interpretation can in part be rationalization. But this condition applies to conservatives no less than to liberals, and conservative Court majorities in earlier days were just as prone to manipulating the Constitution's text.

Ideals or Interests? The apportionment cases were attacked on what appeared to be a lofty philosophical level. "The issue is not a question of the interests of rural versus city people," said the head of the American Farm Bureau Federation, "but of whether we are to maintain our time-tested system of representative government." Should the states be permitted to order their own legislative affairs, or should the judicial arm of the national government intrude its unwanted presence into this arena? The Court's defenders asserted that judicial intervention is called for when a state is found to have abridged individual rights. Those employing the rhetoric of reform have had a real advantage. "Opponents of legislative malapportionment have enjoyed a virtual monopoly in ideological warfare," one commentator pointed out in a symposium in the *Yale Law Journal*. "The criterion almost invariably employed by analysts and publicists is . . . the persistent reiteration of the incompatibility of malapportionment with widely shared democratic values."

Yet it was also clear that high political stakes were involved in the controversy because systems of representation inherently involve systems of distributing political power and influence. Under reapportionment, power would be shifted from one group of voters to another. Since no one is inclined to come straight out and say "I like the power I now have and I don't want to give it up," the tendency is to invoke philosophical principles that indirectly justify the status quo. This already complex issue became clouded because opponents of reapportionment such as Senator Everett Dirksen were willing to gamble that urban voters in a state would be prepared to support a system under which they themselves would remain underrepresented; hence his amendment, which called for—and presumably expected—popular approval of apportionment plans which favored rural areas to some degree.

  Is the Court on Trial?—"American society has . . . a surface covering of democracy, beneath which the old aristocratic colors sometimes peep out." So wrote Alexis de Tocqueville more than a century ago, referring to the bench and the bar. Quite obviously even so "aristocratic" a body as the Supreme Court cannot expect immunity from criticism in a democratic society. The reactions to the apportionment decisions certainly demonstrated that many groups and individuals felt free to attack the Court, which makes evident the vulnerability of judicial authority in the American setting. But whether the Justices should acknowledge or remain oblivious to the angry murmurings of their opponents is a decision that each must ultimately make for himself. A show of icy indifference may in fact augment the Court's "aristocratic" stature, strengthening its authority against those wishing to limit its powers and jurisdiction. Yet it is not inconceivable that a day of reckoning may come, at which time accumulated anger and exasperation will culminate in a rewriting of the role of the Supreme Court. But no matter what the ultimate resolution, it is clear that the tensions over the judicial presence will extend through the coming generation, continuing the permanent "trial" of the Court which has been characteristic of American political history since the nation's inception.

Sources

Some of the material appearing in this case study was originally published in Andrew Hacker, *Congressional Districting: The Issue of Equal Representation* (Washington, D.C.: The Brookings Institution, 1964), and permission to reprint those passages is gratefully acknowledged.

Further Reading

The full opinions of the Supreme Court in various apportionment cases can be found at the following citations: *Baker v. Carr* (369 U.S. 186), *Reynolds v. Sims* (377 U.S. 533), *Lukas v. 44th General Assembly of Colorado* (377 U.S. 713), *Colegrove v. Green* (328 U.S. 549), and *Colegrove v. Barrett* (330 U.S. 804). The District Court opinion in *Baker v. Carr* is in 179 F. Supp. 824. And the quotations from the oral argument before the Supreme Court are in the *United States Law Week*, Vol. 29, pp. 3313–3316.

Comprehensive coverage of the political repercussions following the apportionment decisions can be found in the issues of the *Congressional Quarterly Weekly Report* from 1962 through 1968.

For detailed analyses of the reapportionment question, two collections of articles containing a wide variety of viewpoints are recommended: Malcolm E. Jewell (ed.), *The Politics of Reapportionment* (New York: Atherton Press, 1962); and "The Problem of Malapportionment: A Symposium on *Baker v. Carr*," *Yale Law Journal*, Vol. 72, Number 1 (November, 1962).

A historical treatment of the Supreme Court, generally sympathetic to both the liberal and the activist postures, is Leo Pfeffer, *This Honorable Court* (Boston: Beacon Press, 1965). For an opposing view, with emphasis on the controversial decisions of the past decade, see L. Brent Bozell, *The Warren Revolution* (New Rochelle: Arlington House, 1966). A more systematic analysis employing behavioral methods is Glendon R. Schubert, *The Judicial Mind: Attitudes and Ideologies of Supreme Court Justices, 1946–1963* (Evanston: Northwestern University Press, 1965).

Editor's Epilogue:
Some Questions and Comments

The author of each case study in this volume has sought to raise questions germane to an understanding of its focus and, more broadly, of how American government works. The observations and queries briefly advanced in this editor's section are intended to complement those earlier questions, but by no means to exhaust the range of inquiries. Indeed, the reader is encouraged to formulate and probe for himself still other issues suggested by these studies. It is only by such pointed exploitation of case analyses, after all, that knowledge of the particular builds to comprehension of the general.

The chapters treating Vietnam, antipoverty, and Medicare policy demonstrate that the presidency is the major source of policy and legislative initiatives in modern American government. The "in-party"—the one in control of the White House—thus has a basic advantage over the "out-party." Peabody's study provides rich details on the competitive handicaps of the out-party and on its inability to develop an authoritative and unifying leadership analogous to that of the in-party's president. Does the growing authority of the president promote such an imbalance between the major parties as to jeopardize the maintenance of an effective two-party system?

When evaluating a president's incumbency in our time, both the public and the professionals emphasize his skill in leading the Congress. This talent is sometimes measured mechanistically by the box-score device of ascertaining what fraction of a president's program, especially of its innovative parts, was adopted by the Congress. The limits of such a measure should be apparent in the case studies here. Consider several general questions evoked by the study on the evolution of Medicare policy. Cannot a president play a critical role in projecting a new issue to public attention, even though the Congress at that time rejects the policy (Truman, 1948, and the initial failing attempt to enact Medicare)? May not a president avoid promoting contentious legislation, and thus simultaneously limit his real political leadership while inflating his box score based on congressional support of his declared program (Eisenhower, 1952–1960, and Medicare)? And how does one determine whether a president whose new policy was legislatively endorsed in fact secured as innovative a policy as the circumstances permitted (Johnson, 1963–1968, and the adoption of Medicare)?

The events of 1968 provide special force to this point. President Johnson clearly amassed an enviable record in initiating and winning congressional endorsement of new and significant domestic legislation. Yet, to his bewilderment and sorrow, he found all that eclipsed by rising and intense public dissatisfaction with the seemingly endless and deepening American involvement in the Vietnamese war. Thus the landslide victor of 1964 saw his popular support so profoundly eroded that in early 1968 he withdrew his candidacy for re-election. Historians will long debate, as Eidenberg observes in his study, the soundness of Johnson's Vietnam policies, but there can be little doubt that LBJ's political standing was seriously undermined by that issue. Assessments of the quality of a president's political leadership thus must go well beyond simply measuring the legislative support afforded his declared program.

Today's conventional wisdom has it that the source of innovative policy lies mostly within the executive branch. The case studies in this volume suggest, however, a greater complexity meriting the reader's second thoughts. The genesis of antipoverty policy squares with the preceding expectation, but the confusions and misperceptions on the policy within the executive branch—as delineated in Blumenthal's essay—implicitly qualify the thesis. Moreover, even allowing for the political motives behind Representative Mills' actions on Medicare as detailed in Marmor's study, the Congress proved more creative than the bureaucracy in carving the final contours of Medicare legislation. And, as elaborated in Hacker's chapter, there is the example of judicial innovation on reapportionment, a controversial problem which both legislatures and executives had carefully ignored for decades. Should not, then, any easy equating of innovation with bureaucracy be subjected to re-examination?

Receptivity to innovative law is by no means uniform, even when the law emerges from so prestigious and respected a body as the Supreme Court of the United States. As Hacker indicates in his study, the Court necessarily operates in a political no less than a judicial context. Contrast the uneven acceptance of Court decisions banning religious activities in public schools, the slow progress of educational desegregation in the South since 1955, and the rather rapid and high conformity to Court-enunciated standards of state legislative reapportionment. What characteristics of disputes or of Court decisions help account for this variance?

Conflict and manipulation of deeply held political values are associated with the disagreements treated in these five studies. The rhetoric of the quarrels often takes the time-honored form of urging different distributions of power among the units of a federal system. Thus the reapportionment controversy emphasizes federalistic problems, and the representation of the poor on antipoverty councils provokes charges that the national government is bypassing local government officials and structures. Disagreements as to the meaning of our federal system are important in their own right, but these disputes can better be comprehended as reflecting other and often more basic concerns; the resort to federalistic rhetoric is more disguise than reality.

Such disputes frequently pivot on the ability of the side seeking change to link the change to some compelling political value seen as superior to the claims of states' rights in a federal system, e.g., the one man, one vote value in the reapportionment quarrel. Above all, the pragmatic political style of most Americans makes it likely that criteria related to needs and results will become controlling, e.g., the demonstrated need for some version of Medicare ultimately won out over the otherwise receptive anxieties of the public about "socialized medicine." Still, as Marmor remarks in comparing American and European medical welfare policy, our prevailing political values continue to delimit and shape even the most innovative of American policies.

These case studies show that although the separation of powers retains great vitality, little understanding is to be gained by treating each component in isolation. Quite the contrary. The interplay among the president, the administrative branch, the political parties and interest groups, the Congress, and the judiciary provides the setting and the action for each case study. Further, divisions within each component add to the diversity of influence and the uncertainty of outcome. The impression we are left with is one of uneasy collaboration and conflict among shifting parts and subparts of the political world. Some feel that this diffusion of political power is the chief weakness of American government; others see it as the cornerstone of the protection of diversity and individual liberty. So slippery are the usual forms of this dispute, the reader could profit from a sustained examination of which of these fundamental perspectives on American government comes closer to his own views.